Housmans Peace Diary 2025

with World Peace Directory

72nd Edition ISSN 0957-0136

Published and distributed by

HOUSMANS BOOKSHOP
5 Caledonian Road, Kings Cross, London N1 9DX, UK
(tel +44-20-7837 4473; email diary@housmans.com)

ISBN 978 0 85283 288 2

Editor — Albert Beale
Cover design & month illustrations — Karen Leahy
(k-design-uk.com)
Quotations research — Sara Davidson
Lay-out & production — Chris Booth (formandfunction.coop)

Directory from Housmans Peace Resource Project,
editor Albert Beale (www.housmans.info)

Copyright © 2024 Housmans Bookshop Ltd

Printed by Artisan Print Solutions, Oxfordshire, on FSC paper

Personal Notes

Name

Address

Telephone

___

EXPLANATORY NOTES

National public holidays in the UK, Republic of Ireland, Canada and the USA are noted by the abbreviation HOL, followed by abbreviations for relevant countries: ENG – England, NI – Northern Ireland, SCOT – Scotland, W – Wales; UK – United Kingdom (ie all the preceding four); IRE – Republic of Ireland; CAN – Canada; US – United States. We regret that we are not able to show holidays in other countries.

Dates of moon phases, solstices and equinoxes are for GMT; users in other time zones will find that the local date is different in some cases.

The places of historical events referred to in the Peace Diary – whether in articles or in anniversary notes – are as at the date of the event, regardless of subsequent changes in name, frontiers etc.

Similarly, the **dates** are recorded in the form that was applicable at the relevant period in that place, that is in Old Style where relevant, New Style being disregarded – hence in some cases we are noting nominal anniversaries rather than mathematically correct ones.

ORDERING INFORMATION

Copies of the Diary may be ordered from:
Housmans, 5 Caledonian Road, Kings Cross, London N1 9DX, UK
(tel +44-20-7837 4473; email orders@housmans.com)

Introduction

This is the 72nd edition of the *Housmans Peace Diary*, which is intended to be both a resource and an inspiration for campaigners around the world.

This year's feature pages are mostly taken up with the story of a notorious British conspiracy trial which took place exactly 50 years ago, when 14 peace campaigners were threatened with periods of imprisonment – quite lengthy ones in some cases – because they wanted to communicate with soldiers. The state's sensitivity was particularly because this was in the context of British involvement in Northern Ireland.

The story of how threatened the authorities felt (and of the international outpouring of support and solidarity for the 14 at the time) is now largely forgotten.

The 2025 Diary includes a new selection of weekly quotations and daily anniversaries – to amuse and enthuse users, and to provoke thought. Centenaries noted this year include the refusal of the British government to sign a Geneva Protocol on the peaceful settlement of disputes; the founding of the Berlin Anti-Kriegs Museum; Dick Sheppard (who later founded the PPU) arranging a memorial event to replace the post-WW1 "Victory Ball" at London's Albert Hall; and the Locarno treaties.

We also mark the 50th anniversaries of the Convention Prohibiting Biological Weapons, of the Khmer Rouge coup d'état in Cambodia, and of the Indonesian invasion of East Timor. And there are the 30th anniversaries of the ending of military conscription in Belgium, of the legal recognition of the right to conscientious objection in Bermuda, and of the death of Humphrey Moore (founding editor of *Peace News*). The 20th anniversaries noted include the death of Gay Firth, Northern Ireland reconciliation activist, and the killing of 52 people in four suicide bomb attacks on public transport in London.

This publication is a non-profit service for fellow activists, largely produced by volunteers; we're grateful for the support which makes its production possible. Help to promote the Peace Diary is always welcome – contact Housmans Diary Group, 5 Caledonian Road, London N1 9DX (e-mail diary@housmans.com).

HOUSMANS DIARY GROUP

When pacifists talked to soldiers

Fifty years ago, a group of 14 pacifists and anti-militarists found themselves thrown together courtesy of Britain's political police. They were in the dock alongside one another in the Old Bailey, charged with being part of a conspiracy to talk to soldiers. The wonders of the British common law charge of conspiracy were such that even though some of them had never met one another prior to their arrests, that was no impediment to them all being charged with conspiring with one another. The trial was the culmination of a two-year struggle between those wanting to communicate, and the state's attempts to close down such a threatening activity.

"You seem to have left your door unlocked"

"You seem to have left your door unlocked last night, sir." Hearing these weasel words was what woke up a young pacifist activist in north London very early on a September morning in 1974. They were spoken by one of a group of police — some uniformed, some in plain clothes — standing at the end of his bed clutching a crowbar. Campaigners in other cities faced similar scenarios that morning.

June 1973: *Peace News* calls for British withdrawal from Northern Ireland

The Special Branch dawn raids related to activities in support of the British Withdrawal from Northern Ireland

Campaign (BWNIC), which had been launched in 1973 against the background of "The Troubles" in Northern Ireland. The campaign's perspective was that British involvement in the province was an impediment to the de-escalation of the underlying conflict and the mistrust between people from different traditions, and that the reconciliation that would have to happen one day could not be imposed from outside. In particular, the campaign's view was that adding more men with guns into the equation would inevitably make matters worse; hence BWNIC's call, specifically, for the withdrawal of British troops.

BWNIC wasn't the only campaign trying to end British involvement in Northern Ireland in that era. There was also the Troops Out Movement (TOM). But whereas TOM was rooted primarily in the Republican and socialist movements, BWNIC supporters were drawn more from anti-militarist and anarchist traditions; one result of this different political culture was that BWNIC's campaign included (amongst more traditional political campaigning) producing leaflets addressed specifically to British soldiers.

Leaflets for soldiers

The backdrop to the September 1974 police raids was the imprisonment, earlier that year, of BWNIC supporter Pat Arrowsmith. She had been arrested while distributing copies of a BWNIC leaflet, *Information for British Soldiers*, to members of the armed forces. She was charged under the 1934 Incitement to Disaffection Act — a law itself based on the Incitement to Mutiny Act of 1797. The 1934 Act was severely criticised at the time of its passing, and had been very rarely used since then.

Pat's arrest and imprisonment — she was sentenced to 18 months, though the Appeal Court subsequently cut her sentence — was clearly intended as a warning to BWNIC campaigners trying to communicate with soldiers. However, outrage at Pat's treatment led, if anything, to more people distributing the leaflets.

A slightly amended version of the leaflet — ensuring that its non-directive nature was clearer — was produced, and it was also given a slightly different name

SOME INFORMATION FOR DISCONTENTED SOLDIERS

This information has been compiled by supporters of the British Withdrawal from Northern Ireland Campaign who hope that it will be of some use to soldiers who have decided not to go to Northern Ireland. We are not recommending any particular course of action. There is no easy way out of the Army, but we hope that by one means or another you will avoid taking part in the killing in Northern Ireland.

IF YOU ARE A CONSCIENTIOUS OBJECTOR
that is, if since joining up you have developed a religious or moral objection to taking part in any war, you have a *legal right* to be discharged on these grounds.

—you are advised to contact:
The Central Board for Conscientious Objectors, c/o 6 Endsleigh St, London WC1. Tel: 01-352 7906.
This organisation publishes a step-by-step guide to procedure for application for a discharge on grounds of conscience. Members also offer individual advice and support throughout the whole process and have considerable experience in giving this form of help.

IF YOU INTEND TO APPLY FOR A DISCHARGE ON OTHER GROUNDS
the following organisations may be able to help:
At Ease, c/o Release, 1 Elgin Ave, London W9. Tel: 01-837 9794.
'At Ease' was recently opened to deal with enquiries about all legal ways of leaving the armed forces.
Counsellors (who include ex-servicemen) are available at this address every Thursday evening from 7.30 to 9.30 pm. The help of sympathetic lawyers and social workers can be obtained if necessary. Advice is confidential. No representations will be made to anyone without your permission. No pressure will be applied, whatever you decide to do. 'At Ease' also deals with enquiries by post.
If it is impossible for you to call in person, 'At Ease' can sometimes arrange for preliminary counselling to be given near to where-you are based.

The National Council for Civil Liberties, 186 Kings Cross Rd, London WC1. Tel: 01-278 4575.
Open daily - office hours.
This organisation has considerable experience in giving legal advice to servicemen and representing them to military authorities.

IF YOU HOPE THE ARMY WILL DISCHARGE YOU
—on **political grounds**, you may be interested in the wide selection of peace literature available from:
The Peace Centre, 18 Moor Street Ringway, Birmingham 4. Tel: 021-643 0996.
Housmans Bookshop, 5 Caledonian Rd, London N1. Tel: 01-837 4473.
—on **sexual grounds**, you may wish to contact:
The Campaign for Homosexual Equality, National Office, 28 Kennedy St, Manchester 2,
or their London Information Centre, 22 Great Windmill St, London W1. Tel: 01-437 7363. Open from 6 pm.
or phone **Icebreakers**, 01-274 9590 from 7.30 pm to 10.30 pm.

—on **health grounds**, we would advise you **not** to mutilate yourself, feign mental illness or take dangerous drugs. Some soldiers are doing so in desperation. If you have a genuine health problem, contact 'At Ease' (address above).

"Some information for Discontented Soldiers", the leaflet that led to the trial.

(as much, it was said, to help BWNIC campaigners from being confused, as it was to try to confuse the police!). It was this version, *Some Information for Discontented Soldiers*, which was being widely distributed at army shows, and at army bases and army married quarters, in the summer of 1974. And it was this leaflet which was at the heart of the Special Branch raids in September that year.

Following the raids, and subsequent arrests, a total of 14 campaigners ended up charged with possession of leaflets which could incite disaffection, and in most cases with possessing them with the intention of inciting disaffection. Unlike in Pat's case, however, the accusations weren't simply of contravening the 1934 Act — all 14 were accused of *conspiring together* to contravene the Act.

The use of the common law offence of conspiracy gave the prosecution advantages over the earlier case: it enabled less specific evidence to be used, and it covered simply planning to do something, even if it was not carried out. Hence convictions were easier to obtain — the prosecution didn't even need to prove that any particular defendant ever gave out a leaflet, nor that anyone was actually "disaffected". It also made things worse for the accused in another way — there was (at the time) no upper limit to the prison sentence that could be imposed for conspiracy, irrespective of the maximum sentence for the substantive offence concerned.

Committal of the committed

In the era of the BWNIC trials, any case serious enough to go to a Crown Court, with judge and jury, went first to a Magistrates' Court for a Committal Hearing; here, the prosecution outlined the evidence to demonstrate there was a case strong enough to go to trial. The Committal Hearing for the 14 was planned for London's main Magistrates' Court, Bow Street. However, needing a courtroom with a big enough dock for 14 people, and given the hearing might last a couple of weeks (much longer than the norm),

Street theatre at Lambeth Magistrates' Court, as the committal proceedings begin

imposed too much pressure on one of London's busiest courts.

So it was moved to Lambeth Magistrates' Court, a historic building which had not long before been mothballed as surplus to requirements. It was specially re-opened for the 14, though controversy was caused when a carpenter was brought in to extend one of the docks (none was big enough), given the historic nature of the structure.

The hearing, over a fortnight in March 1975, was a dress rehearsal for the prosecution's presentation of the evidence, and also a dress rehearsal for the defence campaign. The fortnight was enlivened by imaginative street theatre — that by a student group from Cambridge being notable for its perceptive wit about the nature of conspiracy charges in the case of people who'd never met…

> Prosecutor to Police witness: *So how did they all react to being told they were charged with conspiracy?*
> Police witness: *Well sir, they all proved the point by having exactly the same thought at the same time.*
> Prosecutor: *And what was that?*
> Police witness: *Complete surprise.*

Drop the charges!

The indefatigable BWNIC Defence Campaign, operating from the Peace News building in London, was busy rallying support for the defendants, as well as opposition to the trial happening at all. But meanwhile there were more arrests of BWNIC leafleters around the country (the campaign was still continuing of course) — six by the time of the main conspiracy trial, with more arrested while the trial was underway, meaning extra work for the defence campaign.

Although BWNIC campaigning did continue, inevitably a lot of energy was diverted into the defence campaign. There was also the problem that bail conditions for those charged and awaiting trial meant there were legal risks if any of the 14 were deemed to be compounding their "offence". This led to the somewhat melodramatic use of a "safe house" and a pair of rubber gloves when one of the 14 was stuffing envelopes with BWNIC bulletins for posting to supporters. And it also led to the absurd situation where another of the 14, happening to share a train compartment one day with someone in the Royal Navy, had their bail taken away because he had simply told the sailor that he was due on trial for talking to a soldier. It took a fortnight for lawyers to get him out of prison and his bail restored.

Defence activity took place around the world with the help of War Resisters' International (WRI). In the US, there were pickets of British consulates and British Airways offices, with well-known people (such as Joan Baez and Noam Chomsky) speaking out in support of the 14. Solidarity activity included copies of the "offending" leaflet being distributed at British army bases in West Germany, and to members of the British garrison in West Berlin (part of which was still technically a British-occupied zone).

Amnesty International, which had adopted Pat Arrowsmith as a Prisoner of Conscience (the first time they had done so for a prisoner in Britain), announced that any of the 14 who ended up in prison would also be considered a prisoner of conscience.

Unexpected support

And support came from unexpected quarters. A plain package arrived at the defence campaign, which turned out to be from a police inspector (who had known one of the defendants years earlier, before his policing days). It was an essay he'd written as part of his promotions exam to become an inspector, questioning the logic of conspiracy charges (where you could be convicted without committing the offence itself) carrying so much higher a sentence than if you had actually undertaken the allegedly criminal behaviour.

Charges under the 1934 Act were considered sufficiently serious that they could not be pursued without the express permission of the government's Attorney General. A university lecturer who'd once taught one of the 14 was a relative, by marriage, of the then Attorney General in the Labour government — Sam Silkin. This led to some highly personal lobbying of the AG.

At last, after twelve months of rehearsals, by Royal Command, despite popular non-request and regardless of cost, for an indefinite run at the Old Bailey from September 29 (matinees only, weekdays 10.00 am),

DPP Productions proudly present —

CARRY ON CONSPIRING

An hilarious farce by many authors based upon an original statement by 124 co-signatories.

Characters:

All-Star Chorus	Albert Beale
of 14 Conspirators,	Wendy Butlin
Leafleters, Letter-	Philip Cadbury
Writers, Speakers	William Hetherington
and Friends	Juliet Hornsby
	John Hyatt
	Francis Keeley
	Ronald Lee*
	Christopher Roper
	Paul Seed
	Robert Thomas
	Richard Walker
	Michael Westcott
	Gwyneth Williams
A Truthful Sleuth	Rex Haslett
The Bedroom Investigator	Anthony Shaw
The No-Bail Sergeant	Dennis Gunn
A Constable	Francis Judge
The Sunday Mirror AWOL	Nigel Exelby
A Model Major-General	Basil Coad
A Partially-Sighted Seer	David Brown
A Misled Youth	David Morgan
Two Dutiful Sons	Martin & Michael Wyness
A Sailor	James Woods

Plus 100-strong supporting cast of soldiers, airmen, policemen, policewomen, journalists, housewives, passers-by, strangers and friends, including the first appearance live on stage of the unique and inimitable Fred.

Act One	A Passage to Sweden
Act Two	A Market in Devizes
Act Three	Aldershot Fair
Act Four	Seven against Oswestry
Act Five	Riding down from Caerdydd

Director (of Public Persecutions): *Sir Norman Skelhorn, KBE, QC*

The identity of the colourful and flower-bedecked Master of Ceremonies will be revealed at the Gala Premiere on September 29.

Choreographers to the Chorus: *Louis Blom-Cooper QC, Michael Burton, Anthony (Lord) Gifford, Michael Mansfield, Stephen Solly, Rock Tansey;* assisted by *Lawrence Grant, Anthony Machen* and *William Nash.*

Choreographers to the other Principal Characters: *Brian Leary* and *Michael Coombe* (recovering from a cool reception by the critics at the Court Theatre, Preston).

Wardrobe and Make-Up by *Tenebris Light;* Lyrics by *John Ball* and *Anon;* Special Effects by *Public Participation;* Publicity by *BWNIC Defence Group.*

* Ronald Lee appears by kind permission of the Manager of Wormwood Scrubs Theatre.

"This one will run and run"

Peace News published a "Souvenir Programme" for the opening of the trial

British Quakers are one of a handful of "privileged bodies" who have, for centuries, had a special legal right to petition the monarch, dating from the time when dissenting sects were effectively disenfranchised in terms of direct involvement in public affairs; in recent times, the right was exercised only rarely — mostly on significant occasions such as a change of monarch. In the run-up to the BWNIC trial, the annual meeting of Quakers considered the issue of the 14, with two of the defendants (one a Quaker, the other a staunch atheist) invited to the meeting. As a result, the meeting resolved to attempt to enact the procedure to support the call for the dropping of the charges.

Organisations including the Young Liberals and the Socialist Workers Party took the risk of republishing the controversional leaflet, in solidarity.

Ten weeks in the Old Bailey

So the scene was set for the main event. Finally, just over a year after the dawn raids which for many were the start of the process, the trial date approached. Some defendants went on eve-of-trial visits to old friends they feared they might not get a chance to see again for years. Some were mugging up on the bundles of court papers — especially the four defendants who'd chosen to defend themselves.

The weekend, and the day the trial opened, also saw marches, vigils, and the handing-in of petitions and "complicity statements". There were pickets outside British Embassies, and similar premises, in 11 European cities — as well as in the USA and elsewhere.

Then, on the afternoon of 29 September, the 14 were led into the dock in Court 12, with what seemed like half the radical lawyers in London there on the defence team; the press benches and public gallery were full, and a fine crowd was demonstrating outside.

The hearing started with a legal attempt by defence barristers to have the "conspiracy" aspect thrown out. But the judge (Neil McKinnon) agreed with the prosecutor (Michael Coombe) that the conspiracy charges were appropriate. (McKinnon became an avid reader of *Peace*

> **HOW DO YOU PLEAD?**
>
> "I PLEAD FOR PEACE IN A WORLD OF WAR, LOVE IN A WORLD OF HATE, FREE SPEECH FOR ALL, AND AN END TO POLITICALLY MOTIVATED TRIALS IN THIS COUNTRY"
>
> **I SHALL HAVE TO HAVE A MEDICAL REPORT ON YOU, IF YOU ARE NOT CAREFUL**

Court exchange with Tenebris on the cover of *Peace News*, 10 October 1975

News during the course of the trial — perhaps relying on it as the only source of reliable news from Court 12.)

Besides the Incitement Act charges, two of the 14 were additionally charged with aiding an AWOL (a soldier who was Absent Without Leave) contrary to the Army Act; they didn't deny this.

Then there was the formal "How do you plead?", asked of each defendant in respect of each charge they faced. This led to an exchange which came to characterise the culture clash on display.

> Clerk of the Court: *How do you plead?*
> Tenebris: *I plead for peace in a world of war, love in a world of hate, and an end to politically-motivated trials in this country.*
> Judge: *I shall have to have a medical report on you if you're not careful.*

(Tenebris was charged under his formal name, Michael Westcott.)

Next, a jury had to be empanelled. In those days, any defendant had a right to object to up to seven potential jurors "without cause". The 14 agreed on the need for a jury which seemed as diverse as possible in as many ways as possible — to the extent that one could make judgements in that context. The expectation was not that it was possible to choose a "friendly" jury, but that it was at least possible to reject those seeming more likely to be *un*friendly. So anyone with the demeanour of a retired Brigadier, with a *Daily Telegraph* under their arm, was unlikely to make the cut… Ultimately, more than 70 of the possible 98 defence objections were used.

The prosecution case

The opening speech from the prosecution — which went on for several days — made much of the BWNIC founding statement; though only 6 of the 14 were signatories. And as for those of the 14 who were on trial despite never having been detained in the act of distributing the leaflets, well, those three were obviously the masterminds, directing their agents from their lair in London's Kings Cross!

In some ways, the trial settled into a certain rhythm — the prosecution would bring a military witness who had received a copy of the leaflet; the prosecution would get them to say how outraged they were, and — in some cases — whether they could identify the person on the dock who'd given it to them. (Not that anyone in the dock denied doing any specific thing that they'd done; it became the practice for a relevant defendant to stand up even before they were pointed out.) Then the defence would ask the witness what they knew about the rights of members of the forces, and in particular what rights they had to quit if they wanted. (Of course, they knew very little.)

With the recipients of the leaflets not being very helpful (to the prosecution), they called extra military witnesses to try to vindicate the army. One, in charge of several London recruiting offices, said that it was not a "war" in Northern Ireland. When asked by a defendant how a recruit was informed of the moral and legal situation they were being put into, the judge intervened to say that "to kill somebody other than as an act of war is illegal". The defendant responded, "So the British Amy are murdering people the same as the IRA is".

The prosecution also brought evidence from three men who had gone AWOL and subsequently deserted the army and fled to Sweden; the prosecution claimed that they were helped and encouraged by some of the 14.

The main gist of the prosecution case was that the British Withdrawal from Northern Ireland Campaign was formed primarily to "seduce soldiers from their duty or allegiance", hence anyone involved with the campaign — or at least those who the prosecuting authorities had decided to select from the much wider number of BWNIC supporters available — was therefore part of a criminal conspiracy. What the trial was *not* about, insisted the prosecution, was government policy or army conduct in Northern Ireland, nor the way the military treat their employees, nor whether the laws being used in this case were "good" law.

Light relief

The trial was not without its humour on occasions, as well as drama — even if the 14 didn't feel able to fully appreciate the more entertaining aspects at the time.

One defence witness was Harry Mister, a tall and mature fellow with a slight stutter, who was general manager of Housmans Bookshop and of the Peace News building (he was one of the founders of *Peace News* itself). He was called to give evidence as to the arrangements in the building, and the fact that it was a BWNIC address but not an office, and the generally non-conspiratorial nature of the place.

When questioned by the prosecutor, he was asked whether he recognised all the people in the dock. He screwed up his eyes and peered intently, looking slowly up and down the row. "Well," he said, "I think it h-has been my honour to have m-met most of these young p-people at some stage ... except perhaps for that gentleman at the end ... or is he a p-prison officer?"

Defendant Bob Thomas begins his speech in his native Welsh
Drawing by Arthur Horner

Another defence witness was Myrtle Solomon, who had a long-time involvement in the WRI and the Peace Pledge Union (PPU). She was there as a key person from the Central Board for Conscientious Objectors (the CBCO) — essentially a peace movement body, but one recognised by the authorities as having a role in supporting anyone applying for CO status. Her evidence reinforced the defence argument that people in the military were almost universally ignorant of their rights unless people from outside informed them.

Myrtle was a fairly slight woman, in her 50s, who had the demeanour of someone polite and charming. When cross-examining her, the prosecutor, Michael Coombe, at first tried to tar her with the same "subversive" brush as he was using against the 14; it completely failed to work. So before finishing his questioning, he switched tack and tried to elicit answers which would instead draw a clear distinction between her giving respectable legal advice for would-be COs, and out-and-out criminal incitement.

Still not really getting what he wanted, in the face of Myrtle's transparent decency and reasonableness, he gave up. But in that moment he forgot a key barrister's rule: don't ask a question to which you don't know the answer. As he sat down, he said, as much as a throwaway line as an actual question to Myrtle, "But naturally, Miss Solomon, *you've* never harboured an

AWOL." She blinked briefly. "But Mr Coombe, *of course* I have." It took a while for the uproar in the public gallery to die down.

Bullying a defendant

Gwyn Williams, who was defending herself, spent one of the longest times in the witness box when giving her own evidence. And with no barrister representing her, she was prey to hostile questioning by the prosecutor and the judge as a double act (the judge's sympathy with the prosecution was clear from Day 1). One of the defence barristers — for two of the other defendants — was Tony Gifford (he happened, to his own embarrassment, to be a hereditary peer; the judge absolutely hated having to call him "*Lord* Gifford").

At one point, when Gwyn was being persistently bullied by the judge and prosecutor, with no lawyer to intervene on her behalf, Tony Gifford stood up to protest — despite having no formal status enabling him to do so. "Sit *down* Lord Gifford!" the judge bellowed. A pause. Tony's knuckles went white as he gripped the side of his lectern; then, almost as loudly as the judge had addressed him, replied, "I will not sit down while there is injustice in this court." This insubordination stunned the judge, and led to a short break in proceedings; Gwyn got her breath back.

One of Gwyn's more memorable explanations to the court of the nature of army employment laws caught the attention of the press bench. It was included in the *Guardian's* court report that night (press were present right through the trial); and a *Guardian* sub-editor, when writing the headlines for the next morning's front page, was obviously taken with it. So the *Guardian* appeared with this prominent headline: *"Army last relic of medieval bondage" court told*.

Apparently this led to a rift, for some time, in relations between that newspaper and the MoD's press office — even though the court reports were by a political journalist, not by one of the "defence" correspondents.

After all the evidence and the closing speeches, the judge's none-too-coherent summing-up went on for several days. On the morning of Wednesday 10 December, the jury were given their final instructions and retired to consider their verdict. Although most defendants had been on bail during the trial (though one was serving time for a previous animal rights conviction, and brought from custody to the Old Bailey each day), all bail was now rescinded pending the verdict. The 14 were taken down to the cells in the Old Bailey's basement; some of the lawyers followed, to offer moral support.

It was expected that the jury might take some days, given the length of the trial and the amount of evidence; certainly many hours at the very least. There was also the fact that the combination of charges of possessing the leaflets, and of distributing them, and of intending to incite, varied as between defendants — there were 31 verdicts to deliver in all, and not all verdicts might be the same.

Why so fast?

Then suddenly, barely an hour and a half after the jury retired, everyone was summoned back to court. The jury were back; could the verdicts be in already? Was that a bad sign? Quick convictions all round?

The Clerk of the Court asked the jury foreman whether they had reached unanimous verdicts on all 31 counts; they had. Laboriously spelling out each charge against each person, starting with the most serious charge against the person at the top of the indictment, he began: "On Count 1, of conspiring with … with intent to contravene … do you find the defendant Gwyneth Williams Guilty or Not Guilty?" A quick response: "*Not* Guilty!" Uproar in the public gallery, and in the court, with loud cheers and tears. If that was a Not Guilty, surely they all had to be?

Eventually things quietened down enough for the process to be carried through — 30 more questions to the jury, with a firm reply of "Not Guilty" every time.

Someone stood up in the public gallery and announced to everyone that there would be a victory party that night at the PPU offices. In the courtroom,

GWYN WILLIAMS: Found **not guilty** of conspiracy to incite disaffection among members of HM Forces; possession with intent of "Some Information for British Soldiers" at Devizes and of "Some Info for Discontented Soldiers" at Oswestry and when raided, under Section 1 contrary to section 2 of the Act.
Pleaded guilty on two counts of assisting a soldier absent without leave to remain absent, contrary to section 192 (1) (c) of the Army Act, 1955. **Fined £100.**

JOHN HYATT: Found **not guilty** of conspiring to incite disaffection, and of possessing "Some Information for Discontented Soldiers" at 5 Caledonian Rd, London N1.
Pleaded **guilty** to helping a soldier stay absent without leave. **Fined £50.**
"Even if it means going to jail, I will not give evidence against my friends."

CHRIS ROPER: Found **not guilty** of conspiring to incite disaffection, and of possessing "Some Information for Discontented Soldiers" at Aldershot and when raided.
"The army is not peace-keeping: it is keeping the violence at its present high level."

ALBERT BEALE: Found **not guilty** of conspiring to incite disaffection, and of possessing "Some Information for Discontented Soldiers" when raided.
"Nonviolence is a form of action without hatred; it is revolution without guns; it is a very personal thing. Ultimately it's justice without prisons."

WENDY BUTLIN: Found **not guilty** of conspiring to incite disaffection, and of possessing with intent "Some Information for Discontented Soldiers" when raided.
"A soldier is a human being and should not be treated like an automaton."

PHIL CADBURY: Found **not guilty** of conspiring to incite disaffection, and of possessing with intent "Some Information for Discontented Soldiers" at Aldershot and Oswestry.
"I AM an agent of a foreign power ... the power of love, which seems to be foreign to this court."

BILL HETHERINGTON: Found **not guilty** of conspiring to incite disaffection and of endeavouring to seduce a sailor from his duty.
"All my actions have been those of a human being responding to a human situation in a human way."

Peace News profiles and quotes from the acquitted defendants

TENEBRIS LIGHT: Found **not guilty** of conspiring to incite disaffection, and of possessing with intent "Some Information to Discontented Soldiers" at Oswestry.
"A soldier is responsible to himself for what he does, so I feel soldier should be informed."

BOB THOMAS: Found **not guilty** of conspiring to incite disaffection.
"If you think bullets and bombs can bring peace, then I feel an alien amongst you."

JULIET HORNSBY: Found **not guilty** of conspiring to incite disaffection, and of possessing with intent "Some Information for Discontented Soldiers" at Aldershot.
"I am a pacifist and totally opposed to all war-like activities."

RONNIE LEE: Found **not guilty** of conspiring to incite disaffection, and of possessing with intent "Some Information for Discontented Soldiers" at Oswestry.
"Seduction has been shown and a conspiracy has been revealed, not by the defendants, but by the British Army ... and the British State."

RICK WALKER: Found **not guilty** of conspiring to incite disaffection, and of possessing with intent "Some Information for Discontented Soldiers" at Oswestry.
"I shall be continuing to work against militarism, and for a society based on mutual aid, co-operation and voluntary association."

FRANK KEELEY: Found **not guilty** of conspiring to incite disaffection, and of possessing with intent "Some Information for Discontented Soldiers" at Oswestry.
"I do not accept that anybody has any duty or allegiance to anything except their own conscience."

PAUL SEED: Found **not guilty** of conspiring to incite disaffection, and of possessing with intent "Some Information for Discontented Soldiers" at Oswestry.
"The prosecution has not been brought because anybody thinks the leaflet is seductive, but for quite other political reasons."

boundaries between defendants, press and lawyers dissolved. Prosecutor Michael Coombe was heard to mutter, "It's a bad day for the country!"

Finally, proceedings were formally brought to a halt. However, the two defendants who'd pleaded guilty to Army Act charges had to return in the afternoon for sentencing (only fines, it turned out), and the jury, though discharged, returned as well "to keep an eye on McKinnon [the judge]" during the sentencing. Some of the jury even turned up at the party that night, where it became clear that they'd pretty much made up their minds to acquit almost from the outset. If only people had known…

The verdicts made front-page news the next day. The various other cases under the Act were discontinued. And because of the scandal, the law was changed a couple of years later to remove some of the more pernicious aspects of conspiracy law; but it was also changed to limit the rights of defendants to peremptory challenges of potential jurors.

And most important of all, following those acquittals the 1934 Incitement Act has never been used again.

Thanks for help with this article to Diana Shelley, especially for her fortnightly court reports in *Peace News* at the time; many more details of the trial and the issues surrounding it can be found in the *PN*s of that era.

The BWNIC 14 celebrate their acquittal outside the court

Bill Hetherington
1934–2023

Bill Hetherington died late in 2023 — too late to be noted in the 2024 *Peace Diary*. He was a key figure in Peace News Trustees (PNT — parent company of Housmans and *Peace News*). He was also an activist in the Peace Pledge Union and WRI.

His long support for Housmans Bookshop included leading its struggle against legal and financial attacks (from the tax authorities, and libel writs from right-wing activists). At one stage, he put significant finances of his own on the line to stop the shop going under.

And for years, he undertook crucial work for the Diary itself. When changes in shop staff meant there was less of the political and other expertise needed to produce it, and with the publication's existence being a factor persuading PNT to bail out the shop at times of large annual losses, he was concerned to keep it in production. So, with another PNT member, he took on the annual researching and editing work.

Without him, the *Peace Diary* would have ceased to exist many years ago.

December/January

To be truly radical is to make hope possible rather than despair convincing.
Raymond Williams

WEEK 1

MON
30

TUE
31

WED
1

NEW YEAR'S DAY
WORLD DAY OF PEACE
(HOL UK/IRE/CAN/US)

1995 - Abolition of military conscription comes into force, Belgium

(HOL SCOT)

THU
2
1905 - Michael Tippett, pacifist composer, born, Britain

FRI
3
1915 - First use of gas-filled shells, by German forces, Western Front, Europe

SAT
4
1950 - Government asks USA for stockpile of nuclear weapons, Britain

SUN
5
1990 - 50 demand taxes for human needs, not Israeli occupation, at Israeli Embassy, Washington DC, USA

January

My house was called
the house of flowers, because in every cranny
geraniums burst: it was
a good-looking house
with its dogs and children...
And one morning all that was burning

Pablo Neruda

WEEK 2

MON

6

1925 - France & UK announce deferment of planned withdrawal of occupation troops from Rhineland, Germany

TUE

7

1985 - First issue of *Medicine and War*, Britain

WED

8

1885 - Abraham Johannes Muste, US nonviolent activist, born, Zeeland, Netherlands

THU
9
2005 - Death of Gay Firth. activist for N Ireland reconciliation, Britain

FRI
10
1940 - Brethren, Friends & Mennonites ask President for alternative service for COs in event of war, USA

SAT
11
1885 - Alice Paul, first peace picketer of White House, born, USA

SUN
12
2005 - US government ends fruitless search for putative weapons of mass destruction in Iraq

January

They fight a war and they don't know what for. Isn't that crazy? How can one man kill another and not really know the reason why he does it, except that the other man wears a different colour uniform and speaks a different language? And it's me they call mad!

Michael Morpurgo, from *War Horse*, 1982

WEEK 3

MON

13

1985 - Plan to install 758 cruise missiles in 106 submarines announced by USA

TUE

14

1965 - First ever meeting of Prime Ministers of Irish Republic and N Ireland

WED

MARTIN LUTHER KING DAY

15

1990 - National Assembly votes to end Communist Party monopoly of power, Bulgaria

THU
16
1965 - British arms embargo prevents export of Bloodhound missiles to S Africa

FRI
17
1955 - Intention to produce H-bomb announced, Britain

SAT
18
1945 - German defensive forces surrender to USSR army, Budapest, Hungary

SUN
19
1915 - 4 killed in first fatal air raid of WWI, Yarmouth & King's Lynn, Norfolk, Britain

January

In spite of temporary victories, violence never brings permanent peace.
Martin Luther King, from Nobel Lecture, 1964

WEEK 4

MON

MLK DAY OBSERVED
(HOL US)

20

1975 - UN University inaugurated, Tokyo, Japan

TUE

◐

21

1790 - Joseph Guillotin demonstrates device for execution by beheading, Paris, France

WED

22

1905 - "Bloody Sunday" massacre of 100 demonstrators for social reform, outside Winter Palace, St Petersburg, Russia

THU
23
1875 - First disarmament campaign founded, Liverpool, Britain

FRI
24
1985 - Defence Minister personally receives convicted WW2 war criminal on release from prison, Austria

SAT
25
1955 - End of state of war with Germany decreed by USSR

SUN
26
1945 - Liberation of Nazi extermination camp, Auschwitz/Oswiecim, Poland

January/February

What hurts the victim most is not the cruelty of the oppressor, but the silence of the bystander.
Elie Wiesel

WEEK 5

MON
27

2005 - 10 killed in bomb attacks intended to disrupt election to constitutional convention, Iraq

INT'L HOLOCAUST MEMORIAL DAY

TUE
28

1975 - Convention on trade between EC and former colonies signed, Lomé, Togo

WED
29

1926 - German WILPF gives French WILPF fund for "peace" (fruit) trees to be planted in devastated France

●
YUAN TAN
CHINESE NEW YEAR 4723

THU
30
1945 - Death of William Busch, pacifist musician, Britain

FRI
31
1915 - Thomas Merton, pacifist priest, born, USA

SAT
1
1935 - British-German conference on German re-armament opens. London, Britain

SUN
2
1990 - 30-year-long ban on opposition groups lifted, S Africa

February

What's the trouble with you, Spode, is that just because you have succeeded in inducing a handful of half-wits to disfigure the London scene by going about in black shorts, you think you're someone ... you imagine it is the Voice of the People ... What the Voice of the People is saying is.... Did you ever in your puff see such a perfect perisher?
PG Wodehouse, in *The Code of the Woosters*, 1938

WEEK 6
(HOL IRE)

MON

3

2005 - Mass "Make Poverty History" rally, Trafalgar Sq, London, Britain

TUE

4

1945 - UK/USA/USSR conference on post-WW2 treatment of Germany opens, Yalta, Crimea, USSR

WED

☽

5

1985 - Full re-opening of gates to Gibraltar (closed 16 years), La Linea, Spain

THU
6
1985 - Peace camp evicted by army, Molesworth cruise missile base, Britain

FRI
7
1965 - USAF begins saturation bombing, N Vietnam

SAT
8
1725 - John Bellers, Quaker benefactor, author of 1710 plan for European peace, died, London, Britain

SUN
9
1915 - World Union of Women for International Concord founded, Geneva, Switzerland

February

The only way to win the next world war is to prevent it.
Dwight D. Eisenhower, 1956

WEEK 7

MON

10

2005 - Government formally acknowledges possession of nuclear weapons, Pyongyang, N Korea

TUE

11

1985 - Clive Ponting acquitted of breaching official secrets about British sinking Argentinian warship *Belgrano*, London, Britain

WED

○

12

2002 - UN Optional Protocol restricting use of under-18 soldiers comes into force

THU
13
1945 - Over 50,000 killed in Allied fire-bombing, Dresden, Germany

FRI
14
1925 - Ban on Nazi Party lifted, Bavaria, Germany

SAT
15
2003 - Millions march worldwide against war on Iraq

SUN
16
1995 - 2000 leave on peace train to Vavunia from Colombo, Sri Lanka

February

We can learn to work and speak when we are afraid in the same way we have learned to work and speak when we are tired.

Audre Lorde

WEEK 8

PRESIDENTS DAY
(HOL US)

MON

17

1940 - Marches in several towns mark Women's Peace Day, Britain

TUE

18

1934 - Audre Lorde, feminist activist academic, born, USA

WED

19

1965 - Weekend of protests in 30 cities against escalation of Vietnam War, USA

THU
20
1965 - "Letter to a Soldier" distributed, married quarters, Naphill & Dawes Hill army bases, Britain

FRI
21
1990 - After calls for resignation of President, government bans public demonstrations, Kenya

SAT
22
1965 - Freedom Ride to end racial segregation in cinemas & swimming pools, New South Wales, Australia

SUN
23
1945 - Mass bombing by RAF, Pforzheim, Germany

February/March

We speak simply as the women of Wales – the daughters of a nation whose glory it has been to cherish no hatred towards any land or people, and whose desire is for the coming on earth of the reign of fellowship and goodwill.

The Welsh Women's Peace Petition, 1924

WEEK 9

MON
24
1885 - Thoger Thogersens, antimilitarist activist, born, Denmark

TUE
25
2005 - 3 soldiers imprisoned for ill-treating Iraqi prisoners, Britain

WED
26
1965 - European Social Charter comes into force

THU
27
1995 - First substantive meeting of Law of the Sea Assembly, Kingston, Jamaica

FRI
28
2005 - Government resigns as 25,000 call for withdrawal of Syrian troops from country, Martyrs' Sq, Beirut, Lebanon

NUCLEAR-FREE & INDEPENDENT PACIFIC DAY

SAT
1
1915 - Britain declares blockade of Germany

SUN
2
1955 - Defensive alliance formed by Egypt and Syria

March

There is no gate, no lock, no bolt that you can set upon the freedom of my mind.
Virginia Woolf

WEEK 10

MON

3

1905 - Tsar Nicholas II promises consultative assembly in response to public demonstrations, St Petersburg, Russia

TUE

4

1950 - Carl Heath, Quaker penal reformer and pacifist activist, died, Britain

WED

ASH WEDNESDAY

5

1770 - British troops shoot dead five protesters against 1765 Stamp Act, Customs House, Boston, colonial Massachusetts

THU
6
1975 - Nonviolent march for return of democracy, Delhi, India

FRI
7
1965 - First US combat troops sent to S Vietnam

INT'L WOMEN'S DAY

SAT
8
1985 - Public invited by women of E & W Europe to sign petition for complete denuclearisation

SUN
9
1915 - Government proposes legislation to commandeer factories to make munitions, Britain

March

It seems to me that the good lord in his infinite wisdom gave us three things to make life bearable - hope, jokes, and dogs. But the greatest of these was dogs.

Robyn Davidson

WEEK 11

MON

10

1875 - Eleanor May Moores, pacifist activist, born. Australia

TUE

11

1985 - Election of Mikhail Gorbachev as First Secretary of Communist Party opens era of glasnost & perestroika, USSR

WED

12

1925 - Government refuses to sign Oct 1924 Geneva Protocol on peaceful settlement of disputes, Britain

THU
13
1945 - Pax Christi
founded, France

FRI
14
2005 - Parliamentary
report recommends
raising minimum
military recruitment
age to 18, Britain

SAT
15
1985 - 2-1 vote
against building of
nuclear reactor,
Kerm County, USA

SUN
16
1935 - Versailles
Treaty disarmament
repudiated by
Germany

March

And off they went, my two parents
to march against the war in Iraq,
him with his plastic hips. Her with her arthritis … for peace on earth,
for pity's sake, for peace, for peace.
Jackie Kay, from *George Square*

WEEK 12

MON
17

ST PATRICK'S DAY
(HOL NI/IRE)

1625 - *De Jure Belli ac Pacis*, foundational work of international law, published, Paris, France

TUE
18

1955 - Ratification of entry into Western European Union, W Germany

WED
19

1965 - 48 arrested for protesting against loans to South Africa, Chase Manhattan Bank, New York, USA

EQUINOX

THU

20

1815 - Permanent neutrality declared, Switzerland

INT'L DAY FOR ELIMINATION OF
RACIAL DISCRIMINATION

FRI

21

1985 - Police fire on Sharpeville anniversary march, killing 22, Uitenhage, S Africa

◐
SAKA
(INDIAN NEW YEAR 1947)

SAT

22

1990 - Death of Geoffrey Ostergaard, gentle anarchist, Britain

SUN

23

1900 - Erich Fromm, humanistic philosopher, born, Germany

March

For, while the tale of how we suffer, and how we are delighted, and how we may triumph is never new, it always must be heard. There isn't any other tale to tell, it's the only light we've got in all this darkness.

James Baldwin

WEEK 13

MON

24

1879 - Walter Ayles, WWI CO and pacifist parliamentarian, born, Britain

TUE

25

1915 - Sisterhood of International Peace founded, Australia

WED

26

1975 - Convention prohibiting Biological Weapons comes into force

THU
27
1955 - State of emergency declared, Pakistan

FRI
28
1915 - International Socialist Women's Conference calls for peace, Berne, Switzerland

●

SAT
29
1970 - Death of Vera Brittain, WW1 Voluntary Aid Detachment nurse and pacifist author, Britain

BST BEGINS

SUN
30
1995 - Appeal Court recognises conscientious objection, Bermuda

March/April

A liberation movement that is nonviolent sets the oppressor free as well as the oppressed.
Barbara Deming

WEEK 14

MON
31
1985 - 300,000 demonstrate in peace rallies countrywide, Australia

TUE
1
1955 - Boycott of segregated schools, South Africa

WED
2
2014 - Death of Arlo Tatum, US CO and international pacifist activist, Cornwall, Britain

THU
3
1925 - Reparation Recovery Act repealed, Britain

FRI
4
1955 - UK & Australia agree to establish nuclear weapons test ground, Maralinga, S Australia

SAT
5
1795 - Peace between France and Prussia signed, Basle, Switzerland

SUN
6
1985 - Satellite dish is daubed with human blood, Watsonian Army Base, Melbourne, Australia

April

We cannot have peace among men whose hearts delight in killing any living creature. By every act that glorifies or even tolerates such moronic delight in killing we set back the progress of humanity.
Rachel Carson

WEEK 15

MON
7
1917 - Socialist Party votes opposition to WWI, USA

TUE
8
1904 - Entente Cordiale established between Britain and France

WED
9
1940 - Germany invades Denmark and Norway

THU
10
1955 - Death of Jessie Wallace Hughan, co-founder of War Resisters League, USA

FRI
11
1805 - European league for liberation of northern German states set up by Britain & Russia, St Petersburg, Russia

SAT
12
1935 - 60,000 students strike against war throughout USA

SUN
13
1945 - Liberation of Belsen & Buchenwald concentration camps, Germany

April

Dis-le toi désormais
Même s'il est sincère
Aucun rêve jamais
Ne mérite une guerre.

Tell yourself from now on / Even if it is sincere / No dream ever / Is worth a war.

Jaques Brel

WEEK 16

MON

14

1975 - Khmer Rouge coup d'état, Cambodia

TUE

15

1965 - Picket of Biological and Chemical Warfare establishment, Porton Down, Wiltshire, Britain

WED

16

1965 - Vigil at church sequestered by military, Foulness, Essex, Britain

THU
17
1985 - Last S African troops withdrawn from southern Angola

GOOD FRIDAY
(HOL UK/CAN)

FRI
18
1955 - Death of Albert Einstein, pacifist scientist, Princeton, USA

SAT
19
1990 - USSR violently represses independence movement, Lithuania

EASTER DAY

SUN
20
1792 - National Assembly declares war on Austria, France

April

It seems to me that Islam and Christianity and Judaism all have the same god, and he's telling them all different things.
Billy Connolly

WEEK 17

MON

21

1945 - Death of Käthe Kollwitz, artist of peace, Germany

◐
EASTER MONDAY
(HOL ENG/W/NI/IRE/CAN)

TUE

22

1915 - First use of poison gas in war, by German army, Ypres, Belgium

WED

23

1955 - Declaration on World Peace and Co-operation by non-aligned states, Bandung, Indonesia

THU
24
1915 - Massacre/brutal deportation of Armenian population begins, Turkey

ANZAC DAY (AUS/NZ)

FRI
25
1915 - Anglo-French & ANZAC troops land, Gallipoli peninsula, Turkey

SAT
26
1915 - Britain & France promise territorial gain for Italy as reward for joining Allies, in secret treaty, London, Britain

SUN
27
1945 - 3 anarchist editors gaoled 9 months for "incitement to disaffection", London, Britain

April/May

A peace is of the nature of a conquest; for then both parties nobly are subdued, and neither party loser.
William Shakespeare, in *Henry IV, Part 2*

WEEK 18

MON
28
1915 - International Congress of Women meets to discuss peace, The Hague, Netherlands

TUE
29
1915 - Women's International League for Peace & Freedom effectively founded, The Hague, Netherlands

WED
30
1975 - End of Vietnam War

THU
1
1965 - Second Factory for Peace opens, Onllwyn, Dulais Valley, Wales

FRI
2
2005 - Death of Bob Hunter, co-founder of Greenpeace, Toronto, Ontario, Canada

SAT
3
1915 - League of Nations Society founded, Britain

SUN
4
1915 - Triple Alliance with Germany & Austria-Hungary denounced by Italy

May

*The only thing wrong with peace is that
You can't make no money from it.*
Gill Scott Heron

WEEK 19

MON

MAY DAY OBSERVED
(HOL UK/IRE)

5

1955 - International recognition as sovereign state, W Germany

TUE

6

1915 - Sydney Carter, pacifist songwriter, born, London, Britain

WED

7

1915 - 1198 killed by U-boat sinking of civilian liner Lusitania, off southern coast of Ireland

THU
8
1945 - End of World
War 2 in Europe

FRI
9
1955 - Entry into
NATO by
W Germany

SAT
10
1915 - 1 killed in
Zeppelin raid on
Southend, Essex,
Britain

SUN
11
1867 - Declaration
of neutrality,
Luxembourg

May

They asked if I knew what "conscientious objector" meant. I told them that when the white man asked me to go off somewhere and fight and maybe die to preserve the way the white man treated the black man in America, then my conscience made me object.

Malcolm X

WEEK 20

MON

12

1907 - World Demonstration for Peace widely supported in northern hemisphere

TUE

13

1943 - Germany and Italy surrender in North Africa

WED

14

1912 - Parliament authorises new armaments programme, in competition with British naval strength, Germany

INT'L CONSCIENTIOUS OBJECTORS' DAY

THU
15
1899 - First international women's peace rally, The Hague, Netherlands

FRI
16
1915 - 1 killed in Zeppelin raid on Ramsgate, Kent, Britain

SAT
17
1919 - Women's International League for Peace and Freedom formally established, Zurich, Switzerland

SUN
18
1925 - First celebration of International Goodwill Day

May

We will not learn how to live together in peace by killing each other's children.

US President Jimmy Carter

WEEK 21

MON

19

VICTORIA DAY
(HOL CAN)

1918 - 44 killed in German air raid on London, Britain

TUE

20

◐

1957 - Death of Gilbert Murray, peace advocate, Britain

WED

21

1997 - Government announces ban on import, export and production of landmines, Britain

THU
22
1915 - War on Austria-Hungary declared by Italy

FRI
23
1965 - 300,000 in Third Marathon March for peace and justice, Greece

INT'L WOMEN'S DAY FOR DISARMAMENT

SAT
24
1883 - Cecil Cadoux, British pacifist theologian, born, Turkey

SUN
25
1962 - Cathedral consecrated as focus of reconciliation, Coventry, Britain

May/June

It is unconscionable that 10,000 boys have died in Vietnam. If 10,000 American women had mind enough, they could end the war, if they were committed to the task, even if it meant going to jail.

Jeannette Rankin

WEEK 22

MON

MEMORIAL DAY (US)
(HOL UK/US)

26

1935 - 10,000 young people cheer Dick Sheppard's speech against war, Mote Park, Maidstone, Britain

TUE

●

27

1915 - Two killed in Zeppelin raid on Southend, Essex, Britain

WED

28

1996 - President announces abolition of conscription for 1979 generation & after, France

THU
29
1965 - British soldier in uniform arrested as participant in anti-Vietnam War march, London, Britain

FRI
30
1945 - 5000 attend 3 rallies for a constructive peace, London, Britain

SAT
31
1915 - Six killed in Zeppelin raid on outer London, Britain

SUN
1
1047 - Peace of God confirmed by Council of Tuluje

June

Oh! War! How I hate it … Why do they heartlessly kill life-loving young men like Lam, like Ly, like Hung and the thousands of others, who are only defending their motherland with so many dreams?

Dang Thuy Tram, from *Last Night I Dreamed of Peace: The Diary of Dang Thuy Tram*

WEEK 23

MON
(HOL IRE)

2

1907 - Second International Peace Conference opens, The Hague, Netherlands

TUE
◐

3

1964 - Conscientious objection legally recognised, Belgium

WED
INT'L DAY FOR CHILDREN AS VICTIMS OF WAR

4

1975 - Harold Bing, founder member of WRI and PPU, died, Britain

THU
5
1965 - 48-hour fast & picket begins, Chemical & Biological Warfare establishment, Porton Down, Wiltshire, Britain

FRI
6
1915 - 5 killed in Zeppelin raid on East coast, England

SAT
7
1905 - Independence from Sweden obtained nonviolently, Norway

SUN
8
1965 - US forces authorised to begin offensive operations against Vietcong, South Vietnam

June

Those who profess to favour freedom, and yet deprecate agitation, are men who want crops without ploughing up the ground. They want rain without thunder and lightning. They want the ocean without the roar of its mighty waters.

Frederick Douglass

WEEK 24

MON
9
1815 - Permanent neutrality of Switzerland guaranteed by European powers in Final Act of Congress of Vienna, Austria

TUE
10
1917 - Women's Peace Crusade launched, Glasgow, Scotland

WED
11
○

1955 - Fellowship Party founded, London, Britain

THU
12
1935 - Formal truce suspends Chaco War between Bolivia and Paraguay

FRI
13
1985 - 1756 arrested in 150 cities over 2 days in Pledge of Resistance to aid for Nicaraguan Contras, USA

SAT
14
1945 - Supreme Court invalidates compulsory flag salute by schoolchildren, USA

SUN
15
1215 - Magna Carta signed by King John, Runnymede, England

June

Wars will be stopped only when soldiers refuse to fight, when workers refuse to load weapons onto ships and aircraft, when people boycott the economic outposts of Empire that are strung across the globe.
Arundhati Roy

WEEK 25

MON

16

1965 - Speak-out against Vietnam War, Pentagon, Washington DC, USA

TUE

17

1895 - George MacLeod, pacifist pastor, born, Scotland

WED

18

1815 - Battle of Waterloo finally ends Napoleonic hegemony, Belgium

(HOL US)

THU
19
1975 - First UN International Women's Conference opens, Mexico City, Mexico

FRI
20
1985 - 16-year ban on production of chemical weapons lifted, USA

SOLSTICE

SAT
21
1965 - Week of Action begins, Polaris missile base, Scotland

SUN
22
1885 - James Maxton, WWI CO and parliamentary antimilitarist, born, Scotland

June

We got rid of war for good and all on June 26 1945 – before Hiroshima – in the Charter of the United Nations. For half a century, we've been outlawing the hell out of war and look where it got us.

James Cameron

WEEK 26

MON

23

1995 - Widows and mothers rally for peace, Grozny, Chechnya

TUE

24

2014 - Death of Roy Prockter, pacifist accountant & war tax resister, Britain

WED

25

1980 - ETA begins bombing campaign, Spain

MUHARRAM
(ISLAMIC NEW YEAR 1447)
INT'L DAY FOR VICTIMS OF
TORTURE

THU
26

1945 - UN Charter signed by 51 states, War Memorial Hall, San Francisco, California, USA

FRI
27

1918 - Marie Equi, physician & anarchist, arrested for anti-war speech, Portland, Oregon, USA

SAT
28

1935 - League of Nations Union announces result of "Peace Ballot", Britain

SUN
29

1915 - Carl Heinrich Petersen, peace activist, born, Denmark,

June/July

Be nice to whites, they need you to rediscover their humanity.
Desmond Tutu

WEEK 27

MON
30
1935 - Peace marches from N, S, E & W converge, Trafalgar Square, London, Britain

TUE
1
CANADA DAY (HOL CAN)

1935 - Conference of Council of Action for Peace & Reconstruction, Britain

WED
2
2005 - Live8 concerts urging G8 to end global poverty, Berlin, London, Paris, Philadelphia, Rome

THU
3
1945 - Formal setting up of occupation sectors by France, UK, USA, USSR dividing Berlin, Germany

INDEPENDENCE DAY (US)
(HOL US)

FRI
4
1885 - Charles Earle Raven, pacifist priest, born, Britain

SAT
5
1955 - First meeting of Assembly of Western European Union, Strasbourg, France

SUN
6
1993 - Women for a Nuclear Test Ban climb over wall, Buckingham Palace, London, Britain

July

And in the intervals between campaigns, he washes the blood off his hands and works for the universal brotherhood of man, with his mouth.
Mark Twain, from *The Damned Human Race*

WEEK 28

MON

7

2005 - 52 killed in 4 suicide bombing attacks on public transport, London, Britain

TUE

8

1990 - Indian Army takes direct control of Kashmir

WED

9

1955 - Russell-Einstein Manifesto on danger of nuclear war published, London

THU
10
1875 - Edmund Dene Morel, British parliamentarian for peace, born, Paris, France

FRI
11
1995 - Bosnian Serb army captures UN safe area, enabling week-long massacre of 8000 Muslim boys & men, Srebrenica, Bosnia

SAT
12
2005 - 4 killed by suicide bomber, Israeli shopping mall, Tulkarm, West Bank, Palestine

DAY OF COMMEMORATION (IRE)

SUN
13
1925 - French troops begin evacuation of Rhineland, Germany

July

The world is run by brutal men and the surest proof is their armies. If they ask you to stand still, you should dance. If they ask you to burn the flag, wave it. If they ask you to murder, re-create.
Colum McCann

WEEK 29

MON

14

BATTLE OF THE BOYNE
OBSERVED
(HOL NI)

1995 - Massacre of Muslims by Serbs begins, Srebrenica, Bosnia

TUE

15

1955 - 52 Nobel laureates call on all states to renounce force as act of policy, Mainau, W Germany

WED

16

1945 - First nuclear bomb test, "Trinity", Alamogordo, New Mexico, USA

THU
17
2014 - All 298 on board killed as Malaysian airliner is shot down over Donetsk Oblast, Ukraine

FRI
18
1865 - Laurence Housman, pacifist writer, born, Britain

SAT
19
1990 - Iraqi troops start massing on border with Kuwait

SUN
20
1945 - Benjamin Britten hosts "foodless lunch" to publicise hungry in Europe, London, Britain

July

Forget politician-speak about Britain being a tolerant country. Being constantly looked at like an alien in the country you were born in requires true tolerance.

Reni-Eddo Lodge, in *Why I'm No Longer Talking to White People About Race*

WEEK 30

MON
21
1956 - Military conscription re-introduced, W Germany

TUE
22
2005 - Senior police authorise shooting dead (with 7 bullets) unarmed man going to work, Stockwell station, London, Britain

WED
23
1955 - Summit Conference – France, UK, USA, USSR – fails to agree on final German settlement, Geneva, Switzerland

THU
24
1965 - 200 demonstrate against white-only S African test cricket team, Lord's, Middlesex, England

FRI
25
1995 - 7 killed by bomb on Metro, Paris, France

SAT
26
1982 - First World Assembly on Ageing, Vienna, Austria

SUN
27
1955 - Reversion from 4-Power occupation to sovereign state, Austria

July/August

Were the ironies of taxation any better: raising money for schools and hospitals and roads and bridges, and spending it on blowing up schools and hospitals and roads and bridges in self-defeating wars?

Edward St Aubyn

WEEK 31

MON
28
1915 - After revolution previous day, US marines invade Haiti

TUE
29
1920 - No More War demonstrations by disabled veterans, Germany

WED
30
1955 - Military conscription introduced, China

THU
31
1914 - Armies mobilised by Austria-Hungary, Germany and France

FRI
1
1975 - East-West Confidence-Building Measures signed, Helsinki, Finland

SAT
2
1914 - Germany occupies Luxembourg; Russia invades Germany

SUN
3
1914 - War declared on France by Germany

August

I don't believe in carrying a weapon. If somebody wants to shoot me, he'll have to bring his own gun.
Kinky Friedman

WEEK 32
(HOL SCOT/IRE/CAN)

MON
4

1985 - Peace Ribbon made by thousands wrapped around Pentagon, Washington DC, USA

TUE
5

1914 - War declared on Austria-Hungary by Montenegro

WED

HIROSHIMA DAY

6

1945 - Atomic bomb dropped by Allies on Hiroshima, Japan

THU
7
1990 - US troops land, against possible Iraqi invasion, Saudi Arabia

FRI
8
1945 - War declared on Japan by USSR

○ NAGASAKI DAY

SAT
9
1945 - Atomic bomb dropped by Allies on Nagasaki, Japan

SUN
10
2024 - Bradford Peace Museum reopened, Salts Mill, Saltaire, Britain

August

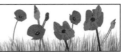

There is nothing in which the birds differ more from man than the way in which they can build and yet leave a landscape as it was before.
Robert Lynd

WEEK 33

MON

11

1980 - Second Review Conference of Nuclear Non-Proliferation Treaty opens, Geneva, Switzerland

TUE

12

1945 - USSR occupies Kurile Islands, Japan

WED

13

1890 - Stuart Morris, pacifist activist, born, Britain

THU
14
1815 - Peace Society founded, New York, USA

FRI
15
1995 - Death of Humphrey Moore, founding editor of *Peace News*, Britain

SAT
16
1945 - Treaty demarcating new Soviet-Polish frontier signed by USSR and Poland

SUN
17
1875 - Kurt Hiller, co-founder of Revolutionary Pacifists, born, Germany

August

What is hateful to you, do not do to your neighbour. This is the whole Torah; all the rest is commentary.
Hillel the Elder

WEEK 34

MON

18

1990 - UN Security Council demands freeing of detainees by Iraq

TUE

19

1990 - Western nationals taken from Kuwait are forced to serve as "human shields" at military bases, Iraq

WED

20

1915 - War declared on Turkey by Italy

THU
21
1965 - Demonstration against white-only S African test cricket team, Edgbaston, Warwickshire, England

INT'L DAY FOR VICTIMS OF VIOLENCE BASED ON RELIGION OR BELIEF

FRI
22
1915 - David Dellinger, pacifist activist, born, Wakefield, Massachusetts, USA

SAT
23
1995 - Senate condemns French and Chinese nuclear tests, Australia

SUN
24
1945 - Death of Alfred Salter, pacifist parliamentarian, Britain

August

I went into the British Army believing that if you want peace you must prepare for war. I believe now that if you prepare thoroughly and efficiently for war, you get war.
Sir John Frederick Maurice

WEEK 35
(HOL E/W/NI)

MON
25
1990 - UN Security Council declares embargo against Iraq

TUE
26
1985 - Death by accident of Samantha Smith, child peace envoy, USA

WED
27
1945 - Letter from Victor Gollancz in *News Chronicle* launches Save Europe Now, Britain

THU
28
1955 - Death of Devere Allen, journalist for peace, USA

FRI
29
1945 - Death of W G Dugan, CO volunteer for infantile paralysis experiments, Yale Medical School, USA

SAT
30
1915 - Under pressure from USA, warships ordered to warn passenger vessels before sinking them, Germany

SUN
31
1925 - US marines end 10-year occupation of Haiti

September

Establishing lasting peace is the work of education; all politics can do is keep us out of war.
Maria Tecla Artemisia Montessori

WEEK 36

MON

LABOUR DAY
(HOL CAN/US)

1

1965 - China purports to incorporate Tibet

TUE

2

1945 - Formal Japanese surrender marks end of WW2, USS Missouri, Tokyo Bay, Japan

WED

3

1990 - Second UN Conference on Less Developed Countries

THU
4
1965 - Death of Albert Schweitzer, Nobel Peace laureate, Lambarene, Gabon

FRI
5
1905 - Peace treaty signed between Russia and Japan, Portsmouth, USA

SAT
6
1915 - Military alliances with Germany and Turkey signed by Bulgaria

SUN
7
1985 - 52 killed as guerillas shoot down airliner, Kandahar, Afghanistan

September

Don't worry about the world coming to an end today. It's already tomorrow in Australia.
Charles M Schulz

WEEK 37

MON

8

1915 - 20 killed in Zeppelin raid on London, Britain

TUE

9

1995 - Demobilisation of army's civilian auxiliary announced, Guatemala

WED

10

1974 - Police dawn raids on homes of pacifists who communicated with soldiers, Britain

THU
11
1895 - Vinoba Bhave, Gandhian disciple and land reformer, born, India

FRI
12
1990 - 4 Allies-2 Germanies peace treaty signed – penultimate step before end of WW2 – Moscow, USSR

SAT
13
1935 - 5000 at rally on Peace & Sanctions, Central Hall, Westminster, Britain

SUN
14
2005 - Protest at Defence Systems & Equipment International arms fair, London, Britain

September

Kate: *Well, for someone who has nothing nice to say about lawyers, you certainly have plenty of them around.*
Larry: *They're like nuclear warheads. They have theirs, so I have mine. Once you use 'em, they fuck everything up.*

"Larry the Liquidator", from the film *Other People's Money*, May 2014

WEEK 38

MON

15

1935 - Hitler announces Nuremberg Laws to deprive Jews of civil rights, Germany

TUE

16

1955 - Military-led uprising, Cordoba, Argentina

WED

17

1978 - Egypt and Israel agree framework for peace, Camp David, USA

THU
18
1970 - Vietnam Moratorium rallies countrywide, Australia

FRI
19
1985 - Government announces 270m purchase of British military equipment, Amman, Jordan

SAT
20
1995 - French nuclear tests condemned by European Parliament

● UN INT'L DAY OF PEACE
INT'L DAY OF PRAYER FOR PEACE

SUN
21
1974 - Inaugural meeting of Campaign Against Arms Trade, Britain

September

In the wake of 9/11, we were desperate to bring those responsible for the brutal attacks to justice. But even that urgency did not justify torture.
Dianne Feinstein

WEEK 39

MON
22

EQUINOX
ROSH HASHANAH
(JEWISH NEW YEAR 5786)

1985 - Premier admits 11 July sinking of Greenpeace ship *Rainbow Warrior* in New Zealand was by French agents, Paris, France

TUE
23

1915 - Army mobilised, Greece

WED
24

1985 - Wojciech Jankowski resists conscription – later gaoled 3 years – Gdansk, Poland

THU
25
1555 - Peace of Religion signed, Augsburg, Germany

INT'L DAY FOR TOTAL ELIMINATION OF NUCLEAR WEAPONS

FRI
26
1815 - Holy Alliance for control of Europe formed between Austria, Prussia & Russia

SAT
27
2023 - Pat Arrowsmith, pacifist, feminist and direct actionist anti-war campaigner, died, Britain

SUN
28
1995 - Accord intended to end Israeli occupation of West Bank signed by PLO and Israel

September/October

War is a quarrel between two thieves too cowardly to fight their own battle; therefore they take boys from one village and another village, stick them into uniforms, equip them with guns, and let them loose like wild beasts against each other.

Attributed to Thomas Carlyle by Emma Goldman

WEEK 40

MON
29
1975 - Trial begins of BWNIC 14 for incitement of troops to disaffection, Old Bailey, London, Britain

TUE
30
1915 - WILPF section founded, Britain

◐
NATIONAL DAY FOR TRUTH
AND RECONCILIATION
(HOL CAN)

WED
1
1925 - Anti-Kriegs Museum, first museum for peace, founded by Ernst Friedrich, Berlin, Germany

INT'L DAY OF NONVIOLENCE

THU
2
1995 - Thousands rally for withdrawal of US troops, Okinawa, Japan

FRI
3
1935 - From colonial Eritrea, Italy invades Abyssinia

SAT
4
1944 - Army officer William Douglas-Home gaoled 1 year for refusing to attack Le Havre, France

SUN
5
1915 - In support of Serbia, Allies land at Salonika, neutral Greece

October

I am a negro of the African race, born in Jamaica ... My country is divided up among the European Powers (now fighting against each other) who in turn have oppressed and tyrannised over my fellow-men. ... In view of these circumstances, and also the fact that I have a moral objection to all wars, I would sacrifice my rights rather than fight ...

Isaac Hall's court martial statement

WEEK 41

MON
6
1915 - Declaration of support for Central Powers by Bulgaria

TUE
7
1915 - Austria-Hungary invades Serbia

WED
8
1895 - Sydney Silverman, WWI CO and successful campaigner against death penalty, born, Britain

THU
9
1964 - "Letter to a soldier" inviting conscientious objection, published, Hampstead Committee of 100, London, Britain

FRI
10
1964 - Programme for Peace & International Co-operation agreed by non-aligned states, Cairo, Egypt

SAT
11
1940 - Campaign of individual satyagraha begins, India

SUN
12
1915 - Edith Cavell, British nurse, shot by German firing squad, Brussels, Belgium

October

I was more of a stranger to my daughter and son than any stranger and I missed out on the best years of my life and what went will never come back. But I am sure that the world without freedom, equality and peace is not worth living or even watching.

Nages Mohamedi (Nobel Peace Laureate, imprisoned in Iran)

WEEK 42

MON
13
1915 - 41 killed in Zeppelin raid on London, Britain

THANKSGIVING (CAN)
COLUMBUS DAY (US)
(HOL CAN/US)

TUE
14
1915 - War declared against Bulgaria by Britain

WED
15
1965 - Envoys from Hague International Congress of Women to Governments of Europe & USA issue Manifesto, New York, USA

THU
16
1940 - "Day of National Mourning" for loss of freedom by conscription, USA

FRI
17
1910 - Death of Julia Ward Howe, feminist pacifist, Oak Glen, Rhode Island, USA

SAT
18
1895 - Brotherhood of the Co-operative Commonwealth founded, Warren, Maine, USA

SUN
19
1923 - War Resisters League founded, USA

October

"Look", said the old soldier.
"This War Memorial is necessary,
It reminds us that people have died for our country."
"Look", said the old pacifist,
"This peace garden is unnecessary but
It reminds us that people want to live for our country."

Benjamin Zephaniah

WEEK 43

MON
20
1990 - Rallies against Gulf War in 22 cities, USA

TUE
21
1995 - 85,000 rally for withdrawal of US bases, Okinawa, Japan

WED
22
1960 - Inaugural meeting of Committee of 100, Britain

THU
23
1945 - Death of Pierre Ceresole, founder of IVS/SCI, Switzerland

UNITED NATIONS DAY

FRI
24
1945 - United Nations Charter comes into force

SAT
25
1945 - Peace Council established, Norway

BST ENDS

SUN
26
1945 - Laurence Housman opens Housmans Bookshop, Shaftesbury Avenue, London, Britain

October/November

INTERNATIONAL DISARMAMENT WEEK 24–30 OCTOBER
Called for in the Final Document of the Tenth UN Special Session on
Disarmament in 1978, Disarmament Week is a time for pressing
governments and arms manufacturers on the urgent need for
disarmament of all kinds weapons.

Contact: Your nearest national UNA (see World Peace Directory)

WEEK 44

MON
(HOL IRE)

27

1995 - Third in new series of French nuclear tests, Mururoa Atoll, Pacific

TUE

28

1945 - People's Peace Crusade launched by PPU, Britain

WED

29

1765 - Delegates from 9 colonies at Stamp Act Congress draw up declaration of rights and liberties, New York City, British N America

THU
30
1910 - Death of Henry Dunant, founder of Red Cross, Heiden, Switzerland

FRI
31
1950 - United Nations Children's' Fund (UNICEF) established

SAT
1
1975 - British doctor Sheila Cassidy arrested and held while tortured, Chile

SUN
2
1965 - Norman Morrison immolates himself for peace in Vietnam, Pentagon, Washington DC, USA

November

It is clearly no function of a Peace Diary to exclude, by implication, "Guilty Children Victims of Defence" – children have no place in war either as participants or victims.

Bill Hetherington, when "correcting" the title of the UN's "International Day of Innocent Children Victims of Aggression" to this publication's preferred designation, the International Day for Children as Victims of War.

WEEK 45

MON

3

1945 - Death of D A Crowe, pacifist surgeon, Britain

TUE

4

1995 - Death of Paul Eddington, pacifist "Prime Minister", Britain

WED   ○

5

2023 - Bill Hetherington, pacifist activist, without whom the *Peace Diary* wouldn't still exist, died, Sheffield, Britain

THU
6
1950 - China allies with North in war in Korea

FRI
7
1945 - Death of Cecil Wilson, pacifist parliamentarian, Britain

SAT
8
1992 - 350,000 protest against racist violence, Berlin, Germany

REMEMBRANCE SUNDAY (UK)

SUN
9
1955 - Withdrawal from UN General Assembly by S Africa

November

I felt then, as I feel now, that the politicians who took us to war should have been given the guns and told to settle their differences themselves, instead of organising nothing better than legalised mass murder.
Harry Patch

WEEK 46

MON
10

WORLD SCIENCE DAY FOR
PEACE & DEVELOPMENT

1995 - Ken Saro-Wiwa & 8 other environmental activists hanged, Ogoniland, Nigeria

TUE
11

VETERANS' DAY (US)
REMEMBRANCE DAY (CAN)
(HOL CAN/US)

1925 - Dick Sheppard arranges memorial service to replace Victory Ball, Albert Hall, London, Britain

WED
12

1995 - 200,000 in "Enough death" rally, Tel Aviv, Israel

THU
13
1963 - 3 injured in spontaneous combustion of nuclear weapons components, Medina Base, Texas, USA

FRI
14
1965 - Russell Tribunal on Vietnam War opens, Sweden

SAT
15
2004 - Inquest jury finds conscript involved in 1953 nerve gas experiment unlawfully killed, Trowbridge, Wiltshire, Britain

SUN
16
1980 - National Peace Week begins, W Germany

November

An emigrant is a human being who commits suicide in the hope of coming back to life in a better reality.
Sami Michael

WEEK 47

MON

17

1980 - 115 arrested in Women's Pentagon Action, Washington DC, USA

TUE

18

1982 - Alternative service for COs increased from 16 to 20 months, W Germany

WED

19

1995 - 300 in day-long hunger strike against US Bases, Okinawa, Japan

UNIVERSAL CHILDREN'S DAY

THU

20

1975 - Death of Francisco Franco brings restoration of democracy, Spain

FRI

21

1995 - Balkan leaders agree to end 43-month war in Bosnia

SAT

22

1965 - UN Development Programme set up

SUN

23

1972 - UNESCO World Heritage Treaty signed

November

One moment of darkness will not blind you forever.
Sophia Huang Xueqin (feminist activist, imprisoned in China)

WEEK 48

MON
24

1915 - Henry Ford announces chartering of Peace Ship *Oscar II* for diplomatic mission to Europe, New York City, USA

TUE
25

INT'L DAY FOR ELIMINATION OF VIOLENCE AGAINST WOMEN

1925 - 12 gaoled for incitement to mutiny, London, Britain

WED
26

1945 - "Save Europe from Starvation" rally, London, Britain

THANKSGIVING (US)
(HOL US)

THU
27
1915 - First convention of No-Conscription Fellowship, Britain

◐

FRI
28
1975 - UN World Food Programme reconstituted

SAT
29
2013 - Death of Howard Clark, British nonviolent activist and writer, Spain

ST ANDREW'S DAY

SUN
30
1934 - Mass lobby against Incitement to Disaffection Bill, Parliament, London, Britain

December

No one regrets more than I do that it has been necessary to punish the conscientious objectors. But it is obvious that unless something were done, consciences would develop to an abnormal degree.

Sir James Allen, First World War "Defence" Minister, New Zealand

WEEK 49

MON

1

PRISONERS FOR PEACE DAY
ST ANDREW'S DAY OBSERVED
(HOL SCOT)

1925 - Locarno Treaties, guaranteeing French/Belgian/German borders and demilitarised Rhineland, signed, London, Britain

TUE

2

2005 - 1000th US execution since 1976 restoration of capital punishment, N Carolina, USA

WED

3

1925 - After long deliberation, existing provisional Northern Ireland frontier confirmed by UK and Irish Free State

THU
4
1865 - Edith Cavell, for whom patriotism was not enough, born, Britain

FRI
5
1915 - 15,000 watch Henry Ford Peace Ship *Oscar II* sailing to Europe from Hoboken, New Jersey, USA

SAT
6
1979 - Report of Brandt Commission on North-South issues published

SUN
7
1975 - Indonesia invades East Timor

December

Dear Mr Andropov,
My name is Samantha Smith. I am ten years old. Congratulations on your new job. I have been worrying about Russia and the United States getting into a nuclear war. Are you going to vote to have a war or not? If you aren't please tell me how you are going to help to not have a war.
Samantha Smith (aged 10), writing to Soviet leader, 1982

WEEK 50

MON

8

1980 - John Lennon murdered, New York, USA

TUE

9

1975 - UN Declaration on Rights of the Disabled

WED

HUMAN RIGHTS DAY

10

1975 - 14 acquitted of "incitement to disaffection" of soldiers over Northern Ireland, London, Britain

THU
11
1932 - "No Force Declaration", renouncing force for settling differences, made by Britain, France, Germany & Italy

FRI
12
1991 - 200 reservists collectively leave Vukovar front and return to Kragujevac, Serbia

SAT
13
1995 - Current series of French nuclear tests condemned by UN General Assembly

SUN
14
1995 - Bosnia peace accord signed, Paris, France

December

*The place where we are right
is hard and trampled / like a yard.
But doubts and loves
dig up the world
like a mole, a plough
And a whisper will be heard in the place
where the ruined / house once stood.*

Yehuda Amichai

WEEK 51

MON

15

1815 - Convention of New England States recommends protection of citizens from possible draft, Hartford, Connecticut, USA

TUE

16

1955 - NATO agrees to equip forces with nuclear weapons

WED

17

2010 - In 1st sitting for 14 years, Advisory Committee on COs rejects navy medic's application for CO discharge, Britain

THU
18
1915 - Henry Ford Peace Ship *Oscar II* arrives, Oslo, Norway

FRI
19
1965 - Demonstrations against Vietnam War, worldwide

SAT
20
1990 - Reservist Yolanda Huet-Vaughan refuses orders for Gulf War, Kansas, USA

SOLSTICE

SUN
21
1965 - UN Convention on Elimination of Racial Discrimination adopted

December

*Don't ever be surprised
to see a rose shoulder up
among the ruins of the house:
This is how we survived.*

Mosab Abu Toha

WEEK 52

MON
22
1965 - Henry House is first soldier court-martialled for protesting against Vietnam War, USA

TUE
23
1947 - President Harry Truman pardons 1523 out of 15,805 WW2 draft refusers, USA

WED
24
1990 - Gulf Peace Team sets up camp, Judayyidat Ar'ar, Iraq

THU 25

CHRISTMAS DAY
(HOL UK/IRE/CAN/US)

1875 - Jessie Wallace Hughan, co-founder of War Resisters League, born, USA

FRI 26

ST STEPHEN'S DAY
(HOL UK/IRE/CAN)

1970 - Anti-NATO street theatre outside Danish Embassy, London, Britain

SAT 27

◐

1815 - Peace Society founded, Massachusetts, USA

SUN 28

1915 - Government decides in principle to introduce military conscription, Britain

December/January

Ring out, wild bells, to the wild sky, …
Ring out false pride in place and blood,
The civic slander and the spite;
Ring in the love of truth and right,
Ring in the common love of good …
Ring out the thousand wars of old,
Ring in the thousand years of peace.

Alfred, Lord Tennyson

WEEK 1 (2026)

MON
29
1940 - Heavy German bombing raid on London, Britain

TUE
30
1985 - British government announces sending of 500 "spearhead" troops to N Ireland

WED
31
NEW YEAR'S EVE

1915 - Fellowship of Reconciliation section founded, USA

THU
1
2026 - Suggested dates (and quotations) for future diaries welcome anytime

FRI
2

SAT
3
○

SUN
4

Forward Planner 2026

	January		February		March	
Mon						
Tue						
Wed						
Thu	1	1				
Fri	2					
Sat	3					
Sun	4		1		1	
Mon	5	2	2	6	2	10
Tue	6		3		3	
Wed	7		4		4	
Thu	8		5		5	
Fri	9		6		6	
Sat	10		7		7	
Sun	11		8		8	
Mon	12	3	9	7	9	11
Tue	13		10		10	
Wed	14		11		11	
Thu	15		12		12	
Fri	16		13		13	
Sat	17		14		14	
Sun	18		15		15	
Mon	19	4	16	8	16	12
Tue	20		17		17	
Wed	21		18		18	
Thu	22		19		19	
Fri	23		20		20	
Sat	24		21		21	
Sun	25		22		22	
Mon	26	5	23	9	23	13
Tue	27		24		24	
Wed	28		25		25	
Thu	29		26		26	
Fri	30		27		27	
Sat	31		28		28	
Sun					29	
Mon					30	14
Tue					31	

Forward Planner 2026

	April		May		June	
Mon					1	23
Tue					2	
Wed	1				3	
Thu	2				4	
Fri	3		1		5	
Sat	4		2		6	
Sun	5	Easter	3		7	
Mon	6	15	4	19	8	24
Tue	7		5		9	
Wed	8		6		10	
Thu	9		7		11	
Fri	10		8		12	
Sat	11		9		13	
Sun	12		10		14	
Mon	13	16	11	20	15	25
Tue	14		12		16	
Wed	15		13		17	
Thu	16		14		18	
Fri	17		15		19	
Sat	18		16		20	
Sun	19		17		21	
Mon	20	17	18	21	22	26
Tue	21		19		23	
Wed	22		20		24	
Thu	23		21		25	
Fri	24		22		26	
Sat	25		23		27	
Sun	26		24		28	
Mon	27	18	25	22	29	27
Tue	28		26		30	
Wed	29		27			
Thu	30		28			
Fri			29			
Sat			30			
Sun			31			

Forward Planner 2026

	July		August		September	
Mon						
Tue					1	
Wed	1				2	
Thu	2				3	
Fri	3				4	
Sat	4		1		5	
Sun	5		2		6	
Mon	6	**28**	3	**32**	7	**37**
Tue	7		4		8	
Wed	8		5		9	
Thu	9		6		10	
Fri	10		7		11	
Sat	11		8		12	
Sun	12		9		13	
Mon	13	**29**	10	**33**	14	**38**
Tue	14		11		15	
Wed	15		12		16	
Thu	16		13		17	
Fri	17		14		18	
Sat	18		15		19	
Sun	19		16		20	
Mon	20	**30**	17	**34**	21	**39**
Tue	21		18		22	
Wed	22		19		23	
Thu	23		20		24	
Fri	24		21		25	
Sat	25		22		26	
Sun	26		23		27	
Mon	27	**31**	24	**35**	28	**40**
Tue	28		25		29	
Wed	29		26		30	
Thu	30		27			
Fri	31		28			
Sat			29			
Sun			30			
Mon			31	**36**		

Forward Planner 2026

	October		November		December	
Mon						
Tue					1	
Wed					2	
Thu	1				3	
Fri	2				4	
Sat	3				5	
Sun	4		1		6	
Mon	5	41	2	45	7	50
Tue	6		3		8	
Wed	7		4		9	
Thu	8		5		10	
Fri	9		6		11	
Sat	10		7		12	
Sun	11		8		13	
Mon	12	42	9	46	14	51
Tue	13		10		15	
Wed	14		11		16	
Thu	15		12		17	
Fri	16		13		18	
Sat	17		14		19	
Sun	18		15		20	
Mon	19	43	16	47	21	52
Tue	20		17		22	
Wed	21		18		23	
Thu	22		19		24	
Fri	23		20		25	
Sat	24		21		26	
Sun	25		22		27	
Mon	26	44	23	48	28	53
Tue	27		24		29	
Wed	28		25		30	
Thu	29		26		31	
Fri	30		27			
Sat	31		28			
Sun			29			
Mon			30	49		

Calendar 2024

JANUARY
MON 1 8 15 22 29
TUE 2 9 16 23 30
WED 3 10 17 24 31
THU 4 11 18 25
FRI 5 12 19 26
SAT 6 13 20 27
SUN 7 14 21 28

FEBRUARY
MON 5 12 19 26
TUE 6 13 20 27
WED 7 14 21 28
THU 1 8 15 22 29
FRI 2 9 16 23
SAT 3 10 17 24
SUN 4 11 18 25

MARCH
MON 4 11 18 25
TUE 5 12 19 26
WED 6 13 20 27
THU 7 14 21 28
FRI 1 8 15 22 29
SAT 2 9 16 23 30
SUN 3 10 17 24 31

APRIL
MON 1 8 15 22 29
TUE 2 9 16 23 30
WED 3 10 17 24
THU 4 11 18 25
FRI 5 12 19 26
SAT 6 13 20 27
SUN 7 14 21 28

MAY
MON 6 13 20 27
TUE 7 14 21 28
WED 1 8 15 22 29
THU 2 9 16 23 30
FRI 3 10 17 24 31
SAT 4 11 18 25
SUN 5 12 19 26

JUNE
MON 3 10 17 24
TUE 4 11 18 25
WED 5 12 19 26
THU 6 13 20 27
FRI 7 14 21 28
SAT 1 8 15 22 29
SUN 2 9 16 23 30

JULY
MON 1 8 15 22 29
TUE 2 9 16 23 30
WED 3 10 17 24 31
THU 4 11 18 25
FRI 5 12 19 26
SAT 6 13 20 27
SUN 7 14 21 28

AUGUST
MON 5 12 19 26
TUE 6 13 20 27
WED 7 14 21 28
THU 1 8 15 22 29
FRI 2 9 16 23 30
SAT 3 10 17 24 31
SUN 4 11 18 25

SEPTEMBER
MON 2 9 16 23
TUE 3 10 17 24
WED 4 11 18 25
THU 5 12 19 26
FRI 6 13 20 27
SAT 7 14 21 28
SUN 1 8 15 22 29

OCTOBER
MON 7 14 21 28
TUE 1 8 15 22 29
WED 2 9 16 23 30
THU 3 10 17 24 31
FRI 4 11 18 25
SAT 5 12 19 26
SUN 6 13 20 27

NOVEMBER
MON 4 11 18 25
TUE 5 12 19 26
WED 6 13 20 27
THU 7 14 21 28
FRI 1 8 15 22 29
SAT 2 9 16 23 30
SUN 3 10 17 24

DECEMBER
MON 2 9 16 23 30
TUE 3 10 17 24 31
WED 4 11 18 25
THU 5 12 19 26
FRI 6 13 20 27
SAT 7 14 21 28
SUN 1 8 15 22 29

Calendar 2025

JANUARY
- **MON** 6 13 20 27
- **TUE** 7 14 21 28
- **WED** 1 8 15 22 29
- **THU** 2 9 16 23 30
- **FRI** 3 10 17 24 31
- **SAT** 4 11 18 25
- **SUN** 5 12 19 26

FEBRUARY
- **MON** 3 10 17 24
- **TUE** 4 11 18 25
- **WED** 5 12 19 26
- **THU** 6 13 20 27
- **FRI** 7 14 21 28
- **SAT** 1 8 15 22
- **SUN** 2 9 16 23

MARCH
- **MON** 3 10 17 24 31
- **TUE** 4 11 18 25
- **WED** 5 12 19 26
- **THU** 6 13 20 27
- **FRI** 7 14 21 28
- **SAT** 1 8 15 22 29
- **SUN** 2 9 16 23 30

APRIL
- **MON** 7 14 21 28
- **TUE** 1 8 15 22 29
- **WED** 2 9 16 23 30
- **THU** 3 10 17 24
- **FRI** 4 11 18 25
- **SAT** 5 12 19 26
- **SUN** 6 13 20 27

MAY
- **MON** 5 12 19 26
- **TUE** 6 13 20 27
- **WED** 7 14 21 28
- **THU** 1 8 15 22 29
- **FRI** 2 9 16 23 30
- **SAT** 3 10 17 24 31
- **SUN** 4 11 18 25

JUNE
- **MON** 2 9 16 23 30
- **TUE** 3 10 17 24
- **WED** 4 11 18 25
- **THU** 5 12 19 26
- **FRI** 6 13 20 27
- **SAT** 7 14 21 28
- **SUN** 1 8 15 22 29

JULY
- **MON** 7 14 21 28
- **TUE** 1 8 15 22 29
- **WED** 2 9 16 23 30
- **THU** 3 10 17 24 31
- **FRI** 4 11 18 25
- **SAT** 5 12 19 26
- **SUN** 6 13 20 27

AUGUST
- **MON** 4 11 18 25
- **TUE** 5 12 19 26
- **WED** 6 13 20 27
- **THU** 7 14 21 28
- **FRI** 1 8 15 22 29
- **SAT** 2 9 16 23 30
- **SUN** 3 10 17 24 31

SEPTEMBER
- **MON** 1 8 15 22 29
- **TUE** 2 9 16 23 30
- **WED** 3 10 17 24
- **THU** 4 11 18 25
- **FRI** 5 12 19 26
- **SAT** 6 13 20 27
- **SUN** 7 14 21 28

OCTOBER
- **MON** 6 13 20 27
- **TUE** 7 14 21 28
- **WED** 1 8 15 22 29
- **THU** 2 9 16 23 30
- **FRI** 3 10 17 24 31
- **SAT** 4 11 18 25
- **SUN** 5 12 19 26

NOVEMBER
- **MON** 3 10 17 24
- **TUE** 4 11 18 25
- **WED** 5 12 19 26
- **THU** 6 13 20 27
- **FRI** 7 14 21 28
- **SAT** 1 8 15 22 29
- **SUN** 2 9 16 23 30

DECEMBER
- **MON** 1 8 15 22 29
- **TUE** 2 9 16 23 30
- **WED** 3 10 17 24 31
- **THU** 4 11 18 25
- **FRI** 5 12 19 26
- **SAT** 6 13 20 27
- **SUN** 7 14 21 28

Calendar 2026

JANUARY
- **MON** 5 12 19 26
- **TUE** 6 13 20 27
- **WED** 7 14 21 28
- **THU** 1 8 15 22 29
- **FRI** 2 9 16 23 30
- **SAT** 3 10 17 24 31
- **SUN** 4 11 18 25

FEBRUARY
- **MON** 2 9 16 23
- **TUE** 3 10 17 24
- **WED** 4 11 18 25
- **THU** 5 12 19 26
- **FRI** 6 13 20 27
- **SAT** 7 14 21 28
- **SUN** 1 8 15 22

MARCH
- **MON** 2 9 16 23 30
- **TUE** 3 10 17 24 31
- **WED** 4 11 18 25
- **THU** 5 12 19 26
- **FRI** 6 13 20 27
- **SAT** 7 14 21 28
- **SUN** 1 8 15 22 29

APRIL
- **MON** 6 13 20 27
- **TUE** 7 14 21 28
- **WED** 1 8 15 22 29
- **THU** 2 9 16 23 30
- **FRI** 3 10 17 24
- **SAT** 4 11 18 25
- **SUN** 5 12 19 26

MAY
- **MON** 4 11 18 25
- **TUE** 5 12 19 26
- **WED** 6 13 20 27
- **THU** 7 14 21 28
- **FRI** 1 8 15 22 29
- **SAT** 2 9 16 23 30
- **SUN** 3 10 17 24 31

JUNE
- **MON** 1 8 15 22 29
- **TUE** 2 9 16 23 30
- **WED** 3 10 17 24
- **THU** 4 11 18 25
- **FRI** 5 12 19 26
- **SAT** 6 13 20 27
- **SUN** 7 14 21 28

JULY
- **MON** 6 13 20 27
- **TUE** 7 14 21 28
- **WED** 1 8 15 22 29
- **THU** 2 9 16 23 30
- **FRI** 3 10 17 24 31
- **SAT** 4 11 18 25
- **SUN** 5 12 19 26

AUGUST
- **MON** 3 10 17 24 31
- **TUE** 4 11 18 25
- **WED** 5 12 19 26
- **THU** 6 13 20 27
- **FRI** 7 14 21 28
- **SAT** 1 8 15 22 29
- **SUN** 2 9 16 23 30

SEPTEMBER
- **MON** 7 14 21 28
- **TUE** 1 8 15 22 29
- **WED** 2 9 16 23 30
- **THU** 3 10 17 24
- **FRI** 4 11 18 25
- **SAT** 5 12 19 26
- **SUN** 6 13 20 27

OCTOBER
- **MON** 5 12 19 26
- **TUE** 6 13 20 27
- **WED** 7 14 21 28
- **THU** 1 8 15 22 29
- **FRI** 2 9 16 23 30
- **SAT** 3 10 17 24 31
- **SUN** 4 11 18 25

NOVEMBER
- **MON** 2 9 16 23 30
- **TUE** 3 10 17 24
- **WED** 4 11 18 25
- **THU** 5 12 19 26
- **FRI** 6 13 20 27
- **SAT** 7 14 21 28
- **SUN** 1 8 15 22 29

DECEMBER
- **MON** 7 14 21 28
- **TUE** 1 8 15 22 29
- **WED** 2 9 16 23 30
- **THU** 3 10 17 24 31
- **FRI** 4 11 18 25
- **SAT** 5 12 19 26
- **SUN** 6 13 20 27

HOUSMANS
World Peace Directory
● 2025 ●

This Directory is provided for the *Peace Diary* by the **Housmans Peace Resource Project**, and edited by Albert Beale. **To make the best use of it, please read the next two pages.**

There is a difficult balance to be struck between the usefulness, for many people, of the information in this format, and the fact that the full World Peace Database — from which this Directory is derived — is available on-line at **www.housmans.info/wpd**. Your feedback about this is encouraged.

Groups omitted from this printed version tend to be the more localised or specialised groups — and those which are least efficient at responding to communications from the database editor! The complete on-line information is searchable, and it is also possible to obtain your own copy of the full database.

To keep the database up to date, organisations are contacted from time to time by post, and also (where possible) by e-mail. But we rely on other input as well: if your group changes any of its contact details, please send the information without waiting to be asked. There is never a wrong time to send information.

This Directory is copyright © Housmans Peace Resource Project, 2024. Even where non-profit organisations are allowed to re-use sections of the Directory at nominal charge, permission must be obtained first.

Disclaimer: Organisations listed are not necessarily responsible for their inclusion, nor for the way they are described, nor for the terminology used to describe their country.

All correspondence about the Directory should be sent to: **Housmans Peace Resource Project, 5 Caledonian Road, London N1, UK** (tel +44-20-7278 4474; e-mail worldpeace@gn.apc.org). Information is preferred in writing.

Directory Introduction

This is the 72nd Peace Directory to be published with the Housmans Peace Diary. It is intended to help people find contact points for issues which interest them, and also to be a day-to-day reference resource for activists.

What's in the Directory?

The 2025 Directory lists over 1400 national and international organisations, covering the breadth of the peace movement – with the emphasis on grassroots, non-governmental groups – as well as major bodies in related fields such as environmental and human rights campaigning.

How to find things in the Directory

Check both the national and international listings if necessary. If you can't find exactly what you want, try a less specialised organisation which might include what you're looking for. (And see the previous page for the availability of further information.)

International organisations are listed alphabetically. The national listings are in alphabetical order of English-language country name; the organisations are then arranged alphabetically within each country. Organisations' names (and addresses) are generally in the language of the country concerned.

Whilst aware of political sensitivities, we use commonly accepted postal and administrative divisions of the world to decide what is or isn't a "country". This doesn't mean we support or oppose countries' divisions or mergers – we just want the Directory to be easy to use.

In the national listings we don't repeat the country name at the end of each address, so you will need to add it.

How the entries are set out

The organisation's name is in **bold print**; or, if the name is that of a magazine, in ***bold italics***. Any common abbreviation is shown [in square brackets], in **bold** or ***bold italics*** as appropriate. Most organisations then have codes (in round brackets) giving an indication of their politics and activities (**see Note 1**). The address is shown next. Then we give (in brackets) any telephone number (**see Note 2**), fax number (**see Note 3**), electronic mail address (**see Note 4**), and web site address (**see Note 4**). Magazines published by the organisation are then shown in *italics*. Where the listing is itself a publication, details of frequency etc may be given next (**see Note 5**). There may be brief additional information where necessary.

The **Notes**, including our standard abbreviations, are given opposite.

Notes

1. Codes used to explain something about the listed organisation are as follows. The codes for international bodies in the left-hand column are used to show an official link to tbe body (or to one of its national affiliates in the country concerned). If these are not sufficient, the general codes on the right are used.

   AI Amnesty International
   FE Friends of the Earth International
   FR International Fellowship of Reconciliation
   GP Greenpeace International
   IB International Peace Bureau
   IP International Physicians for the Prevention of Nuclear War
   PC Pax Christi International
   SC Service Civil International
   SE Servas International
   SF Society of Friends (Quakers)
   UN World Federation of United Nations Associations
   WL Women's International League for Peace and Freedom
   WP World Peace Council
   WR War Resisters' International

   AL Alternativist / Anarchist
   AT Arms Trade / Conversion
   CD Citizen Diplomacy / People-to-People
   CR Conflict Resolution / Mediation
   DA Disarmament / Arms Control
   EL Environmental / Ecological
   HR Equality / Minority & Human Rights
   ND Nuclear Disarmament
   PA Anti-Militarist / Pacifist
   PO Positive Action / Lifestyle
   RA Radical Action / Direct Action
   RE Research into Peace, Conflict / Peace Education
   RP Religious Peace Group
   SD Social Defence / Civilian-Based Defence
   TR War Tax Resistance / Peace Tax Campaigning
   TW Development / Liberation / Third World
   WC International Workcamps
   WF World Federalists / World Citizens

2. Telephone numbers are given in standard international format: +[country code]-[area code]-[local number]. The "+" indicates the international access code used in the country you're phoning from. The area code (if there is one) is given without any national trunk prefix digit(s) that are used in the country concerned – for calls *within* the country you must add them if they exist. Exceptionally, a few countries without area codes still require an extra digit (generally 0) at the start of their national number for internal calls; the main culprits are Belgium, France, Switzerland, South Africa and Thailand. Note that for calls between neighbouring countries there are often non-standard codes outside the normal system.

3. The telephone number of a facsimile (telefax) machine is given without repeating codes which are the same as in the preceding ordinary telephone number; "fax" alone means the fax number is identical to the phone number. Because many groups share a fax machine, always start your message by saying clearly which person and organisation it is meant for.

4. The e-mail and web site addresses are given in standard internet format. (The e-mail address is the one with the "@" in it.) The "http://" which, by definition, starts every web address is **not** repeated each time here.

5. Abbreviations used in connection with publications are:

dly daily	**x yrly** x per year	**ea** each
wkly weekly	**annl** annual	**pa** per annum
ftly fortnightly	**irreg** irregular	**ftm** free to members
mthly monthly	**occl** occasional	**nfp** no fixed price / donation

INTERNATIONAL ORGANISATIONS

Abolition 2000 International Secretariat (ND EL), c/o IPB, Marienstr 19/20, 10117 Berlin, Germany (+49-30-2065 4857) (secretariat@abolition2000.org) (www.abolition2000.org).
Global network to eliminate nuclear weapons.

Alliance Against Genocide (HR), c/o Genocide Watch, 1405 Cola Drive, McLean, VA 22101, USA (+1-202-643 1405) (communications@genocidewatch.org) (www.genocidewatch.com).
Formerly Alliance Against Genocide.

Alternatives to Violence Project International (CR), PO Box 164, Purchase, NY 10577, USA (avp.international).
International network of national AVP organisations. AVP groups organise training to aid creative responses to potentially violent situations.

Amnesty International - International Secretariat [AI] (HR RE), Peter Benenson House, 1 Easton St, London WC1X 0DW, Britain (+44-20-7413 5500) (fax 7956 1157) (contactus@amnesty.org) (www.amnesty.org).
Newsletter, *Annual Report*.
East Asia office (Hong Kong) +852-3963 7100; Southern Africa office (Johannesburg) +27-11-283 6000; Middle East and North Africa office (Beirut) +961-1-748751.

Arab Coalition Against the Death Penalty (HR), c/o Amman Center for Human Rights Studies, Al Abdali, Al Sharaf Building - 4th Floor, 212524 Amman, Jordan (+962-6-465 5043) (fax) (achrs@achrs.org) (achrs.org).

Architects & Planners for Justice in Palestine [APJP] (HR), c/o 100 Whitchurch Lane, Edgware, Middx HA8 6QN, Britain (info@apjp.org) (apjp.org).

Asian Legal Resource Centre [ALRC] (HR), G/F, 52 Princess Margaret Rd, Ho Man Tin, Kowloon, Hong Kong (+852-2698 6339) (fax 2698 6367) (alrc@alrc.asia) (alrc.asia).
Raises issues at regional and international fora, emphasising linkage between rule of law and human rights. Provides information for use by Asian Human Rights Commission.

Association of World Citizens [AWC] (WF CD RE), 60 Traverse des Passets, 07140 Gravières, France (rene.wadlow@gmail.com) (awcunited.com).

Association pour la Prévention de la Torture / Association for the Prevention of Torture [APT] (HR), BP 137, 1211 Genève 19, Switzerland (+41-22 919 2170) (fax 22 919 2180) (apt@apt.ch) (www.apt.ch).
Works to improve legal frameworks and detention monitoring, to prevent torture and other ill-treatment.

Bellona Foundation (EL), Vulkan 11, 0178 Oslo, Norway (+47-2323 4600) (fax 2238 3862) (info@bellona.no) (bellona.org).
Other international office in Brussels. Offices also in Russia (Murmansk and St Petersburg).

Center for Global Nonkilling [CGNK] (RE PA), 3653 Tantalus Dr, Honolulu, HI 96822-5033, USA (+1-808-536 7442) (info@nonkilling.org) (nonkilling.org).
To promote change towards the measurable goal of a killing-free world.

Child Rights International Network [CRIN] (HR), Unit 4, Old Paradise Yard, 20 Carlisle Lane, London SE1 7LG, Britain (info@crin.org) (home.crin.org).
Supports UN Convention on rights of children. Work includes opposing mutilation of children.

Church and Peace (SF FR PC), Mittelstr 4, 34474 Diemlstadt-Wethen, Germany (+49-5694-990 5506) (fax 1532) (IntlOffice@church-and-peace.org) (www.church-and-peace.org).
Theology and Peace / Théologie et Paix / Theologie und Frieden.
European ecumenical network.

Climate Action Network International [CAN] (EL), Khaldeh, Dakdouk Bldg - 3rd floor, Mount Lebanon, Lebanon (+961-1-447192) (fax 448649) (administration@climatenetwork.org) (www.climatenetwork.org).
Network of 1300 organisations in 120 countries.

Co-ordinating Committee for International Voluntary Service [CCIVS] (SC TW WC EL HR), UNESCO House, 1 rue Miollis, 75732 Paris Cedex 15, France (+33-14568 4936) (fax 14568 4934) (secretariat@ccivs.org) (www.ccivs.org).

Coalition for Peace in Africa / Coalition pour la Paix en Afrique [COPA] (CR RE), PO Box 61753, 00200 Nairobi, Kenya (+254-20-386 6686) (www.copafrica.org).

Coalition Mondiale Contre la Peine de Mort / World Coalition Against the Death Penalty [WCADP] (HR), 69 rue Michelet, 93100 Montreuil, France (+33-18089 4505) (fax 14870 2225) (contact@worldcoalition.org) (worldcoalition.org).

Discover Peace in Europe (CD RE), c/o Konfliktkultur, Breitenfeldergasse 2/14, 1080 Wien, Germany (office@discoverpeace.eu) (www.discoverpeace.eu).
Outdoor learning; Peace Trails.

Ecumenical Accompaniment Programme in Palestine and Israel [EAPPI] (RP HR CD

INTERNATIONAL ORGANISATIONS

CR SF), c/o World Council of Churches (Public Witness section), PO Box 2100, 1211 Genève 2, Switzerland (+41-22 791 6108) (fax 22 791 6122) (eappi@wcc-coe.org) (www.eappi.org).
Accompanying Palestinians and Israelis in non-violent actions; advocacy to end occupation. Also: PO Box 741, Jerusalem 91000 (+972-2-626 2458).

European Bureau for Conscientious Objection [EBCO] (WR SC), 35 Rue Van Elewyck, 1050 Bruxelles, Belgium (+32-2 648 5220) (ebco@ebco-beoc.org) (www.ebco-beoc.org).

European Institute of Peace [EIP] (RE), Rue des deux Églises 25, 1000 Bruxelles, Belgium (+32-2 430 7360) (info@eip.org) (www.eip.org).
Independent, "augmenting EU's peace agenda".

European Network Against Arms Trade [ENAAT] (AT), Anna Spenglerstr 71, 1054 NH Amsterdam, Netherlands (+31-20-616 4684) (info@stopwapenhandel.org) (www.enaat.org).

European Peacebuilding Liaison Office [EPLO] (RE), Ave de Tervueren 12, 1040 Bruxelles, Belgium (+32-2 233 3737) (office@eplo.org) (eplo.org).
Network of NGOs and others involved in peacebuilding work, promoting relevant policies at EU level.

Every Casualty (RE), 86-90 Paul St, London EC2A 4NE, Britain (team@everycasualty.org) (www.everycasualty.org).
Systematic documentation of conflict casualties. Aims to ensure that the full cost of conflict is known and can be understood.

Fédération Internationale de l'Action des Chrétiens pour l'Abolition de la Torture [FIACAT] (HR), 96 Boulevard de la Libération, 94300 Vincennes, France (+33-15864 1047) (fiacat@fiacat.org) (www.fiacat.org).
Also UN office, Geneva (fiacat.onu@fiacat.org).
EU office, Brussels (fiacat.europe@fiacat.org).

Fédération Internationale des Ligues des Droits de l'Homme [FIDH] (HR), 17 Passage de la Main d'Or, 75011 Paris, France (+33-14355 2518) (fax 14355 1880) (contact@fidh.org) (www.fidh.org).
International Federation of Human Rights Leagues.
At EU: +32-2 609 4423. At UN: +1-646-395 7103. At ICC: +31-70-356 0259.

Friends of the Earth International [FoEI] (EL), PO Box 19199, 1000 GD Amsterdam, Netherlands (+31-20-622 1369) (fax 639 2181) (www.foei.org).
Europe office in Brussels (+32-2 893 1000) (www.foeeurope.org).

Friends World Committee for Consultation [FWCC] (SF), 173 Euston Rd, London NW1, Britain (+44-20-7663 1199) (world@friendsworldoffice.org) (fwccworld.org).
Also 4 regional offices. Africa: PO Box 41946, Nairobi, Kenya; Americas: 1506 Race St, Philadelphia, PA 19102, USA; Asia & West Pacific: PO Box 6063, O'Connor, ACT 2602, Australia; Europe & Middle East: PO Box 1157, Histon CB24 9XQ, Cambs, Britain.

Gesellschaft für Bedrohte Völker - International (HR TW), Postfach 2024, 37010 Göttingen, Germany (+49-551-499060) (fax 58028) (info@gfbv.de) (www.gfbv.de). *Pogrom*.
Society for Threatened Peoples. Campaigns against genocide and ethnocide.

Global Anabaptist Peace Network (RP), c/o Mennonite World Conference, 50 Kent Ave - Suite 206, Kitchener, ON, N2G 3R1, Canada (+1-519-571 0060) (fax 226-647 4224) (Kitchener@mwc-cmm.org).

Global Campaign Against US/NATO Military Bases (ND CD), c/o Peace and Neutrality Alliance, 17 Castle St, Dalkey, Co Dublin, Ireland, Republic of (contact@noUSNATOBases.org) (nousnatobases.org).
Worldwide network.

Global Campaign on Military Spending - Co-ordination Office [GCOMS] (DA AT), c/o Centre Delàs d'Estudis per la Pau, c/ Erasme de Janer 8 - entresol - despatx 9, 08001 Barcelona, Spain (+34-93-441 1947) (coordination.gcoms@ipb.org) (demilitarize.org).
Organise Global Day of Action on Military Spending. A project of the International Peace Bureau; main IPB office in Berlin (+49-30-1208 4549).

Global Initiative to End All Corporal Punishment of Children (HR), The Foundry, 17 Oval Way, London SE11, Britain (+44-20-7713 0569) (info@endcorporalpunishment.org) (www.endcorporalpunishment.org).

Global Network Against Weapons and Nuclear Power in Space (PA EL RA), PO Box 652, Brunswick, ME 04011, USA (+1-207-607 4255) (globalnet@mindspring.com) (www.space4peace.org).

For explanation of codes and abbreviations, see introduction

INTERNATIONAL ORGANISATIONS

Global Partnership for the Prevention of Armed Conflict [GPPAC] (RE CR), Alexanderveld 5, 2585 DB Den Haag, Netherlands (+31-70-311 0970) (info@gppac.net) (www.gppac.net).

GRAIN (EL HR PO), Casanova 118 - escalera derecha 1ºB, 08036 Barcelona, Spain (+34-93-301 1381) (grain@grain.org) (grain.org). Supports small farmers and social movements in struggle for community-controlled and biodiversity-based food systems.

Greenpeace International (EL), Ottho Heldringstr 5, 1066 AZ Amsterdam, Netherlands (+31-20-718 2000) (fax 718 2002) (info.int@greenpeace.org) (www.greenpeace.org/international).

Housmans Peace Resource Project [HPRP] (CD RE), 5 Caledonian Rd, London N1, Britain (+44-20-7278 4474) (fax 7278 0444) (worldpeace@gn.apc.org) (www.housmans.info).
Housmans World Peace Database & Directory.

Human Rights in China [HRIC] (HR), 110 Wall St, New York, NY 10005, USA (+1-212-239 4495) (hrichina@hrichina.org) (www.hrichina.org). Hong Kong Office (+852-2710 8021) (hrichk@hrichina.org).

Human Rights Watch [HRW] (HR), Empire State Building - 34th Floor, 350 5th Ave, New York, NY 10118-3299, USA (+1-212-290 4700) (fax 736 1300) (www.hrw.org). EU liaison office in Brussels (+32-2 732 2009) (fax 2 732 0471). Offices also in: Britain, Canada, France, Germany, Netherlands, South Africa.

Humanists International (HR PO), The Foundry, 17 Oval Way, Vauxhall, London SE11 5RR, Britain (+44-20-3923 0244) (humanists.international). Formerly International Humanist and Ethical Union.

Institute for Economics and Peace (RE), 205 Pacific Hwy, St Leonards, Sydney, NSW 2065, Australia (+61-2-9901 8500) (info@economicsandpeace.org) (economicsandpeace.org). Office also in USA (+1-646-963 2160).

International Action Network on Small Arms [IANSA] (AT DA), 777 United Nations Plaza - 3E, Nww York, NY 10017, USA (communication@iansa.org) (www.iansa.org).

International Association of Lawyers Against Nuclear Arms [IALANA] (IB ND AT DA), Marienstr 19/20, 10117 Berlin, Germany (+49-30-2065 4857) (fax 2065 3837) (office@ialana.info) (www.ialana.info). UN office: c/o LCNP, +1-212-818 1861; Pacific office: +64-9-524 8403.

International Campaign for Boycott, Disinvestment and Sanctions Against Israel (HR RA), c/o PACBI, PO Box 1701, Ramallah, West Bank, Palestine (bdsmovement.net).

International Campaign to Abolish Nuclear Weapons [ICAN] (ND), 150 Route de Ferney, 1211 Genève 2, Switzerland (+41-22 788 2063) (info@icanw.org) (www.icanw.org). Asia Pacific office, Australia (+61-3-9023 1958).
Launched by IPPNW and others in 2007. Promotes implementation of nuclear ban treaty.

International Coalition to Ban Uranium Weapons [ICBUW] (AT DA), Marienstr 19-20, 10117 Berlin, Germany (+49-30-2065 4857) (info@icbuw.eu) (www.icbuw.eu).

International Fellowship of Reconciliation [IFOR] (RP IB), Postbus 1528, 3500 BM Utrecht, Netherlands (+31-30-303 9930) (office@ifor.org) (www.ifor.org).

International Friendship League [IFL] (CD), PO Box 217, Ross-in-Wye HR9 9FD, Britain (+44-1989-566745) (info@iflworld.org) (iflworld.org). *Courier.*

International Network of Engineers and Scientists for Global Responsibility [INES] (DA ND), Marienstr 19-20, 10117 Berlin, Germany (+49-30-3199 6686) (fax 3199 6689) (office@inesglobal.net) (www.inesglobal.net).

International Network of Museums for Peace [INMP] (IB RE), c/o Kyoto Museum for World Peace, 56-1 Toji-in Kitamachi, Kita, Kyoto 603-8577, Japan (inmpoffice@gmail.com) (tinyurl.com/INMPMuseumsForPeace). Worldwide network of peace museums, gardens, and other peace-related sites, centres and institutions, which share the desire to build a culture of peace.

International Network on Explosive Weapons [INEW] (DA), c/o Article 36, The Coalface - Runway East, 46 Clifton Terrace, London N4, Britain (www.inew.org). Works for prohibition of and restrictions on uses of explosive weapons in populated areas.

International Peace Bureau [IPB] (AT TW RE ND TR), Marienstr 19-20, 10117 Berlin, Germany (+49-30-1208 4549) (info@ipb-office.berlin) (www.ipb.org). *IPB News.*
Main programme: disarmament for development. Work includes Global Campaign on Military Spending. Most broadly-based international peace networking body. Also office in Geneva; and GCOMS co-ordination office in Barcelona.

INTERNATIONAL ORGANISATIONS

International Peace Institute [IPI] (RE DA CR), 777 United Nations Plaza, New York, NY 10017-3521, USA (+1-212-687 4300) (fax 983 8246) (ipi@ipinst.org) (www.ipinst.org).
Supports multilateral disarmament negotiations. Independent think-tank - "promoting the prevention and settlement of conflict".
Offices also in Austria and Bahrain.

International Peace Research Association [IPRA] (RE), c/o Risk and Conflict Network, Dept of Media & Communication Design, Northumbria University, Newcastle-upon-Tyne NE1 8ST, Britain (+44-191-227 3567) (info@iprapeace.org) (www.iprapeace.org).

International Physicians for the Prevention of Nuclear War [IPPNW] (ND RE TW), 339 Pleasant St - Third floor, Malden, MA 02148, USA (+1-617-440 1733) (ippnwbos@ippnw.org) (ippnw.org).

International Tibet Network (HR), 1310 Fillmore St - Suite 401, San Francisco, CA 94115, USA (+1-988-225 5516) (mail@tibetnetwork.org) (www.tibetnetwork.org).
Links 180 groups around the world. Local Tibet support groups also via www.tibet.org.

Interpeace (CR), 2E Chemin Eugène-Rigot, 1202 Genève, Switzerland (+41-22 404 5900) (fax 22 404 5901) (info@interpeace.org) (www.interpeace.org).
Set up by UN; now independent peacebuilding group. Supports societies to build lasting peace.
Regional offices: Nairobi, Abidjan, Guatemala City, New York, Brussels.

Mayors for Peace (CD ND DA), c/o Hiroshima Peace Culture Foundation, 1-5 Nakajima-cho, Naka-ku, Hiroshima 730-0811, Japan (+81-82-242 7821) (fax 242 7452) (mayorcon@pcf.city.hiroshima.jp) (www.mayorsforpeace.org).
Mayors for Peace Newsletter.

Middle East Treaty Organisation [METO] (ND CD), 62 Traps Lane, New Malden KT3 4SE, Britain (meto@wmd-free.me) (www.wmd-free.me).
Civil society network. Seeks to rid Middle East of weapons of mass destruction.

NATO Watch (DA ND RE), The Bothy, 29 Erradale, Gairloch IV21 2DS, Britain (+44-1445 771086) (idavis@natowatch.org) (natowatch.org).
Observatory.
Collates information about NATO. Provides regular briefings.

Network for Religious and Traditional Peacemakers (RP), c/o Finn Church Aid, PO Box 210, 00131 Helsinki, Finland (www.peacemakersnetwork.org).

Network of European Peace Scientists [NEPS], c/o Arzu Kibris, Rm E2.08, University of Warwick, Coventry CV4 7AL, Britain (info@europeanpeacescientists.org) (www.europeanpeacescientists.org).

No First Use Global (ND), c/o Prague Vision, Ostrovského 253/3 - Suite 4061, 15000 Praha 5, Czech Republic (info@nofirstuse.global) (www.nofirstuse.global).
Coalition for adoption of no-first-use policy by nuclear-armed states.

No to War - No to NATO / Na i Ryfel! - Na i NATO / Não à Guerra - Não à NATO (RA DA ND), c/o IALANA, Marienstr 19-20, 10117 Berlin, Germany (+41-30-2065 4857) (fax 2065 3837) (info@no-to-nato.org) (www.no-to-nato.org).
International network to delegitimise NATO. Co-ordination of groups in many NATO states; organises actions against NATO events. Also c/o Arielle Denis, Mouvement de la Paix, in France (Arielle.Denis@mvtpaix.org).

Nonviolence International (IB PA), PO Box 39127, Friendship Station NW, Washington, DC 20016, USA (+1-202-244 0951) (info@nonviolenceinternational.net) (www.nonviolenceinternational.net).
Links resource centres promoting use of nonviolent action.

Nonviolent Peaceforce [NP] (CR HR), Rue de Lausanne 81, 1202 Genève, Switzerland (+41-22-552 6610) (headoffice@nonviolentpeaceforce.org) (www.nonviolentpeaceforce.org).
Office in USA (+1-612-871 0005).

Northeast Asia Regional Peacebuilding Institute [NARPI] (RE CR), 25 Goongchon-ro, Wabu-eup, Namyangju-si, Gyeonggi-do 12669, Korea, South (+82-70-8817 8690) (fax -31-521 8695) (admin@narpi.net) (narpi.net).

Organisation for the Prohibition of Chemical Weapons [OPCW] (DA), Johan de Wittlaan 32, 2517 JR Den Haag, Netherlands (+31-70-416 3300) (fax 360 3535) (public.affairs@opcw.org) (www.opcw.org).

Orthodox Peace Fellowship [OPF] (FR), Kanisstr 5, 1811 GJ Alkmaar, Netherlands (+31-72-515 4180) (office@incommunion.org) (incommunion.org).
In Communion.

For explanation of codes and abbreviations, see introduction

INTERNATIONAL ORGANISATIONS

Palestinian Return Centre [PRC] (HR), 100 H Crown House, 60 North Circular Rd, London NW10 7PN, Britain (+44-20-8453 0919) (fax 8453 0994) (info@prc.org.uk) (www.prc.org.uk).

Parliamentarians for Nuclear Non-proliferation and Disarmament [PNND] (ND), c/o Prague Vision Institute for Sustainable Security, Lipanská 4, 13000 Praha 3, Czech Republic (+420-773 638867) (alyn@pnnd.org) (pnnd.org).
Europe office, Basel; UN office, New York. Also London office.
Provides parliamentarians with information on nuclear weapons policies; helps them become engaged in nuclear non-proliferation and disarmament.

Pax Christi International (RP IB CD RE CR), Ave de la Reine 141, 1030 Bruxelles, Belgium (+32-2 502 5550) (fax 2 502 4626) (hello@paxchristi.net) (www.paxchristi.net).
Network of autonomous organisations - Catholic.

Peace Brigades International / Brigadas Internacionales de Paz / Brigades de Paix Internationales [PBI] (HR CD CR RE), Village Partenaire, Rue de Fernard Bernier 15, 1060 Bruxelles, Belgium (+32 2 543 4443) (admin@peacebrigades.org) (www.peacebrigades.org).
Projects in Colombia, Guatemala, Mexico, Honduras, Kenya, Indonesia.

Peace Research Institute Oslo / Institutt for Fredsforskning [PRIO] (RE CR), PO Box 9229, Grønland, 0134 Oslo, Norway (+47-2254 7700) (fax 2254 7701) (info@prio.no) (www.prio.no).
Journal of Peace Research; *Security Dialogue*. Journals from: SAGE Publications, 6 Bonhill St, London EC2, Britain (+44-20-7374 0645).

Peacebuilding Support Office of the United Nations (CR RE), UN Secretariat - 30th Floor, New York, NY 10017, USA (+1-212-963 9999) (www.un.org/en/peacebuilding). Formerly United Nations Peacebuilding Commission.

PEN International (HR), Unit A, Koops Mill Mews, 162-164 Abbey St, London SE1 2AN, Britain (+44-20-7405 0338) (info@pen-international.org) (www.pen-international.org).
Includes Writers in Prison Committee, Writers for Peace Committee.

People to People International [PTPI] (CD), 2405 Grand Blvd - Suite 500, Kansas City, MO 64108, USA (+1-816-531 4701) (fax 561 7502) (ptpi@ptpi.org) (www.ptpi.org).

Principles for Peace [P4P] (RE), c/o Interpeace, Maison de la Paix, 2E Chemin Eugène-Rigot, 1201 Genève, Switzerland (+41-22-404 5900) (fax 404 5901) (principlesforpeace.org).
Bridging gap betweeen policy and action.

Privacy International (HR), 62 Britton St, London EC1, Britain (+44-20-3422 4321) (info@privacyinternational.org) (www.privacyinternational.org).
For data protection, and control of surveillance.

Pugwash Conferences on Science and World Affairs (ND EL RE TW), 1211 Connecticut Ave NW - Suite 800, Washington, DC 20036, USA (+1-202-478 3440) (pugwashdc@aol.com) (pugwash.org).
Offices also in Rome (+39-06-687 8376), Geneva (+41-22 907 3667), London (+44-20-7405 6661).

Quaker Council for European Affairs [QCEA] (SF HR PA EL AT), Square Ambiorix 50, 1000 Brussel, Belgium (+32-2 234 3061) (office@qcea.org) (www.qcea.org).

Quaker UN Office - Geneva [QUNO] (SF HR TW EL CR), 13 Av du Mervelet, 1209 Genève, Switzerland (+41-22 748 4800) (fax 22 748 4819) (quno@quno.ch) (www.quno.org).
Geneva Reporter.

Registry of World Citizens [WCR] (WF IB WP RE), Les Nids, 49190 St Aubin de Luigné, France (abc@recim.org) (www.recim.org).

Religions for Peace (RP IB RE CR TW), 777 United Nations Plaza, New York, NY 10017, USA (+1-212-687 2163) (fax 983 0098) (info@rfp.org) (religionsforpeace.org).
Formerly World Conference of Religions for Peace.
Regional offices in Asia, Europe, Latin America, Africa.

Resist China (HR), c/o International Tibet Network, 1310 Fillmore St, San Francisco, CA 94115, USA (campaigns@tibetnetwork.com) (resistchina.org).
Links campaigns resisting authoritarian regime. Works in relation to Tibet, Hong Kong, Uyghurs, Mongolian culture, threats to Taiwan.

Schengen Peace Foundation & World Peace Forum (RE), 14 rue Mathias Hardt, 1717 Luxembourg, Luxembourg (+352-223294) (info@worldpeaceforum.org) (www.worldpeaceforum.org).

School Day of Non-Violence and Peace / Día Escolar de la No-Violencia y la Paz [DENIP] (RE), Apdo Postal 77, 11510 Puerto

INTERNATIONAL ORGANISATIONS

Real, Spain (denip.pax@gmail.com) (denip.webcindario.com). (30 January, anniversary of Mahatma Gandhi's death).

Science4Peace [S4P] (CD RE DA), c/o Dr Hannes Jung, DESY - Bldg 01B/EG.213, Notkestr 85, 22603 Hamburg, Germany (+49-40-8998 3741) (fax 8994 3741) (hannes.jung@desy.de).

Sea Shepherd (EL RA), PO Box 8628, Alexadria, VA 22306, USA (+1-818-736 8357) (fax -360-370 5651) (info@seashepherd.org) (seashepherd.org). Nature conservation on the high seas. Use direct action to confront those attacking the ecosystem.

Search for Common Ground - Brussels Office (RE CD CR), Rue Belliard 205 - bte 13, 1040 Bruxelles, Belgium (+32-2 736 7262) (fax 2 732 3033) (brussels@sfcg.org) (www.sfcg.org). Conflict transformation projects in 34 countries.
Washington DC Office (+1-202-265 4300); West Africa Office, Freetown (+232-22-223479).

Servas International [SI] (CD PO), c/o Jonny Sågänger, Reimersholmsgatan 47 - plan 2, 11740 Stockholm, Sweden (helpdesk@servas.org) (www.servas.org). World hospitality network for peace and goodwill. Building understanding by facilitating personal contacts between people of different nationalities.

Service Civil International - International Office [SCI] (WC PA TW PO HR), Belgiëlei 37, 2018 Antwerpen, Belgium (+32-3 226 5727) (info@sciint.org) (sci.ngo).

Service International pour les Droits de l'Homme / International Service for Human Rights (HR), CP 16, 1211 Genève 20, Switzerland (+41-22 919 7100) (information@ishr.ch) (www.ishr.ch). Runs project to protect human rights defenders.
Also New York office (+1-212-490 2199) (information.ny@ishr.ch).

Stay Grounded (EL), c/o Periskop, Neustiftgasse 36, 1070 Wien, Austria (info@stay-grounded.org) (stay-grounded.org). Campaigns for elimination of most aviation. For transition to mobility justice.

Stockholm International Peace Research Institute [SIPRI] (RE), Signalistgatan 9, 16972 Solna, Sweden (+46-8-655 9700) (sipri@sipri.org) (www.sipri.org). *SIPRI Yearbook.*

Stop the War in Ukraine (DA CR), c/o CND, 162 Holloway Rd, London N7 8DQ, Britain (www.peaceinukraine.org). International network. Opposing both Russian invasion and NATO expansion. Supporting ceasefire and negotiations rather than any "victory".

Third World Network [TWN] (TW), 131 Jalan Macalister, 10400 Penang, Malaysia (+60-4-226 6728) (fax 226 4505) (twn@twnetwork.org) (www.twn.my). *Third World Resurgence; Third World Network Features.*
Latin America Secretariat: ITEM, Av 18 de Julio 2095/301, Montevideo 11200, Uruguay. Africa Secretariat: 9 Ollenu St, PO Box AN 19452, Accra-North, Ghana (fax +233-21-511188).
Also publishes *South-North Development Monitor* (SUNS).

Transnational Institute [TNI] (HR ND RE TW EL), PO Box 14656, 1001 LD Amsterdam, Netherlands (+31-20-662 6608) (fax 675 7176) (tni@tni.org) (www.tni.org). *Transnational Institute Series.*
Research in support of social movements.

UN Non-Governmental Liaison Service (New York Office) [UN-NGLS] (EL HR PO TW), Room DC1-1106, United Nations, New York, NY 10017, USA (+1-212-963 3125) (fax 963 8712) (info@un-ngls.org) (www.un-ngls.org).

UN Research Institute for Social Development [UNRISD] (HR TW EL), Palais des Nations, 1211 Genève 10, Switzerland (+41-22 917 3020) (fax 22 917 0650) (info.unrisd@un.org) (www.unrisd.org). *UNRISD News.*
Research on social dimensions of problems affecting development. Research programmes include: Social Policy and Development; Sustainable Development; Gender and Development.

Unfold Zero (ND), c/o Basel Peace Office, University of Basel, Petersgraben 27, 4051 Basel, Switzerland (info@unfoldzero.org) (www.unfoldzero.org).
Network for nuclear weapons abolition. Focus on action through UN system. Joint project of various disarmament campaigns.

UNICEF, 3 United Nations Plaza, New York, NY 10017, USA (+1-212-326 7000) (fax 887 7465) (aaltamirano@unicef.org) (www.unicef.org).

United Nations Department for Disarmament Affairs (AT CR ND DA), UN Headquarters Bldg (Rm DN25-12), New York, NY 10017, USA (+1-212-963 1570) (fax 963 4066) (www.un.org/disarmament).

For explanation of codes and abbreviations, see introduction

INTERNATIONAL ORGANISATIONS

United Nations Institute for Disarmament Research [UNIDIR] (RE), Palais des Nations, 1211 Genève 10, Switzerland (+41-22 917 1141) (fax 22 917 0176) (unidir@un.org) (www.unidir.org).

Universala Esperanto-Asocio [UEA] (HR CD PO), Nieuwe Binnenweg 176, 3015 BJ Rotterdam, Netherlands (+31-10-436 1044) (fax 436 1751) (uea@co.uea.org) (www.uea.org).
Esperanto; *Kontakto*.

Unrepresented Nations and Peoples Organization [UNPO] (HR CR EL), Rue du Pépin 54, Bruxelles 1000, Belgium (+32-2 513 1459) (unpo@unpo.org) (unpo.org).

War Resisters' International [WRI] (PA RA HR TR CR), 5 Caledonian Rd, London N1 9DX, Britain (+44-20-7278 4040) (info@wri-irg.org) (wri-irg.org).
The Broken Rifle; *CO Update*; *War Profiteers News*.
Network of organisations of nonviolent activists, pacifists, conscientious objectors, etc.

Women's International League for Peace and Freedom [WILPF] (PA HR AT ND), CP 28, 1 rue de Varembé, 1211 Genève 20, Switzerland (+41-22 919 7080) (fax 22 919 7081) (secretariat@wilpf.ch) (www.wilpf.org).
WILPF UN Office: 777 UN Plaza - 6th Floor, New York, NY 10017, USA (+1-212-682 1265) (fax 286 8211).
Projects of UN office include (www.peacewomen.org) and (www.reachingcriticalwill.org).

World Congress of Faiths (RP), 21 Maple St, London W1T 4BE, Britain (+44-1935-864055) (enquiries@worldfaiths.org) (www.worldfaiths.org).

World Federalist Movement - Institute for Global Polivy [WFM-IGP] (WF HR RE TW), 708 3rd Ave - Suite 1715, New York, NY 10017, USA (+1-212-599 1320) (fax 599 1332) (info@wfm-igp.org) (www.wfm-igp.org). Also: Bezuidenhoutseweg 99A, 2594 AC Den Haag, Netherlands (+31-70-363 4484).

World Federation of United Nations Associations / Fédération Mondiale des Associations pour les NU [WFUNA/FMANU] (TW HR), 1 United Nations Plaza - Room 0240, New York, NY 10017, USA (+1-212-963 5610) (info@wfuna.org) (wfuna.org).

World Future Council Foundation (WF EL), Dorotheenstr 15, 22301 Hamburg, Germany (+49-40-3070 91420) (fax 3070 91414) (info@worldfuturecouncil.org) (www.worldfuturecouncil.org).
Promotes sustainable future. Other offices: UN (Geneva) (+41-22 555 0950); UK (+44-20-3356 2771) (info.uk@worldfuturecouncil.org); China (+86-10-6500 8172) (info.china@worldfuturecouncil.org).

World Goodwill (RP PO), Suite 54, 3 Whitehall Court, London SW1A 2EF, Britain (+44-20-7839 4512) (fax 7839 5575) (worldgoodwill.uk@lucistrust.org) (www.worldgoodwill.org). *Newsletter*.
Also: Lucis Trust, Rue du Stand 40, 1204 Genève, Switzerland (geneva@lucistrust.org); 866 UN Plaza - Suite 482, New York, NY 10017, USA (worldgoodwill.us@lucistrust.org).

World Information Service on Energy [WISE] (EL ND RA), Postbus 59636, 1040 LC Amsterdam, Netherlands (+31-20-612 6368) (info@wiseinternational.org) (www.wiseinternational.org).
WISE/NIRS Nuclear Monitor.
Grassroots-oriented anti-nuclear information. Works with NIRS in USA.

World Orchestra for Peace [WOP] (CD UN PO), c/o Charles Kaye, 26 Lyndale Ave, London NW2 2QA, Britain (+44-20-7317 8433) (ckconsult19@gmail.com) (www.worldorchestraforpeace.com). Also tel +44-7967-108974. Established 1995. Designated UNESCO Artist for Peace in 2010.

World Peace Council / Consejo Mundial de la Paz [WPC] (ND TW), Othonos St 10, 10557 Athinai, Greece (+30-210 3316 326) (fax 210 3251 576) (wpc@otenet.gr) (www.wpc-in.org).

World Rainforest Movement (EL HR), Avenida General María Paz 1615 - Of 3, 11400 Montevideo, Uruguay (+598-2-605 6943) (fax) (wrm@wrm.org.uy) (wrm.org.uy).

World Service Authority [WSA] (WF HR PA CD), 5 Thomas Circle NW - Suite 300, Washington, DC 20005, USA (+1-202-638 2662) (fax 638 0638) (info@worldservice.org) (www.worldservice.org). *World Citizen News*.

World Student Christian Federation - Inter-Regional Office [WSCF] (TW RP HR), Ecumenical Centre, BP 2251, 1211 Genève 2, Switzerland (+41-22 791 6358) (fax 22 791 6221) (wscf@wscf.ch) (www.wscfglobal.org). *Federation News*; *Student World*.

Youth for Exchange and Understanding [YEU] (CD), Ave du Suffrage Universel 49, 1030 Bruxelles, Belgium (+32-2 649 2048) (fax) (info@yeu-international.org) (www.yeu-international.org).
Also Portugal office (+351-289-813074).

NATIONAL ORGANISATIONS

AFGHANISTAN
Revolutionary Association of the Women of Afghanistan [RAWA] (HR), see under Pakistan (www.rawa.org).

ALBANIA
Albanian Human Rights Group [AHRG] (HR), St Ibrahim Rugova - 2/39, Green Park, Tiranë (+355-42-225060) (el.ballauri@gmail.com) (www.ahrg-al.org).

Fondacioni Shqiptar Zgjidhja e Konflikteve dhe Pajtimi i Mosmarrëveshjeve [AFCR] (RE CR), Rr "Him Kolli" - Pall PF Trade - Nr 5, Tiranë (+355-4-226 4681) (fax 226 4837) (mediationalb@abcom.al) (www.mediationalb.org). *Pajtimi*.

ARGENTINA
Fundación Servicio Paz y Justicia [SER-PAJ] (FR IB HR), Piedras 730, 1070 Buenos Aires (+54-11-4361 5745) (secinstitucional@serpaj.org.ar) (serpaj.org.ar).

Greenpeace Argentina (GP), Zabala 3873, 1427 Buenos Aires (activismo@infogreenpeace.org.ar) (www.greenpeace.org/argentina).

ARMENIA
Civil Society Institute [CSI] (HR), 43 Aygestan 11th St, Yerevan 0025 (+374-10-574317) (csi@csi.am) (www.csi.am).

United Nations Association of Armenia (UN), 17 Nalbandyan Str - 7/1, Yerevan 0010 (+374-10-565595) (info@auna.am) (www.auna.am).

AUSTRALIA
Act for Peace [AFP] (RP RE TW DA), c/o National Council of Churches in Australia, Locked Bag Q199, Sydney, NSW 1230 (+61-2-8259 0800) (www.actforpeace.org.au).

Amnesty International Australia (AI), Locked Bag 23, Broadway, NSW 2007 (+61-2-8396 7600) (fax 9217 7663) (supporter@amnesty.org.au) (www.amnesty.org.au).

Anabaptist Association of Australia and New Zealand (RP), 190 Magpie Hollow Rd, South Bowenfels, NSW 2790 (+61-2-6351 2896) (aaanz.info@gmail.com) (www.anabaptist.asn.au).

Anglican Pacifist Fellowship - Australia [APF] (RP), c/o Philip Huggins, 5 Docker St, Richmond, Vic 2121 (phuggins@melbourne.anglican.com.au).

Anti-Nuclear Alliance of Western Australia [ANAWA] (ND EL), 5 King William St, Bayswater, WA 6053 (+61-8-9272 4252) (admin@anawa.org.au) (www.anawa.org.au).

Australia East Timor Friendship Assocaiation - South Australia [AEFTA-SA] (HR), PO Box 240, Goodwood, SA 5034 (+61-8-8344 3511) (www.aetfa.org.au).

Australia West Papua Association (HR), PO Box 105, Bunbury, WA 6231 (ash@freewestpapua.org) (www.freewestpapuaperth.org).

Australian Anti-Bases Campaign Coalition [AABCC] (IB WP AT ND RA), PO Box A899, Sydney South, NSW 1235 (+61-4-1829 0663) (denis@anti-bases.org) (www.anti-bases.org).

Centre for Peace Studies (RE EL SD), University of New England, Armidale, NSW 2351 (+61-2-6773 2442) (fax 6773 3350) (hware@une.edu.au) (www.une.edu.au/study/peace-studies). Organise annual Nonviolence Film Festival.

Coalition for Justice & Peace in Palestine [CJPP] (HR), PO Box 144, Glebe, NSW 2037 (cjpp@coalitionforpalestine.org) (www.coalitionforpalestine.org).

Conflict Resolution Network [CRN] (CR UN RE), PO Box 1016, Chatswood, NSW 2057 (+61-2-9419 8500) (crn@crnhq.org) (www.crnhq.org).

Ecumenical Accompaniment Programme in Palestine and Israel - Australia (RP HR), c/o National Council of Churches in Australia, Locked Bag Q199, Sydney, NSW 1230 (+61-2-8259 0800) (www.ncca.org.au/eappi).

Footprints for Peace (ND EL), PO Box 632, Fremantle South, WA 6162 (marcus@footprintsforpeace.org) (www.footprintsforpeace.net).

Friends of the Earth (FE RA PO), PO Box 222, Fitzroy, Vic 3065 (+61-3-9419 8700) (fax 9416 2081) (foe@foe.org.au) (www.foe.org.au).

Greenpeace Australia Pacific (GP), GPO Box 2622, Sydney, NSW 2001 (support.au@greenpeace.org) (www.greenpeace.org).

Independent and Peaceful Australia Network [IPAN] (PA DA), PO Box 573, Coorparoo, Qld 4151 (+61-431-597256) (ipan.australia@gmail.com) (ipan.org.au). Opposes overseas military bases.

Institute for Social Ecology (EL AL RA), PO Box 5208, West End, Brisbane, Qld 4101 (+61-4-2179 4776).

International Volunteers for Peace [IVP] (SC), 103A Goldsmith St, Goulburn, NSW 2580 (+61-2-4821 3350) (admin@ivp.org.au) (www.ivp.org.au).

Just Peace, PO Box 573, Coorparoo, QLD 4151 (+61-4-3159 7256) (JustPeaceQld@gmail.com).

Medical Association for Prevention of War [MAPW] (IP), PO Box 1379, Carlton, Vic 3053 (+61-3-9023 1958) (mapw@mapw.org.au) (www.mapw.org.au).

AUSTRALIA

Nonlethal Security for Peace Campaign (DA RE WF), PO Box 724, Avalon Beach, NSW 2107 (info@tamingwar.com) (tamingwar.com). Formerly the Non-Lethal Weapons for Peace Campaign.

Pax Christi (PC IB), PO Box 31, Carlton South, Vic 3053 (+61-3-9893 4946) (mscjust@smartchat.net.au) (www.paxchristi.org.au). *Disarming Times.* Also NSW (+61-2-9550 3845).

People for Nuclear Disarmament (NSW) [PND] (ND RE), 499 Elizabeth St, Surry Hills, Sydney, NSW 2010 (+61-2-9319 4296) (johnhallam2001@yahoo.com.au). *Peace Action.*

People for Nuclear Disarmament - Western Australia [PND] (IB ND), 5 King William St, Bayswater, WA 6053 (+61-8-9272 4252) (jovall@iinet.net.au).

People's Charter to Create a Nonviolent World (PA TW EL), PO Box 68, Daylesford, Vic 3460 (flametree@riseup.net) (thepeoplesnonviolencecharter.wordpress.com).

Quaker Service Australia (SF TW), Unit 14, 43-53 Bridge Rd, Stanmore, NSW 2048 (+61-2-8054 0400) (administration@qsa.org.au) (www.qsa.org.au). *QSA Newsletter.*

Religions for Peace Australia (RP), 71 Wellington St, Flemington, Vic 3031 (+61-4-3999 5761) (wcrpaust@iinet.net.au) (religionsforpeaceaustralia.org.au).

Reprieve Australia (HR), PO Box 4296, Melbourne, VIC 3001 (+61-3-9670 4108) (contact@reprieve.org.au) (www.reprieve.org.au). Campaigns against death penalty.

SafeGround (DA), PO Box 2143, Morphettville, SA 5043 (info@safeground.org.au) (safeground.org.au). *SafeGround Memorandum.* Work to reduce impact of explosive remnants of war.

Schweik Action Wollongong (SD), PO Box U129, Wollongong, NSW 2500 (+61-2-4228 7860) (fax 4221 5341) (brian_martin@uow.edu.au) (www.bmartin.cc/others/SAW.html).

Tasmanian Peace Trust (RE), PO Box 451, Hobart, TAS 7002.

Tasmanian Quaker Peace & Justice Committee [TQPJC] (SF PA), PO Box 388, North Hobart, Tas 7002 (+61-400-925385).

United Nations Association of Australia (UN), Suite 206, Griffin Centre, 20 Genge St, Canberra City, ACT 2601 (admin@unaa.org.au) (www.unaa.org.au).

Universal Peace Federation - Australia [UPF] (RP), PO Box 642, Burwood, NSW 1805 (oceaniahq@gmail.com) (www.upf.org).

Vision of Humanity (RE), PO Box 42, St Leonards, NSW 1590 (+61-2-9901 8500) (info@visionofhumanity.org) (www.visionofhumanity.org).

War Resisters' League [WRL] (WR AL HR), PO Box 451, North Hobart, Tas 7002 (+61-3-6278 2380) (pdpjones1943@gmail.com).

Women's International League for Peace and Freedom [WILPF] (WL ND), PO Box 934, Dickson, ACT 2602 (wilpf.australia@wilpf.org.au) (wilpf.org.au). *Peace & Freedom.*

World Citizens Association (Australia) [WCAA] (WF), PO Box 6318, University of New South Wales, Sydney, NSW 1466 (C.Hamer@unsw.edu.au) (www.worldcitizens.org.au).

AUSTRIA

Amnesty International Österreich (AI), Möringgasse 10, 1150 Wien (+43-1-78008) (fax 780 0844) (office@amnesty.at) (www.amnesty.at).

Arbeitsgemeinschaft für Wehrdienstverweigerung und Gewaltfreiheit [ARGE WDV] (WR), Schotteng 3A/1/4/59, 1010 Wien (+43-1-535 9109) (fax 532 7416) (argewdv@verweigert.at) (www.verweigert.at).

Bürgermeister für den Frieden in Deutschland und Österreich (CD ND DA), see under Germany.

Begegnungszentrum für Aktive Gewaltlosigkeit / Centre for Encounter and Active Nonviolence [BFAG] (WR TW EL), Wolfgangerstr 26, 4820 Bad Ischl (+43-6132-24590) (info@begegnungszentrum.at) (www.begegnungszentrum.at). *Rundbrief.*

Franz Jägerstätter House (PC), St Radegund 31, 5121 Ostermiething (+43-6278-8219) (pfarre.stradegund@dioezese-linz.at).

Global 2000 (FE), Neustiftgasse 36, 1070 Wien (+43-1-812 5730) (fax 812 5728) (office@global2000.at) (www.global2000.at).

Greenpeace Central and Eastern Europe (GP), Wiedner Haupstr 120-124, 1050 Wien (+43-1-545 4580) (fax 5454 58098) (office@greenpeace.at) (www.greenpeace.at). Previously Greeenpeace Austria.

Internationaler Versöhnungsbund [IVB] (FR), Lederergasse 23/III/21, 1080 Wien (+43-1-408 5332) (fax) (office@versoehnungsbund.at) (www.versoehnungsbund.at).

Österreichische Gesellschaft für Aussenpolitik und die Vereinten Nationen [OEGAVN] (UN), Reitschulgasse 2/2, Hofburg/Stallburg, 1010 Wien (+43-1-535 4627) (office@oegavn.org) (www.una-austria.org).

Österreichisches Netzwerk für Frieden und Gewaltfreiheit (RE), c/o IVB, Lederergasse 23/III/27, 1080 Wien (www.friedensnetzwerk.at).

Österreichisches Studienzentrum für Frieden und Konfliktlösung [ÖSFK/ASPR] (HR PA RE CR), Rochusplatz 1, 7461 Stadtschlaining, Burg (+43-3355-2498) (fax 2662) (aspr@aspr.ac.at) (www.aspr.ac.at).
Study Centre for Peace and Conflict Resolution.

Pax Christi Österreich [PXÖ] (PC), Kapuzinerstr 84, 4020 Linz (+43-732-7610 3254) (office@paxchristi.at) (www.paxchristi.at). *Pax.*

Peace Museum Vienna (RE), Blutgasse 3/1, 1010 Wien (office@peacemuseumvienna.com) (www.peacemuseumvienna.com).
Includes Windows for Peace project in city streets.

Service Civil International - Österreichischer Zweig [SCI-A] (SC PA), Schottengasse 3a/1/59, 1010 Wien (+43-1-535 9108) (fax 532 7416) (office@sci.or.at) (www.sciaustria.org).

Vienna Center for Disarmament & Non-Proliferation [VCDNP] (ND RE), Andromeda Tower - 13th Floor, Donau-City Str 6, 1220 Wien (+43-1-236 9482) (fax 269 9124) (info@vcdnp.org) (vcdnp.org).

AZERBAIJAN

Azerbaijan Institute for Democracy and Human Rights (HR), Nakhchivani Street 4B - flat 64, 1130 Baku (office@aidhr.org) (www.aidhr.org).

Azerbaijan Peace and Development Alliance (IB), 3/6 S Rustanov St - kv 65, Baku 370001 (+994-12-492 7920) (elmira@awdc.baku.az).

Azerbaycan Insan Huquqlarini Mudafie Merkezi / Human Rights Centre of Azerbaijan [AIHMM/HRCA] (HR), PO Box 31, Baku 1000 (+994-12-492 1369) (fax) (eldar.hrca@gmail.com) (penitentiary.ucoz.ru).
Human Rights in Azerbaijan.

BANGLADESH

Bangladesh Interreligious Council for Peace and Justice [BICPAJ] (FR IB PC CR EL), 14/20 Iqbal Rd, Mohammadpur, Dhaka 1207 (+880-2-914 1410) (fax 812 2010) (bicpaj@bijoy.net) (www.bicpaj.org).

Bangladesh Peace Council [BDC] (WP), Flat 3A1 - House No 8, Road No 6 - Block C, Banani, Dhaka 1213 (+88-2-882 7007) (dr.maguassem@gmail.com) (www.bd-pc.org).

Peace For All (IB CR HR), GPO Box 3448, Dhaka 1000 (+880-2-956 5907) (peaceforallbd@yahoo.com).

Service Civil International [SCI] (SC), 57/15 East Razabazar, Panthapath West, Dhaka 1215 (+880-2-935 3993) (scibangladesh@gmail.com) (scibangladesh.org).

BARBADOS

Barbados Inter-Religious Organisation [BIRO] (RP), c/o Roman Catholic Diocese of Bridgetown, PO Box 1223, Bridgetown (vincentblackett@hotmail.com).
Affiliated to Religions for Peace International.

BELARUS

Mizhnarodniy Tsenter Gramadsyanskich Initsiyatu "Nash Dom" / International Centre of Civil Initiatives (WR HR), see under Lithuania (+370-60-765718) (feedack@nash-dom.info) (nash-dom.info).

BELGIUM

ACAT Belgique (HR), Rue Brogniez 44, Anderlecht (acat.belgique@gmail.com).

Agir pour la Paix (WR), 35 rue van Elewyck, Ixelles, 1050 Bruxelles (+32-2 648 5220) (info@agirpourlapaix.be) (agirpourlapaix.be).

Amis de la Terre / Friends of the Earth Belgium (Wallonia and Brussels) [AT] (FE PO), Rue Nanon 98, 5000 Namur (+32-81 390639) (fax 81 390638) (contact@amisdelaterre.be) (www.amisdelaterre.be).

Amnesty International Belgique Francophone [AIBF] (AI), Rue Berckmans 9, 1060 Bruxelles (+32-2 538 8177) (fax 2 537 3729) (aibf@aibf.be) (www.amnesty.be).
Libertés!.

Amnesty International Vlaanderen (AI), Kerkstr 156, 2060 Antwerpen (+32-3 271 1616) (fax 3 235 7812) (amnesty@aivl.be) (www.aivl.be).

Artsen Voor Vrede [AVV] (IP), Karel Van de Woesti St 18, 9300 Aalst.
Gezondheidszorg en Vredesvraagstukken.

Association Médicale pour la Prévention de la Guerre Nucléaire [AMPGN] (IP), 51 Ave Wolvendael, 1180 Bruxelles (de.salle.philippe@skynet.be) (ampgn-belgium.be).

BePax (PC HR), Chaussée Saint-Pierre 208, 1040 Bruxelles (+32-2 896 9500) (info@bepax.org) (www.bepax.org).

Brigades de Paix Internationales [BPI/PBI] (HR CR CD RE), 23 rue Lt F Wampach, 1200 Bruxelles (+32-473 878136) (info@pbi-belgium.org) (pbi-belgium.org).

Climaxi - Friends of the Earth (Flanders & Brussels) (FE ND HR), Groenlaan 39, 9550 Herzele (info@climaxi.org) (www.climaxi.org).

Commission Justice et Paix - Belgique francophone (RP), Rue Maurice Liétart 31/6, 1150 Bruxelles (+32-2 738 0801) (fax 2 738 0800) (info@justicepaix.be) (www.justicepaix.be).

BELGIUM

Flemish War and Peace Museum (RE), IJzertoren, IJzerdijk 49, 8600 Diksmuide (+32-51 500286) (info@aandeijzer.be) (www.museumaandeijzer.be).
Greenpeace (GP), Haachtsesteenweg 159, 1030 Brussel (+32-2 274 0200) (fax 2 274 0230) (info@be.greenpeace.org) (www.greenpeace.org/belgium/).
Groupe Interconfessionnel de la Réconciliation / Kinshasa [GIR] (FR), Route de Longchamp 26, 1348 Louvain-la-Neuve (buangajos@hotmail.com).
I Stop the Arms Trade (AT RA PA), c/o Vredesactie, Patriottenstr 27, 2600 Berchem (+32-3 281 6839) (ikstopwapenhandel@vredesactie.be) (istopthearmstrade.eu). Non-violent direct action against EU arms trade.
Intal Globalize Solidarity (WP TW), 53 Chaussée de Haecht, 1210 Bruxelles (+32-2 209 2350) (fax 2 209 2351) (info@intal.be) (www.intal.be).
Pax Christi Vlaanderen [PCV] (PC RE CD ND CR), Italiëlei 98A, 2000 Antwerpen (+32-3 225 1000) (paxchristi@paxchristi.be) (www.paxchristi.be). *Koerier.*
Pax Christi Wallonie-Bruxelles [PCWB] (PC), Rue Maurice Liétart 31/1, 1150 Bruxelles (+32-2 738 0804) (fax 2 738 0800) (info@paxchristiwb.be) (www.paxchristiwb.be). *Signes des Temps.*
Register van Wereldburgers / Registry of World Citizens [RW] (WF PA TW), Vredestr 65, 2540 Hove (+32-3 455 7763) (verstraeten.jean@belgacom.net) (www.recim.org/cdm/).
Say No (PA), A Beermaerstr 28a, 1170 Brussel (+32-497 934716) (info@desertie.be) (www.sayno.be). Anti-militarist choral project.
Servas - Belgium & Luxembourg (SE), c/o Rita Dessauvage, Kloosterweg 30, 1652 Beersel-Alsemberg (belgium@servas.org) (belgium.servas.org).
Service Civil International [SCI] (SC), Rue van Elewyck 35, 1050 Bruxelles (+32-2 649 0738) (sci@scibelgium.be) (www.scibelgium.be).
Sortir de la Violence [SDV] (FR CR RE), 205 Chaussée de Wavre, 1050 Bruxelles (+32-2 679 0644) (info@sortirdelaviolence.org) (www.sortirdelaviolence.org).
ViA (SC WC), Belgiëlei 37, 2018 Antwerpen (+32-3 707 1614) (via@viavzw.be) (www.viavzw.be).
Vlaams Vredesinstituut / Flemish Peace Institute (RE), Leuvenseweg 86, 1000 Brussel (+32-2 552 4591) (fax 2 552 4408) (vredesinstituut@vlaamsparlement.be) (www.vlaamsvredesinstituut.eu). Also www.flemishpeaceinstitute.eu.
Vredesactie (WR AT ND), Breughelstr 31, 2018 Antwerpen (+32-3 281 6839) (contact@vredesactie.be) (www.vredesactie.be). *Vredesactie.*
Vrouwen in 't Zwart / Femmes en Noir / Women in Black [WiB] (PA DA HR), c/o Ria Convents, Vismarkt 8, 3000 Leuven (+32-16 291314) (marianne.vandegoorberg@telnet.be) (snellings.telenet.be/womeninblackleuven).

BENIN

ACAT Bénin (HR), 03 BP 0394, Cotonou (acat_coordbnin@yahoo.fr). Action by Christians for the Abolition of Torture.

BERMUDA

Amnesty International Bermuda (AI), PO Box HM 2136, Hamilton HM JX (+1441-296 3249) (fax) (director@amnestybermuda.org).

BHUTAN

People's Forum for Human Rights (HR), see under Nepal.

BOSNIA-HERZEGOVINA

Centar za Zivotnu Sredinu / Centre for the Environment [CZZS] (FE), Miša Stupara 5, 78000 Banja Luka (+387-5143 3140) (fax 5143 3141) (info@czzs.org) (czzs.org).
Centar za Nenasilnu Akciju / Centre for Nonviolent Action [CNA] (CD CR PA RE), Kranjcevicerva 33, 71000 Sarajevo (+387-3326 0876) (fax 3326 0875) (cna.sarajevo@nenasilje.org) (www.nenasilje.org). See also in Serbia.
Fondacaa Mirovna Akademija (RE), Porodice Ribar 8, 71000 Sarajevo (+387-3395 0902) (fax) (info@mirovna-akademija.org) (www.mirovna-akademija.org).
Mreza za Izgradnju Mira / Network for Building Peace (CD CR), Marka Marulica 2, 71000 Sarajevo (+387-3374 1080) (fax 3374 1081) (info@mreza-mira.net) (www.mreza-mira.net). Network of peace and human rights organisations.
Nansen Dialogue Centre Sarajevo [NDC Sarajevo] (CR), Hakije Kulenovica 10, 71000 Sarajevo (+387-33-556846) (fax 556845) (ndcsarajevo@nansen-dialogue.net) (www.ndcsarajevo.org).
WhyNjet / Why Not (WR), Dzemala Bijedica 309, 71000 Sarajevo (+387-33-618461) (info@zastone.ba) (www.zastone.ba). Supports conscientious objection.

BRAZIL

ACAT Brasil (HR), Praça Clovis Bevilaqua 351 - sala 701, 01018-001 São Paulo - SP (+55-11-3101 6084) (acatbrasil.international@gmail.com). Action by Christians for the Abolition of Torture.
Amigos da Terra - Brasil (FE), Rua Olavo Bilac 192 - Azenha, 90040-310 Porto Alegre - RS (+55-51-3332 8884) (www.amigosdaterrabrasil.org.br).

Associação das Nações Unidas - Brasil [ANUBRA] (UN), Av Brigadeiro Faria Lima 1485 - North Tower - 19th Floor, 01452-002 São Paulo - SP (+55-11-3094 7984) (fax) (unab@unab.org.br) (www.unab.org.br).

Centro Brasileiro de Solidariedade aos Povos e Luta pela Paz [CEBRAPAZ] (WP CD SD ND), Rua Marconi 34 - Conj 51, República, 01047-000 São Paulo - SP (+55-11-3223 3469) (cebrapaz@cebrapaz.org.br) (cebrapaz.org.br).

Commissão Pastoral da Terra [CPT] (PC), Edificio Dom Abel - 1º andar, Rua 19 - Nº 35, 74030-090 Centro Goiânia, Goiás (+55-62-4008 6466) (fax 4008 6405) (cpt@cptnacional.org.br) (www.cptnacional.org.br).

Instituto Brasileiro do Não Matar / Brazilian Institute for Nonkilling (PA), Rua Uruguai 472 - Ed J Philipps - Apto 1002, Centro - Itajaí, Santa Catarina 88302-202 (+55-47-3349 6601) (info@naomatar.org).

BRITAIN

38 Degrees (EL HR TW), Moor Place, 1 Fore St, London EC2Y (+44-20-7846 0093) (emailtheteam@38degrees.org.uk) (38degrees.org.uk). Organises internet lobbying on progressive issues.

Acronym Institute for Disarmament Diplomacy (RE), Werks Central, 15-17 Middle St, Brighton BN1, Sussex (+44-1273 737219) (info@acronym.org.uk) (acronym.org.uk).

Action by Christians Against Torture [ACAT-UK] (HR), c/o 25 Higher Woolbrook Park, Sidmouth EX10 9ED, Devon (uk.acat@gmail.com) (www.acatuk.org.uk).

Action on Armed Violence (AT DA TW HR), 405 Mile End Rd, Bow, London E3 (info@aoav.org.uk) (aoav.org.uk).

Afghanistan Peace Project [APP] (PA CR), 31 Carisbrooke Rd, St Leonards-on-Sea TN38 0JN, Sussex (web@afghanistanpeaceproject.co.uk) (www.vcnv.org). Formerly Voices for Creative Non-Violence UK.

Alternatives to Violence Project - Britain [AVP Britain] (CR PO), 28 Charles Sq, London N1 6HT (+44-20-7324 4755) (info@avpbritain.org.uk) (www.avpbritain.org.uk).

Amnesty International - UK Section [AIUK] (AI), Human Rights Action Centre, 17-25 New Inn Yard, London EC2A 3EA (+44-20-7033 1500) (fax 7033 1503) (sct@amnesty.org.uk) (www.amnesty.org.uk).

Anglican Pacifist Fellowship [APF] (WR IB RP), Peace House, 19 Paradise St, Oxford OX1 1LD (enquiries@anglicanpeacemaker.org.uk) (www.anglicanpeacemaker.org.uk). *The Anglican Peacemaker*.

Archbishop Desmond Tutu Centre for War and Peace Studies (RE CR), Liverpool Hope University - Hope Park Campus, Liverpool L16 9JD (tutu@hope.ac.uk) (tutu.hope.ac.uk).

Article 36 (DA), The Coalface / Runway East, 46 Clifton Terrace, London N4 3JP (info@article36.org) (www.article36.org). Working to change law relating to weapons.

Baby Milk Action (TW PO EL), 4 Brooklands Ave, Cambridge CB2 8BB (+44-1223-464420) (info@babymilkaction.org) (www.babymilkaction.org). *BMA Update*.

Balkans Peace Park Project - UK Committee [B3P] (CD EL), c/o Rylstone Lodge, Rylstone, Skipton BD23 6LH, N Yorks (+44-1756-730231) (A.T.I.Young@bradford.ac.uk) (www.balkanspeacepark.org).

Baptist Peace Fellowship [BPF] (FR), c/o 21 Kingshill, Cirencester GL7 1DE, Gloucestershire (bobgardiner@yahoo.co.uk) (www.baptist-peace.org.uk). *BPF Newsletter*.

Before You Sign Up, 11 Manor Rd, Stratford-upon-Avon, Warwickshire CV37 (info@beforeyousignup.info) (www.beforeyousignup.info). For people thinking of joining the armed forces.

Bloomsbury Ad Hoc Committee [BADHOC] (EL HR PA), c/o 26 Museum Chambers, Little Russell St, London WC1A 5PD (badhoc@activist.com).

Boycott Israel Network [BIN] (HR TW), c/o PSC, Box BM PSA, London WC1N 3XX (info@boycottisraelnetwork.net) (www.boycottisraelnetwork.net).

Bradford University Department of Peace Studies (RE CR TW), Bradford BD7 1DP, West Yorks (+44-1274-235235) (fax 235240) (www.brad.ac.uk/acad/peace/).

Brighton Peace & Environment Centre [BPEC] (RE EL), 39-41 Surrey St, Brighton BN1, Sussex (+44-1273-766610) (info@bpec.org) (www.bpec.org).

British American Security Information Council [BASIC] (RE AT ND), The Founndry, 1 Oval Way, Vauxhall, London SE11 (+44-20-3488 6974) (basicuk@basicint.org) (basicint.org).

British Shalom-Salaam Trust [BSST] (CD CR RE), c/o 28 Huddleston Rd, London N7 0AG (bsst@bsst.org.uk) (bsst.org.uk). Supporting cross-community grassroots projects in Israel-Palestine.

Building Bridges for Peace (CR), c/o 2 Crossways, Cott Lane, Dartington, Totnes TQ9 6HE, Devon (joberry@buildingbridgesforpeace.org) (buildingbridgesforpeace.org). Conflict transformation through empathy.

For explanation of codes and abbreviations, see introduction

BRITAIN

Burma Campaign UK (HR EL TW), Unit 110, The Bon Marche Centre, 241-251 Ferndale Rd, London SW9 (info@burmacampaign.org.uk) (www.burmacampaign.org.uk).

Campaign Against Arms Trade [CAAT] (WR AT IB RA), Unit 1.9, The Green House, 244-254 Cambridge Heath Rd, London E2 9DA (+44-20-7281 0297) (enquiries@caat.org.uk) (www.caat.org.uk). *CAAT News*.

Campaign against Climate Change [CCC] (EL RA), Top Floor, 5 Caledonian Rd, London N1 9DX (+44-20-7833 9311) (info@campaigncc.org) (www.campaigncc.org).

Campaign Against Criminalising Communities [CAMPACC] (HR), c/o 44 Ainger Rd, London NW3 (+44-20-7586 5892) (estella24@tiscali.co.uk) (www.campacc.org.uk).

Campaign for Better Transport [CBT] (EL), 70 Cowcross St, London EC1M 6EJ (+44-20-3746 2225) (info@bettertransport.org.uk) (www.bettertransport.org.uk).

Campaign for Earth Federation / World Federalist Party (WF), c/o Ian Hackett, 1 Kenilworth Rd, London W5 5PB (worldfederalistparty@gmail.com) (www.federalunion.org).

Campaign for Freedom of Information [CFI] (HR), Free Word Centre, 60 Farringdon Rd, London EC1 (+44-20-7324 2519) (admin@cfoi.org.uk) (www.cfoi.org.uk).

Campaign for Homosexual Equality [CHE] (HR), c/o London Friend, 86 Caledonian Rd, London N1 9DN (+44-7941-914340) (info@c-h-e.org.uk) (www.c-h-e.org.uk).

Campaign for Human Rights in the Philippines [CHRP UK] (HR), c/o Bahay Housing Association, Hackney CVS, The Adiaha Antigha Centre, 24-30 Dalston Lane, London E8 (info@chrp.org.uk) (www.chrp.org.uk).

Campaign for Nuclear Disarmament [CND] (IB ND RA RE), 162 Holloway Rd, London N7 8DQ (+44-20-7700 2393) (enquiries@cnduk.org) (www.cnduk.org). *Campaign!*.

Campaign for Nuclear Disarmament Cymru / Yr Ymgyrch dros Ddiarfogi Niwclear [CND Cymru] (ND RA AT DA), c/o 9 Primrose Hill, Llanbadarn Fawr, Aberystwyth SY23 3SE (heddwch@cndcymru.org) (www.cndcymru.org). *Heddwch*.

Campaign for Press and Broadcasting Freedom [CPBF] (HR), 2nd floor, 23 Orford Rd, Walthamstow, London E17 9NL (freepress@cpbf.org.uk) (www.cpbf.org.uk). *Free Press*.

Campaign Opposing Police Surveillance [COPS] (HR), 5 Caledonian Rd, London N1 9DX (info@campaignopposingpolicesurveillance.com) (campaignopposingpolicesurveillance.com)

Campaign to Protect Rural England [CPRE] (EL PO), 15-21 Provost St, London N1 7NH (+44-20-7981 2800) (info@cpre.org.uk) (www.cpre.org.uk). Campaigns include opposing fracking.

Ceasefire Centre for Civilian Rights (DA), 3 Whitehall Court, London SW1A 2EL (contact@ceasefire.org) (www.ceasefire.org). Civilian-led monitoring of rights violations.

Centre for Alternative Technology / Canolfan y Dechnoleg Amgen [CAT] (EL PO AL), Machynlleth, Powys SY20 9AZ (+44-1654-705950) (fax 702782) (info@cat.org.uk) (www.cat.org.uk). *Clean Slate*.

Centre for Good Relations (CR RE), 96 Pendle Gardens, Culcheth, Warrington WA3 4LU (info@centreforgoodrelations.com) (centreforgoodrelations.com). Training, workshops, "civic diplomacy".

Centre for Trust, Peace and Social Relations [CTPSR] (RE), 5 Innovation Village, Coventry University Technology Park, Cheetah Rd, Coventry CV1 2TT (+44-24-7765 1182) (info.ctpsr@coventry.ac.uk) (www.coventry.ac.uk).

Centre of Religion, Reconciliation and Peace (RE RP), University of Winchester, Sparkford Rd, Winchester SO22, Hampshire (+44-1962-841515) (fax 842280) (www.winchester.ac.uk).

Chernobyl Children's Project (UK) (PO EL CD), Kinder House, Fitzalan St, Glossop SK13, Derbyshire (+44-1457-863534) (ccprojectuk@gmail.com) (www.chernobyl-children.org.uk).

Children of Peace (CR HR), 1st Floor, The Roller Mill, Mill Lane, Uckfield TN22 5AA, Sussex (+44-1825-768074) (info@childrenofpeace.org.uk) (www.childrenofpeace.org.uk). Charity working in Israel, Palestine, Jordan.

Christian Aid (TW), 35-41 Lower Marsh, London SE1 (+44-20-7620 4444) (fax 7620 0719) (info@christian-aid.org) (www.christianaid.org.uk).

Christian Campaign for Nuclear Disarmament [CCND] (ND RP), 162 Holloway Rd, London N7 8DQ (+44-20-7700 4200) (christians@cnduk.org) (www.christiancnd.org.uk). *Ploughshare*.

Christian International Peace Service [CHIPS] (RP CR PO WC), Unit 7, Warwick House, Overton Rd, London SW9 7JP (+44-20-7078 7439) (info@chipspeace.org) (chipspeace.org).

Church & Peace (RP CR RE), 39 Postwood Green, Hertford Heath SG13 7QJ (+44-1992-416442) (IntlOffice@church-and-peace.org) (www.church-and-peace.org).

City to Sea (EL PO), 5 York Court, Wilder St, St Paul's, Bristol BS2 8QH (info@citytosea.org.uk) (www.citytosea.org.uk). Campaign to stop plastic pollution at source.

Climate Outreach (EL), The Old Music Hall, 106-108 Cowley Rd, Oxford OX4 1JE (+44-1865-403334) (info@climateoutreach.org) (climateoutreach.org). Formerly Climate Outreach and Information Network.

Close Capenhurst Campaign (EL), c/o News From Nowhere, 96 Bold St, Liverpool L1 (closecapenhurst@gmail.com) (close-capenhurst.org.uk). Opposes uranium enrichment plant in Cheshire.

Co-operation Ireland (GB) (CD), Windy Ridge, Courtlands Hill, Pangbourne RG8, Berkshire (+44-118-976 7790) (fax) (murphy992@btinternet.com) (www.cooperationireland.org).

Commonweal Collection (RE AL PA EL), c/o J B Priestley Library, Bradford University, Bradford BD7 1DP, Yorks (+44-1274-233404) (commonweal@riseup.net) (bradford.ac.uk/library/libraries-and-collections/). Peace library.

Community for Reconciliation [CfR] (RP), Barnes Close, Chadwick, Malthouse Lane, Bromsgrove, Worcs B61 0RA (+44-1562-710231) (fax 710278) (cfrenquiry@aol.com) (www.cfrbarnesclose.co.uk). *Newslink*.

Conciliation Resources (CR), Burghley Yard, 106 Burghley Rd, London NW5 1AL (+44-20-7359 7728) (fax 7359 4081) (cr@c-r.org) (www.c-r.org).

Concord Media (PA EL TW), 22 Hines Rd, Ipswich IP3 9BG, Suffolk (+44-1473-726012) (sales@concordmedia.org.uk) (www.concordmedia.org.uk).

Conflict and Environment Observatory [CEOBS] (DA EL RE), The Chapel, Scout Rd, Mytholmroyd, Hebden Bridge HX7 5HZ, West Yorks (+44-300-302 1130) (ceobs.org).

Conflict Research Society [CRS] (RE), Giles Lane, Canterbury CT2 7NZ, Kent (conflictresearchsociety@kent.ac.uk) (www.conflictresearchsociety.org).

Conscience - Taxes for Peace not War (TR WR HR), c/o PPU, 1 Peace Passage, London N7 0BT (info@conscienceonline.org.uk) (www.conscienceonline.org.uk).

Conway Hall Ethical Society (HR RE), Conway Hall, Red Lion Sq, London WC1 4RL (+44-20-7405 1818) (admin@conwayhall.org.uk) (www.conwayhall.org.uk). *Ethical Record*. Formerly South Place Ethical Society.

Cord (TW CR), Floor 9, Eaton House, 1 Eaton Rd, Coventry CV1 2FJ (+44-24-7708 7777) (info@cord.org) (www.cord.org). International peacebuilding charity.

Corporate Occupation (HR RA TW), c/o Corporate Watch, 84b Whitechapel High St, London E1 7QX (tom@shoalcollective.org) (www.corporateoccupation.org). Opposes occupation of Palestine.

Corporate Watch (EL RA AL), c/o Freedom Press, Angel Alley, 84b Whitechapel High St, London E1 7QX (+44-20-7426 0005) (contact@corporatewatch.org) (www.corporatewatch.org). *News Update*.

Cuba Solidarity Campaign (TW WC), c/o UNITE, 33-37 Moreland St, London EC1V 8BB (+44-20-7490 5715) (office@cuba-solidarity.org.uk) (www.cuba-solidarity.org.uk). *Cuba Si*.

Cumbrians Opposed to a Radioactive Environment [CORE] (EL), Dry Hall, Broughton Mills, Broughton-in-Furness, Cumbria LA20 (+44-1229-716523) (fax) (martin@corecumbria.co.uk) (www.corecumbria.co.uk).

Cymdeithas y Cymod / FoR Wales (FR PA CR), c/o 42 St Patrick's Drive, Pen-y-Bont ar Ogwr / Bridgend, CF31 1RP (cymdeithasycymod@gmail.com) (www.cymdeithasycymod.org.uk).

Cymru dros Heddwch / Wales for Peace (RE DA), c/o Welsh Centre for International Affairs, Temple of Peace, Cathays Park, Cardiff CF10 (+44-29-2082 1051) (janeharries@wcia.org.uk) (www.walesforpeace.org).

Cynghrair Wrth-Niwclear Cymru / Welsh Anti-Nuclear Alliance [CWNC/WANA] (EL), PO Box 90, Llandrindod Wells, Powys LD1 9BP (info@wana.wales) (www.wana.wales).

Darvell Bruderhof (RP PA PO), Brightling Rd, Robertsbridge, Sussex TN32 5DR (+44-1580-883330) (darvell@bruderhof.com) (www.bruderhof.com). Anabaptist community.

Defend the Right to Protest [DTRTP] (HR), BM DTRTP, London WC1N 3XX (info@defendtherighttoprotest.org) (www.defendtherighttoprotest.org).

Demilitarise Education [dED] (RE DA), Partisan Collective, 19 Cheetham Hill Rd, Manchester M4 4FY (hiya@ded1.co) (ded1.co).

Don't Bank on the Bomb Scotland (ND), c/o Scottish CND, PO Box 3620, Glasgow G73 9FQ (nukedivestmentscotland@gmail.com) (nukedivestmentscotland.org). Network campaignng against "nuclear investments".

Drone Campaign Network (DA), c/o Peace House, 19 Paradise St, Oxford OX1 (DroneCampaignNetwork@riseup.net) (www.dronecampaignnetwork.org.uk). Network of organisations and academics.

Drone Wars UK (DA HR RE), Peace House, 19 Paradise St, Oxford OX1 1LD (office@dronewars.net) (www.dronewars.net). Opposes growing British use of armed drones.

BRITAIN

Economic Issues Programme of the Society of Friends (SF HR EL), QPSW, Friends House, 175 Euston Rd, London NW1 2BJ (+44-20-7663 1000) (suzannei@quaker.org.uk) (www.quaker.org.uk/economic-justice). *Earth & Economy* newsletter.

Ecumenical Accompaniment Programme in Palestine and Israel - British and Irish Group [EAPPI] (RP HR SF SD), c/o QPSW, Friends House, 175 Euston Rd, London NW1 2BJ (+44-20-7663 1144) (eappi@quaker.org.uk) (www.quaker.org.uk/eappi).

Edinburgh Peace and Justice Centre (CR ND PA RE HR), 25 Nicolson Sq, Edinburgh EH8 9BX (+44-131-629 1058) (contact@peaceandjustice.org.uk) (peaceandjustice.org.uk). Promotes nonviolence, conflict resolution.

Egypt Solidarity Initiative (HR), c/o MENA Solidarity Network, Unit 193, 15-17 Caledonian Rd, London N1 (campaign@egyptsolidarityinitiative.net) (egyptsolidarityinitiative.net).

Ekklesia (RP RE), 235 Shaftesbury Ave, London WC2 (+44-20-7836 3930) (info@ekklesia.co.uk) (www.ekklesia.co.uk).

End Violence Against Women Coalition (HR), 17-25 New Inn Yard, London EC2 (+44-20-7033 1559) (admin@evaw.org.uk) (www.endviolenceagainstwomen.org.uk).

English PEN (HR), 24 Bedford Row, London WC1R 4EH (enquiries@englishpen.org) (www.englishpen.org). Defend writers at risk; work for freedom of speech.

Environmental Investigation Agency [EIA] (EL), 62/63 Upper St, London N1 (+44-20-7354 7960) (ukinfo@eia-international.org) (www.eia-international.org). Also operates in USA.

Environmental Network for Central America [ENCA] (EL HR), c/o Janet Bye, 5 St Edmund's Place, Ipswich IP1 (+44-20-8769 0492) (enca.info@gmail.com) (www.enca.org.uk). *ENCA*. Works with affected communities.

Esperanto-Asocio de Britio [EAB] (PO HR), Esperanto House, Station Rd, Barlaston, Stoke-on-Trent, Staffs ST12 9DE (+44-1782-372141) (eab@esperanto.org.uk) (www.esperanto.org.uk). *EAB Update*; *La Brita Esperantisto*.

Ethical Consumer Research Association (EL PO AL), Unit 21, 41 Old Birley St, Manchester M15 (+44-161-226 2929) (fax 226 6277) (enquiries@ethicalconsumer.org) (www.ethicalconsumer.org). *Ethical Consumer*.

EuroPal Forum (HR), 21 Chalton St, London NW1 1JD (+44-20-3289 6057) (admin@europalforum.org.uk) (europalforum.org.uk). Mobilises in support of Palestinian rights.

Every Casualty Counts (RE), 86-90 Paul St, London EC2A 4NE (network@everycasualty.org) (www.everycasualty.org). Formerly Every Casualty Project.

Exeter Area CND (ND), The Peace Shop, 31 New Bridge St, Exeter EX4 3AH, Devon (+44-1392-431447) (info@exetercnd.org) (www.exetercnd.org). Formerly South West Region CND.

Extinction Rebellion (EL RA PO), The Exchange, Brick Row, Stroud GL5 1DF, Glos (extinctionrebellion@risingup.org.uk) (www.ExtinctionRebellion.org.uk). Actions for climate and economic justice.

Faith & Resistance Network (RP RA), c/o QPSW, Friends House, 175 Euston Rd, London NW1 (faithandresistanceblog.wordpress.com).

Feedback (EL HR), Office 518, The Archives, Unit 10, The High Cross Centre, Fouyntayne Rd, London N15 4BE (+44-20-3051 8633) (hello@feedbackglobal.org) (feedbackglobal.org). For food which is good for planet and its people.

Fellowship of Reconciliation [FoR] (FR WR), Peace House, 19 Paradise St, Oxford OX1 1LD (+44-1865-250781) (office@for.org.uk) (www.for.org.uk). *Peacelinks*. Covers England and Scotland.

Filia (HR), c/o Drystone Chambers, 35 Bedford Row, London WC1 (info@filia.org.uk) (filia.org.uk). Supporting women's human rights.

Fitnah - Movement for Women's Liberation (HR), BM Box 1919, London WC1N 3XX (fitnah.movement@gmail.com) (www.fitnah.org). *Fitnah*. Opposes misogynist cultural and religious customs.

Fly Kites Not Drones (CD HR PA PO), c/o VCNV-UK, 31 Carisbrooke Rd, St Leonards-on-Sea TN38, Sussex (kitesnotdrones@gmail.com) (www.flykitesnotdrones.org). Non-violence project for young people.

Football for Peace [FFP] (CD), c/o 90 Long Acre, Covent Garden, London WC2E 9DA (44-20-7632 1225) (info@ffpglobal.org) (footballforpeaceglobal.org).

ForcesWatch (PA HR RE), 5 Caledonian Rd, London N1 (+44-20-7837 2822) (office@forceswatch.net) (www.forceswatch.net).

Free Tibet Campaign (HR TW EL), ER82, The Link, Effra Rd, London SW2 1BZ (+44-20-7324 4612) (mail@freetibet.org) (freetibet.org).

Freedom Declared Foundation [FDF] (HR), Office 3, Cathedral House, 63-68 St

Thomas's St, Portsmouth PO1 2HA (freedomdeclaredfoundation.org). Champions universal freedom of conscience.
Freedom from Torture (HR), 111 Isledon Rd, London N7 (+44-20-7697 7777) (fax 7697 7799) (www.freedomfromtorture.org). *Survivor*. Supports survivors of torture.
Friends of the Earth - England, Wales and Northern Ireland [FOE] (FE PO), The Printworks, 1st Floor, 139 Clapham Rd, London SW9 0HP (+44-20-7490 1555) (fax 7490 0881) (info@foe.co.uk) (friendsoftheearth.uk).
Friends of the Earth Cymru / Cyfeillion y Ddaear Cymru (FE), 33 The Balcony, Castle Arcade, Cardiff CF10 1BY (+44-29-2022 9577) (cymru@foe.co.uk) (www.foecymru.co.uk).
Friends of the Earth Scotland (FE), Thorn House, 5 Rose St, Edinburgh EH2 2PR (+44-131-243 2700) (fax 243 2725) (info@foe.scot) (www.foe.scot).
Gandhi Foundation (HR RE PO), Kingsley Hall, Powis Rd, Bromley-by-Bow, London E3 3HJ (contact@gandhifoundation.org) (www.gandhifoundation.org). *The Gandhi Way*.
Gender Action for Peace and Security [GAPS UK] (HR RE AT CR), c/o Saferworld, The Brick Yard, 28 Charles Sq, London N1 6HT (+44-20-7922 7836) (info@gaps-uk.org) (gaps-uk.org). Network of organisations and individual experts.
GeneWatch UK (EL HR), 86 Dedworth Rd, Windsor SL4 5AA, Berks (+44-3300-010507) (mail@genewatch.org) (www.genewatch.org). Monitors genetic engineering.
Global Campaign on Military Spending - UK [GCOMS-UK] (DA AT TW), c/o CND, 162 Holloway Rd, London N7 8DQ (contact@demilitarize.org.uk) (demilitarize.org.uk). Organise UK end of annual international action day.
Global Justice Now (TW HR), 66 Offley Rd, London SW9 0LS (+44-20-7820 4900) (offleyroad@globaljustice.org.uk) (www.globaljustice.org.uk). *Ninety Nine*. Formerly World Development Movement.
Global Witness (EL HR TW CR), Lloyds Chambers, 1 Portsoken St, London E1 (+44-20-7492 5820) (fax 7492 5821) (mail@globalwitness.org) (www.globalwitness.org). Also in USA.
GM Watch (EL), 99 Brentwood Rd, Brighton BN1 7ET, Sussex (editor@gmwatch.org) (www.gmwatch.org). Analyses and counters GM industry propaganda.
GM-Free Cymru (EL), c/o Dyffryn Dwarch, Abermawr, nr Mathry, Pembrokeshire SA62 (gm@caerhys.co.uk) (www.gmfreecymru.org).
GM-free Scotland (EL), c/o 35 Hamilton Drive, Glasgow G12 (gmfreescotland@yahoo.co.uk) (gmfreescotland.blogspot.co.uk).

Greater Manchester & District CND [GM&DCND] (ND), Bridge 5 Mill, 22a Beswick St, Ancoats, Manchester M4 7HR (+44-161-273 8283) (gmdcnd@gn.apc.org) (gmdcnd.org.uk). *Nuclear Alert*.
Green Alliance (EL), 40 Broadway, London SW1H 0BU (+44-20-7233 7433) (ga@green-alliance.org.uk) (www.green-alliance.org.uk). Environmental thinktank.
Green Christian [GC] (EL PO), 97 Plumpton Ave, Hornchurch RM12 6BB, Essex (info@greenchristian.org.uk) (www.greenchristian.org.uk). *Green Christian*.
Green CND (ND), c/o CND, 162 Holloway Rd, London N7 (+44-20-7700 2393).
Green Party of England and Wales (EL ND HR RA), The Biscuit Factory - A Block (201), 100 Clements Rd, London SE16 4DG (+44-20-3691 9400) (office@greenparty.org.uk) (www.greenparty.org.uk). *Green World*.
Greener UK (EL), c/o Green Alliance, 40 Broadway, London SW1H 0BU (amount@green-alliance.org.uk) (greeneruk.org). Tracking environmental implications of BREXIT.
GreenNet (TW HR PO), Oxford House, Derbyshire St, London E2 6HG (+44-330-335 4011) (info@gn.apc.org) (www.gn.apc.org). Internet services for campaigners.
Greenpeace UK (GP), Canonbury Villas, London N1 2PN (+44-20-7865 8100) (info.uk@greenpeace.org) (www.green-peace.org.uk). *Connect*.
Growing Against Violence (CR PO), 18 Stoneleigh Broadway, Epsom, Surrey KT17 2HU (operations@growingagainstviolence.org.uk) (www.growingagainstviolence.org.uk). Against peer-to-peer violence and exploitation.
Gun Control Network (AT RE PO EL), PO Box 11495, London N3 2FE (gcn-uk@btconnect.com) (www.gun-control-network.org).
Housmans Bookshop (WR EL AL HR), 5 Caledonian Rd, Kings Cross, London N1 9DX (+44-20-7837 4473) (fax 7278 0444) (shop@housmans.com) (www.housmans.com). *Peace Diary & World Peace Directory*. Peace/political books, magazines, cards, etc.
Human Rights Watch - London Office (HR), First Floor, Audrey House, 16-20 Ely Place, London EC1 (+44-20-7618 4700) (londonoutreach@hrw.org) (www.hrw.org/london).
Humanists UK (HR PO), 39 Moreland St, London EC1V 8BB (+44-20-7324 3060) (fax 7324 3061) (info@humanists.uk) (humanism.org.uk). Formerly British Humanist Association.

BRITAIN

Humanity United for Universal Demilitarisation [HUFUD] (PA PO DA), 14a Lakeside Rd, London W14 0DU (info.hufud@gmail.com) (www.hufud.org). For universal abolition of militarism and weapons.

Index on Censorship (HR RA TW), 1 Rivington Place, London EC2A 3BA (+44-20-7963 7262) (david@indexoncensorship.org) (www.indexoncensorship.org). *Index on Censorship.*

International Alert Training and Learning (CR RE), 346 Clapham Rd, London SW9 (+44-20-7627 6811) (fax 7627 6900) (vmatovic@international-alert.org) (www.internationalert.org).

International Association for Religious Freedom - British Chapter (HR), c/o Essex Hall, 1 Essex St, London WC2R 3HY (Pejman_Khojasteh@btinternet.com) (www.iarf.net). *IARF World.*

International Campaign to Abolish Nuclear Weapons - UK [ICAN-UK] (ND), c/o MEDACT, 28 Charles Sq, London N1 6HT (infouk@icanw.org) (www.icanw.org/unitedkingdom).

International Centre of Justice for Palestinians [ICJP] (HR), Office 4, 219 Kensington High St, London W8 6ED (info@icjpalestine.com) (www.icjpalestine.com).

International Friendship League - UK (CD), PO Box 578, Northampton NN5 4WY (www.ifl.org.uk).

International Service [UNAIS] (TW UN), Second Floor, Rougier House, 5 Rougier St, York YO1 6HZ (+44-1904-647799) (fax 652353) (contact@internationalservice.org.uk) (www.internationalservice.org.uk).

International Voluntary Service [IVS] (SC), Thorn House, 5 Rose St, Edinburgh EH2 2PR (+44-131-618 0929) (info@ivsgb.org) (ivsgb.org).

Iona Community (FR PA HR), Suite 9, Fairfield, 1048 Govan Rd, Glasgow G51 4XS (+44-141-429 7281) (admin@iona.org.uk) (iona.org.uk). (On Iona: +44-1681-700404).

Iranian and Kurdish Women's Rights Organisation [IKWRO] (HR), PO Box 75229, London E15 9FX (+44-20-7920 6460) (info@ikwro.org.uk) (ikwro.org.uk). Works against "honour"-based violence.

Israeli Committee Against House Demolitions UK [ICAHD UK] (HR RA), BM ICAHD UK, London WC1N 3XX (+44-20-3740 2208) (info@icahduk.org) (www.icahduk.org). Opposes Israeli occupation of Palestinian land.

JD Bernal Peace Library (RE), c/o Marx Memorial Library, 37a Clerkenwell Green, London EC1R 0DU (+44-20-7253 1485) (archives@mml.xyz) (www.marx-memorial-library.org). *Theory and Struggle.*

Jews for Justice for Palestinians [JJP] (HR), 20-22 Wenlock Rd, London N1 7GU (jfjfpexecutive@gmail.com) (jfjfp.com).

Jubilee Debt Campaign (TW), The Grayston Centre, 28 Charles Sq, London N1 6HT (+44-20-7324 4722) (info@jubileedebt.org.uk) (jubileedebt.org.uk). *Drop It!*.

Jubilee Scotland (TW), 41 George IV Bridge, Edinburgh EH1 1EL (+44-131-225 4321) (mail@jubileescotland.org.uk) (www.jubileescotland.org.uk). Successor to Jubilee 2000 Scottish Coalition.

Justice & Peace Scotland / Ceartas agus Sìth (RP), 65 Bath St, Glasgow G2 2BX (+44-141-333 0238) (office@justiceandpeacescotland.org.uk) (justiceandpeacescotland.org).

Khulisa - Breaking the cycle of violence (CD CR PO), Wells House (Unit 7), 5-7 Wells Terrace, London N4 (+44-20-7561 3727) (info@khulisa.co.uk) (www.khulisa.co.uk). Modelled on programmes in South Africa.

Kick Nuclear (EL RA), c/o CND, 162 Holloway Rd, London N7 8DQ (+44-20-7700 2393) (kicknuclearlondon@gmail.com) (kicknuclear.com). Opposes UK's addiction to nuclear power.

Kindness UK (PO), Turpin's Yard, Oaklands Rd, London NW2 6LL (+44-20-8452 8518) (kindnessuk.com).

Labour CND (ND), 162 Holloway Rd, London N7 8DQ (+44-1425-279307) (labourcnd@gmail.com) (www.labourcnd.com).

Land Justice Network (HR EL RA), c/o The Land Magazine, Monkton Wyld Court, Charmouth, Bridport, Dorset DT6 (landjusticeuk@gmail.com) (www.landjustice.uk). Network challenging use and ownership of land.

Lawyers for Palestinian Human Rights (HR TW), c/o Bates Wells & Braithwaite, 10 Queen Street Place, London EC4R 1BE (contact@lphr.org.uk) (lphr.org.uk).

Liberation (HR TW DA CR), 77 St John St, Clerkenwell, London EC1M 4NN (+44-20-7324 2498) (info@liberationorg.co.uk) (www.liberationorg.co.uk). *Liberation.*

Liberty - The National Council for Civil Liberties (HR), Liberty House, 26-30 Strutton Ground, London SW1P 2HR (+44-20-7403 3888) (fax 7799 5306) (www.libertyhumanrights.org.uk).

Living Streets (EL HR PO), 4th Floor, Universal House, 88-94 Wentworth St, London E1 7SA (+44-20-7377 4900) (info@livingstreets.org.uk) (www.livingstreets.org.uk).

Local Futures / ISEC [ISEC-UK] (EL), PO Box 239, Totnes TQ9 9DP (+44-1392-581175) (info@localfutures.org) (www.localfutures.org).

London Catholic Worker [LCW] (RP RA PA AL), 49 Mattison Rd, London N4 (+44-20-8348 8212) (londoncatholicworker@yahoo.co.uk) (www.londoncatholicworker.org). *London Catholic Worker*.

London Mining Network [LMN] (HR EL), Finfuture, 225-229 Seven Sisters Rd, London N4 (contact@londonminingnetwork.org) (www.londonminingnetwork.org).

London Region CND [LRCND] (ND), Mordechai Vanunu House, 162 Holloway Rd, London N7 8DQ (+44-20-7607 2302) (info@londoncnd.org) (www.londoncnd.org).

Low-Level Radiation Campaign [LLRC] (EL), Times Building, South Crescent, Llandrindod Wells, Powys LD1 5DH (+44-1597-824771) (lowradcampaign@gmail.com) (www.llrc.org).

MEDACT (IP IB EL), The Grayston Centre, 28 Charles Sq, London N1 6HT (+44-20-7324 4739) (fax 7324 4734) (office@medact.org) (www.medact.org). *Communiqué*.

Medical Aid for Palestinians [MAP] (HR), 33a Islington Park St, London N1 1QB (+44-20-7226 4114) (fax 7226 0880) (info@map.org.uk) (www.map.org.uk). *Witness*.

Merseyside CND (ND), 151 Dale St, Liverpool L2 2AH (+44-151-229 5282) (mcnd@care4free.net) (www.mcnd.org.uk).

Methodist Peace Fellowship [MPF] (FR), 133 Manchester Rd, Hapton, nr Burnley BB11 5RF (bea_foster@hotmail.com) (www.mpf.org.uk).

Milton Keynes Peace & Justice Network (ND HR DA), 300 Saxon Gate West, Central Milton Keynes, Bucks MK9 2ES (office@mkpeaceandjustice.org.uk) (www.mkpeaceandjustice.org.uk). *MK Network News*.

Mines Advisory Group [MAG] (DA TW PO), Suite 3A, South Central, 11 Peter St, Manchester M2 5QR (+44-161-236 4311) (fax 236 6244) (info@maginternational.org) (www.maginternational.org).

Movement for Compassionate Living [MCL] (PO EL), 105 Cyfyng Rd, Ystalyfera, Swansea SA9 2BT (+44-1639-841223) (mcl.ystalyfera@googlemail.com) (www.MCLveganway.org.uk).

Movement for the Abolition of War [MAW] (IB), 1 Old Mill Place, Vicarage Lane, Haslemere GU27 1NE (+44-20-3397 3019) (info@abolishwar.org.uk) (www.abolishwar.org.uk). *Abolish War*.

Musicians for Peace and Disarmament [MPD] (IB ND DA), 37 Bolton Gdns, Teddington TW11 9AX (info.mpdconcerts@gmail.com) (www.mpdconcerts.org).

National Federation of Atheist, Humanist and Secularist Student Societies [AHS] (HR), 39 Moreland St, London EC1 (communications@ahsstudents.org.uk) (ahsstudents.org.uk).

National Justice & Peace Network [NJPN] (RP), 39 Eccleston Sq, London SW1V 1BX (+44-20-7901 4864) (fax 7901 4821) (admin@justice-and-peace.org.uk) (www.justice-and-peace.org.uk). *Justice and Peace*.

National Secular Society [NSS] (HR), Dutch House, 307-308 High Holborn, London WC1V 7LL (+44-20-7404 3126) (enquiries@secularism.org.uk) (www.secularism.org.uk).

Network for Climate Action (EL RA), c/o LARC, 62 Fieldgate St, London E1 1ES (www.networkforclimateaction.org.uk). Provide resources for climate activists.

Network for Peace [NfP] (DA ND PA), 5 Caledonian Rd, London N1 9DX (mail@networkforpeace.org.uk) (www.networkforpeace.org.uk).

Network of Christian Peace Organisations [NCPO] (RP), c/o FOR, Peace House, 19 Paradise St, Oxford OX1 1LD (+44-1865-250781) (enquiries@ncpo.org.uk) (ncpo.org.uk).

New Economics Foundation [NEF] (EL CD PO), 10 Salamanca Place, London SE1 7HB (+44-20-7820 6300) (info@neweconomics.org) (www.neweconomics.org).

New Economy Organisers Network [NEON] (EL HR PO), 10 Salamanca Place, London SE1 7HB (hello@neweconomyorganisers.org) (neweconomyorganisers.org). Network of organisers.

New Israel Fund UK (HR), Unit 2, Bedford Mews, London N2 9DF (+44-20-7724 2266) (fax 7724 2299) (info@uknif.org) (uknif.org). Supports progressive civil society in Israel.

Nicaragua Solidarity Campaign [NSC] (HR TW WC), 86 Durham Rd, London N7 7DT (+44-20-7561 4836) (nsc@nicaraguasc.org.uk) (www.nicaraguasc.org.uk). *Nicaragua Now*.

Nipponzan Myohoji (RP), Peace Pagoda, Willen, Milton Keynes MK15 0BA, Bucks (+44-1908-663652) (fax). Also in London: +44-20-7228 9620.

No 2 Nuclear Power (EL), c/o Pete Roche, Friends of the Earth Scotland, Thorn House, 5 Rose Street, Edinburgh EH2 (rochepete8@aol.com) (www.no2nuclearpower.org.uk). Provides key website and nuclear information.

No Sweat (HR RA TW), 5 Caledonian Rd, London N1 (admin@nosweat.org.uk) (www.nosweat.org.uk). Against sweatshops; for workers' and TU rights.

BRITAIN

NO2ID (HR), Box 412, 19-21 Crawford St, London W1H 1PJ (+44-20-7340 6077) (office@no2id.net) (www.no2id.net). *NO2ID Newsletter*.
Opposes ID cards and the database state.
Non-Violent Resistance Network [NVRN] (RA ND PA), c/o David Polden, CND, 162 Holloway Rd, London N7 8DQ (+44-20-7700 2393) (davidtrpolden1@gmail.com). *Newsletter*.
Northern Friends Peace Board [NFPB] (SF), Victoria Hall, Knowsley St, Bolton BL1 2AS (+44-1204-382330) (nfpb@gn.apc.org) (nfpb.org.uk). *NFPB Update*.
Nuclear Awareness Group [NAG] (EL), 16 Back St, Winchester SO23 9SB, Hants (+44-1962-890160) (fax) (nuclearawarenessgroup.org.uk). *Newsletter*.
Nuclear Information Service [NIS] (RE ND), 35-39 London St, Reading RG1 4PS (+44-118-327 4935) (fax) (office@nuclearinfo.org) (nuclearinfo.org).
Nuclear Morality Flowchart Project (ND), c/o Martin Birdseye, 88 Fern Lane, Hounslow TW5 0HJ, Middlesex (+44-20-8571 1691) (info@nuclearmorality.com) (nuclearmorality.com). Helps people to think about ethical accountability.
Nuclear Trains Action Group [NTAG] (ND RA), c/o Mordechai Vanunu House, 162 Holloway Rd, London N7 8DR (+44-20-7700 2393) (davidtrpolden1@gmail.com) (www.nonucleartrains.org.uk). *Newletter*.
Working Group of London Region CND.
Nuclear Weapons Financing Research Group (RE ND RP), c/o Christian CND, 162 Holloway Rd, London N7 8DQ (investinginchange.enquiries@gmail.com) (investinginchange.org).
Network of religious peace organisations.
Nuclear-Free Local Authorities Secretariat [NFLA] (ND EL), c/o Manchester City Council, Town Hall, Manchester M60 3NY (+44-161-234 3244) (fax 274 7379) (s.morris4@manchester.gov.uk) (www.nuclearpolicy.info).
Nukewatch (ND RA NDRE), c/o Edinburgh Peace & Justice Centre, 25 Nicholson Sq, Edinburgh EH8 9BX (+44-345 458 8365) (spotters@nukewatch.org.uk) (www.nukewatch.org.uk).
Oasis of Peace UK (CD CR HR), 192B Station Rd, Edgware HA8 7AR, Middx (+44-20-8952 4717) (office@oasisofpeace.org.uk) (www.oasisofpeaceuk.org).
Formerly British Friends of NSWaS.
One World Trust [OWT] (WF), Coombe Head, Tresham, Wotton under Edge, Glos GL12 7RW (info@oneworldtrust.org) (www.oneworldtrust.org).

OneVoice Movement - Europe (CD CR), Unit 4, Benwell Studios, 11-13 Benwell Rd, London N7 7BL (+44-20-8004 6431) (europe@OneVoiceMovement.org.uk) (www.onevoicemovement.org). See also under Israel, Palestine, and USA.
Orthodox Peace Fellowship UK [OPF] (RP), c/o Seraphim Honeywell, "Birchenhoe", Crowfield, nr Brackley NN13 5TW, Northants (oxpeacefp@aol.com) (www.incommunion.org). *In Communion*.
Oxford Network of Peace Studies [OxPeace] (RE), c/o Dept of Politics and International Relations, Manor Road Building, Manor Rd, Oxford OX1 3UQ (+44-1865-278700) (liz.carmichael@sjc.ox.ac.uk).
Promotes study of peacemaking and peacebuilding.
Oxford Research Group (RE CR DA), The Green House, 244-254 Cambridge Heath Rd, London E2 9DA (+44-20-3559 6745) (org@oxfordresearchgroup.org.uk) (www.oxfordresearchgroup.org.uk).
Palestine Solidarity Campaign [PSC] (TW CR), Box BM PSA, London WC1N 3XX (+44-20-7700 6192) (fax 7700 5747) (info@palestinecampaign.org) (www.palestinecampaign.org).
Pax Christi (PC PA RE), Christian Peace Education Centre, St Joseph's, Watford Way, Hendon, London NW4 4TY (+44-20-8203 4884) (fax 8203 5234) (admin@paxchristi.org.uk) (www.paxchristi.org.uk). *Justpeace*.
Pax Christi Scotland (PC), c/o Xaverian Missionaries, Calder Ave, Coatbridge ML5 4JS (admin@paxchristiscotland.org) (www.pax-christiscotland.org).
Peace Brigades International UK [PBI UK] (PA RE HR CD), 29c Oakfield Rd, London N4 4NP (admin@peacebrigades.org.uk) (peacebrigades.org.uk).
Peace Direct (CR RE), Second Floor, 72-74 Mare St, London E8 4RT (+44-20-3422 5549) (info@peacedirect.org) (www.peacedirect.org).
Peace Education Network (RE), c/o Pax Christi, St Joseph's, Watford Way, London NW4 4TY (+44-20-8203 4884) (education@paxchristi.org.uk) (www.peace-education.org.uk).
Peace Hub - Quaker Peace and Justice Centre (SF PO CD), 41 Bull St, Birmingham B4 6AF (+44-121-238 2869) (office@peacehub.org.uk) (peacehub.org.uk).
Peace in Kurdistan (HR), 44 Ainger Rd, London NW3 3AT (+44-20-7586 5892) (estella24@tiscali.co.uk) (www.peaceinkurdistancampaign.com).
Peace Museum UK (RE PA CR), Salts Mill, Victoria Rd, Saltaire BD18 3LA (info@peacemuseum.org.uk) (www.peacemuseum.org.uk).

Peace News - for nonviolent revolution [PN] (WR HR AL RA ND), 5 Caledonian Rd, London N1 9DY (+44-20-7278 3344) (fax 7278 0444) (editorial@peacenews.info) (www.peacenews.info).

Peace One Day (CR PO RE), St George's House, 15 St George's Rd, Richmond, Surrey TW9 (+44-20-8334 9900) (fax 8948 0545) (info@peaceoneday.org) (www.peaceoneday.org).

Peace Party - Non-violence, Justice, Environment (PA HR EL), c/o John Morris, 39 Sheepfold Rd, Guildford GU2 9TT, Surrey (+44-1483-576400) (info@peaceparty.org.uk) (www.peaceparty.org.uk). *Peace*.
Secular pacifist electoral movement.

Peace Pledge Union [PPU] (WR RE), 1 Peace Passage, Brecknock Rd, London N7 0BT (+44-20-7424 9444) (mail@ppu.org.uk) (www.ppu.org.uk). *Peace Matters*.

Peace Tax Seven (TR), c/o Woodlands, Ledge Hill, Market Lavington, Wilts SN10 (info@peacetaxseven.com) (www.peacetaxseven.com).

Peaceful Schools UK (RP), Witch Hazel Cottage, Linden Rd, Headley Down GU35 8EN, Hants (+44-1428-717090) (anna@peacefulschools.org.uk) (peacefulschools.org.uk).
Formerly Peaceful Schools Movement.

People & Planet (TW HR EL), The Old Music Hall, 106-108 Cowley Rd, Oxford OX4 1JE (+44-1865-403225) (people@peopleandplanet.org) (peopleandplanet.org).
National student network.

Police Spies Out of Lives [PSOOL] (HR), c/o 84b Whitechapel High St, London E1 7QX (contact@policespiesoutoflives.org.uk) (policespiesoutoflives.org.uk). Supports women abused by undercover police.

Possible (EL), 8 Delancey Passage, Camden Town, London NW1 7NN (+44-20-7388 6688) (hello@wearepossible.org) (www.wearepossible.org). Formery 10:10 Climate Action.

Practical Action (PO TW), Schumacher Centre for Technology and Development, Bourton Hall, Bourton-on-Dunsmore, Rugby, Warwickshire CV23 9QZ (+44-1926-634400) (fax 634401) (enquiries@practicalaction.org.uk) (www.practicalaction.org.uk).

Public Interest Case Against Trident [PICAT] (ND), 6 Church St, Knighton, Powys LD7 1AG (+44-1547-520929) (reforest@gn.apc.org) (picat.online).

Pugwash Conferences on Science and World Affairs (DA EL RE TW CR), Ground Floor Flat, 63A Great Russell St, London WC1B 3BJ (+44-20-7405 6661) (office@britishpugwash.org) (britishpugwash.org). *Pugwash Newsletter*.
Part of international Pugwash network.

Quaker Concern for the Abolition of Torture [Q-CAT] (SF HR), c/o 38 The Mount, Heswall CH60 4RA, Wirral (+44-151-342 4425) (chasraws@onetel.com) (q-cat.org.uk).

Quaker Peace & Social Witness [QPSW] (SF DA PA), Friends House, 175 Euston Rd, London NW1 2BJ (+44-20-7663 1000) (qpsw@quaker.org.uk) (www.quaker.org.uk/qpsw).

Quaker Sustainability and Peace Programme (SF EL RE DA PA), QPSW, Friends House, 175 Euston Rd, London NW1 2BJ (+44-20-7663 1067) (fax 7663 1001) (survival@quaker.org.uk) (www.quaker.org.uk). Previously Peace and Disarmament Programme.

Radical Routes (AL PO), c/o Cornerstone Resource Centre, 16 Sholebroke Ave, Leeds LS7 3HB (+44-1603-776445) (enquiries@radicalroutes.org.uk) (www.radicalroutes.org.uk).
Network of radical housing, worker & other co-ops.

Redress (HR), 87 Vauxhall Walk, London SE11 (+44-20-7793 1777) (fax 7793 1719) (info@redress.org) (www.redress.org).
Seeks justice for torture survivors.

Religions for Peace UK [WCRP-UK] (RP RE), c/o 18 Little Acres, Ware SG12 9JW, Hertfordshire (+44-1920-465714) (fax) (secretary@religionsforpeace.org.uk) (www.religionsforpeace.org.uk).

Religious Society of Friends in Britain (Quakers) (SF), Friends House, Euston Rd, London NW1 2BJ (+44-20-7663 1000) (fax 7663 1001) (www.quaker.org.uk).
Quaker News; *The Friend*; *Quaker Voices*.

Reprieve (HR), PO Box 72054, London EC3P 3BZ (+44-20-7553 8140) (info@reprieve.org.uk) (www.reprieve.org.uk).

Rethinking Security (RE DA EL), c/o Saferworld, The Grayston Centre, 28 Charles Sq, London N1 (celia@rethinkingsecurity.org.uk) (rethinkingsecurity.org.uk).
Network of academics, activists, organisations.

Rising Tide UK [RTUK] (EL RA AL), c/o London Action Resource Centre, 62 Fieldgate St, Whitechapel, London E1 1ES (info@risingtide.org.uk) (www.risingtide.org.uk).
Direct action for climate justice.

RoadPeace (EL RE HR), Shakespeare Business Centre, 245a Coldharbour Lane, London SW9 8RR (+44-20-7733 1603) (info@roadpeace.org) (roadpeace.org).
Supports road traffic victims and families.

Saferworld (RE AT), The Grayston Centre, 28 Charles Sq, London N1 (+44-20-7324 4646) (fax 7324 4647) (general@saferworld.org.uk) (www.saferworld.org.uk).
Helping people turn away from armed violence.

BRITAIN

Scientists for Global Responsibility [SGR] (RE ND EL AT DA), Unit 2.8, Halton Mill, Mill Lane, Halton, Lancaster LA2 6ND, Lancashire (+44-1524-812073) (info@sgr.org.uk) (www.sgr.org.uk). *SGR Newsletter*.

Scotland's for Peace (ND RE AT), c/o 77 Southpark Ave, Glasgow G12 (+44-141-357 1529) (info@scotland4peace.org) (www.scotland4peace.org). Umbrella body.

Scottish Campaign for Nuclear Disarmament [SCND] (ND), PO Box 3620, Glasgow G73 9FQ (+44-141-357 1529) (scnd@banthebomb.org) (www.banthebomb.org). *Nuclear Free Scotland*.

Scottish Friends of Palestine (HR TW), 31 Tinto Rd, Glasgow G43 2AL (+44-141-637 8046) (info@scottish-friends-of-palestine.org) (www.scottishfriendsofpalestine.org).

Scrap Trident Coalition (ND PA RA), c/o Edinburgh Peace and Justice Centre, 5 Upper Bow, Edinburgh EH1 2JN (+44-131-629 1058) (scraptrident@gmail.com) (scraptrident.org). Network in Scotland.

SCRAP Weapons (DA), Centre for Int'l Studies and Diplomacy, SOAS, University of London, 10 Thornhaugh St, Russell Sq, London WC1H 0XG (+44-20-7898 4322) (scrap.weapons@soas.ac.uk) (www.scrapweapons.com).

Sea Shepherd UK (EL RA), 27 Old Gloucester St, London WC1N 3AX (+44-300-111 0501) (admin@seashepherduk.org) (www.seashepherd.org.uk). Conserving nature on the high seas.

Seeds of Peace (CD CR PO), Suite 1, 3rd Floor, 11-12 St James's Square, London SW1Y 4LB (london@seedsofpeace.org) (www.seedsofpeace.org). Trains people for conflict transformation.

Servas Britain (SE), c/o 1 Wrekin Course, Wellington, Telford TF6 5AJ (www.servas.org.uk).

Shadow World Investigations [SWI] (AT RE), 7 Cavendish Sq, Marylebone, London W1G 0PE (admin@shadowworldinvestigations.org) (shadowworldinvestigations.org). Investigates corruption, especially in arms trade.

Soil Association (EL PO TW), South Plaza, Marlborough St, Bristol BS1 (+44-117-314 5000) (fax 314 5001) (memb@soilassociation.org) (www.soilassociation.org). Scotland office: +44-131-666 2474.

Solidarity with People of Turkey [SPOT] (HR), 22 Moorefield Rd, London N17 6PY (spot@daymer.org) (spotturkey.co.uk).

South Cheshire & North Staffs CND [SCANS CND] (ND), Groundwork Enterprise Centre, Albany Works, Moorland Rd, Burslem, Stoke-on-Trent ST6 1EB, Staffs (+44-1782-829913) (scanscnd@ymail.com) (www.scanscnd.co.uk). *Banner*.

Southdowns Peace Group (DA), c/o Vida, 22 Beaufort Rd, Bedhampton, Havant PO9 3HU (+44-23-9234 6696) (vida.henning@ntlworld.com).

Southern Region CND (ND), 3 Harpsichord Place, Oxford OX4 1BY (+44-1865-248357) (oxfordcnd@phonecoop.coop).

Stop Climate Chaos Scotland [SCCS] (EL), 2nd Floor, Thorn House, 5 Rose St, Edinburgh EH2 2PR (+44-131-243 2701) (info@stopclimatechaosscotland.org) (www.stopclimatechaos.org/scotland). Development, environment, etc, groups' coalition.

Stop Hinkley (EL), 8 The Bartons, Yeabridge, South Petherton TA13 5LW, Somerset (+44-1749-860767) (admin@stophinkley.org) (www.stophinkley.org). Against nuclear power in south-west England.

Stop the War Coalition [STWC], 86 Durham Rd, London N7 (+44-20-7561 4830) (office@stopwar.org.uk) (www.stopwar.org.uk).

Student Christian Movement [SCM] (RP), Grays Court, 3 Nursery Rd, Edgbaston, Birmingham B15 3JX (+44-121-426 4918) (scm@movement.org.uk) (www.movement.org.uk).

Surfers Against Sewage [SAS] (EL), Unit 2, Wheal Kitty Workshops, St Agnes TR5 0RD, Cornwall (+44-1872-553001) (fax 552615) (info@sas.org.uk) (www.sas.org.uk). *Pipeline News*.

Survivors Against Terror (CD CR RE), c/o 21 Keyworth Rd, Gedling, Nottingham NG4 4JD (contact@survivorsagainstterror.org.uk) (survivorsagainstterror.org.uk). Supporting victims and bereaved.

Syria Peace & Justice Group (CR CD AT DA), c/o LARC, 62 Fieldgate St, London E1 (syriapeaceandjustice@gmail.com) (syriapeaceandjustice.wordpress.com). Anti-militarist human rights campaign.

Syrian Human Rights Committee [SHRC] (HR), PO Box 123, Edgware HA8 0XF, Middlesex (fax +44-870-1377678) (walid@shrc.org) (www.shrc.org). Syrian human rights group in exile.

Tapol (HR AT TW RE), Durham Resource Centre, 86 Durham Rd, London N7 (+44-20-7561 7485) (info@tapol.org) (www.tapol.org).

The Climate Coalition (EL), Romero House, 55 Westminster Bridge Rd, London SE1 7JB (+44-20-7870 2213) (admin@theclimatecoalition.org) (www.theclimatecoalition.org).

The Corner House (HR TW EL), Station Rd, Sturminster Newton, Dorset DT10 1BB (+44-1258-473795) (fax) (enquiries@thecornerhouse.org.uk) (www.thecornerhouse.org.uk). *Briefing Papers*.

The Forgiveness Project (CR PO), 10 Buckingham Palace Rd, London SW1W 0QP (+44-20-7821 0035) (fax) (info@theforgivenessproject.com) (www.theforgivenessproject.com).

Tibet Foundation (HR), Hamilton House, Mabledon Place, London WC1H 9BB (+44-20-7930 6001) (info@tibet-foundation.org) (www.tibet-foundation.org).

Tibet Society (HR TW CR), 2 Baltic Place, London N1 5AQ (+44-20-7923 0021) (info@tibetsociety.com) (www.tibetsociety.com). Campaigns for Tibetan self-determination.

Together Against Sizewell C [TASC] (EL), c/o Wood Farm, Westward Ho, Leiston, Suffolk IP16 4HT. (info@tasizewellc.org.uk) (tasizewellc.org.uk). Opposing proposed new nuclear power station.

Town and Country Planning Association [TCPA] (EL), 17 Carlton House Terr, London SW1Y 5AS (+44-20-7930 8903) (fax 7930 3280) (tcpa@tcpa.org.uk) (www.tcpa.org.uk). *Town & Country Planning*.

Trade Justice Movement (TW HR EL), 66 Offley Rd, London SW9 0LS (mail@tjm.org.uk) (www.tjm.org.uk).

Trident Ploughshares (WR ND RA), c/o Edinburgh Peace & Justice Centre, 25 Nicolson Sq, Edinburgh EH8 9BX (+44-345 458 8361) (tp2000@gn.apc.org) (tridentploughshares.org).

Turning the Tide (SF PO RA), Friends House, Euston Rd, London NW1 2BJ (+44-20-7663 1064) (fax 7663 1049) (stevew@quaker.org.uk) (www.turning-the-tide.org). *Making Waves*. Offers workshops, nonviolence training, etc.

Tyne & Wear CND (ND), 1 Rectory Ave, Gosforth, Newcastle-upon-Tyne NE3 1XS (+44-191-285 1290) (rhpg@btinternet.com)

UK Committee for UNICEF [UNICEF UK] (TW HR), UNICEF House, 30a Great Russell St, London EC1 (+44-20-7490 2388) (fax 7250 1733) (www.unicef.org.uk).

UK Friends of the Bereaved Families Forum [FBFF] (CD CR PO), 6 St Pauls Way, London N3 2PP (info@ukfbff.org) (familiesforum.co.uk). (See Parents' Circle - Families' Forum under both Israel and Palestine).

UNA Exchange (UN WC PO), Temple of Peace, Cathays Park, Cardiff CF10 3AP (+44-29-2022 3088) (fax 2022 2540) (info@unaexchange.org) (www.unaexchange.org). *Opinions*.

Unitarian and Free Christian Peace Fellowship [UPF] (RP), c/o Sue Woolley, 5 Martins Rd, Piddinston, Northampton NN7 2DN (+44-1604-870746) (www.unitariansocieties.org.uk/peace).

United Nations Association - UK [UNA-UK] (UN HR RE TW), 3 Whitehall Court, London SW1A 2EL (+44-20-7766 3454) (fax 7000 1381) (info@una.org.uk) (www.una.org.uk).

Uniting for Peace [UfP] (DA ND CD AT RE), 14 Cavell St, London E1 2HP (+44-20-7791 1717) (info@unitingforpeace.com) (unitingforpeace.com). *Uniting for Peace*. Also in Edinburgh (+44-131-446 9545).

Vegan Society (EL TW PO HR), Donald Watson House, 34-35 Ludgate Hill, Birmingham B3 1EH (+44-121-523 1730) (info@vegansociety.com) (www.vegansociety.com). *The Vegan*.

Vegetarian Society of the UK (EL TW PO), Parkdale, Dunham Rd, Altrincham, Cheshire (+44-161-925 2000) (fax 926 9182) (info@vegsoc.org) (www.vegsoc.org). *The Vegetarian*.

Veggies (PO EL), c/o Sumac Centre, 245 Gladstone St, Nottingham NG7 (+44-115-960 8254) (info@veggies.org.uk) (www.veggies.org.uk).

Violence Research Centre (RE), c/o Institute of Criminology, Sidgwick Ave, Cambridge CB3 9DA (+44-1223-335360) (fax 335356) (vrc@crim.cam.ac.uk) (www.vrc.crim.cam.ac.uk). Studies interpersonal violence.

Voluntary Service Overseas [VSO] (TW), 100 London Rd, Kingston-upon-Thames KT2, Surrey (+44-20-8780 7500) (enquiry@vsoint.org) (www.vsointernational.org).

Volunteer Action for Peace [VAP UK] (WC HR EL), 16 Overhill Rd, East Dulwich, London SE22 0PH (action@vap.org.uk) (www.vap.org.uk). Within UK, tel 0844-209 0927.

Volunteering Matters (PO CD), The Levy Centre, 18-24 Lower Clapton Rd, London E5 (+44-20-3780 5870) (information@volunteeringmatters.org.uk) (volunteeringmatters.org.uk). Formerly Community Service Volunteers.

War On Want [WOW] (TW), 44-48 Shepherdess Walk, London N1 7JP (+44-20-7324 5040) (fax 7324 5041) (support@waronwant.org) (www.waronwant.org).

Week of Prayer for World Peace (RP), c/o 126 Manor Green Rd, Epsom KT19 8LN, Surrey (+44-1628-530309) (j.jackson215@btinternet.com) (www.weekofprayerforworldpeace.com).

West Midlands CND [WMCND] (ND), 54 Allison St, Digbeth, Birmingham B5 5TH (+44-121-643 4617) (wmcndall@gmail.com) (www.wmcnd.org.uk).

West Midlands Quaker Peace Education Project [WMQPEP] (SF RE CR), 41 Bull St, Birmingham B4 6AF (+44-121-236 4796) (office@peacemakers.org.uk) (www.peacemakers.org.uk).

BRITAIN

Western Sahara Campaign UK (HR TW), Manora, Cwmystwyth, Aberystwyth SY23 4AF (+44-1974-282214) (coordinator@wsahara.org.uk) (www.wsahara.org.uk)

White Ribbon Campaign (PO), White Ribbon House, 1 New Rd, Mytholmroyd, Hebden Bridge HX7 5DZ (+44-1422-886545) (info@whiteribboncampaign.co.uk) (www.whiteribboncampaign.co.uk).

Women's Environmental Network [WEN] (EL), 20 Club Row, London E2 7EY (+44-20-7481 9004) (info@wen.org.uk) (www.wen.org.uk).

Women's International League for Peace and Freedom [UK WILPF] (WL), 52-54 Featherstone St, London EC1Y 8RT (+44-20-7250 1968) (ukwilpf.peace@gmail.com) (www.wilpf.org.uk). Also Scottish office (scottishwilpf@yahoo.com.uk).

Woodcraft Folk (PA EL PO RE TW), Units 9/10, 83 Crampton St, London SE17 (+44-20-7703 4173) (fax 7358 6370) (info@woodcraft.org.uk) (www.woodcraft.org.uk). *The Courier*. Co-operative children's and youth organisation.

World Future Council - UK Office (WF EL DA ND), 4th Floor, Rex House, 4-12 Regent St, London SW1Y 4PE (info.uk@worldfuturecouncil.org) (www.worldfuturecouncil.org). Promotes sustainable future.

World Harmony Orchestra (CD PO), 12d Princess Crescent, London N4 2HJ (www.worldharmonyorchestra.com). Raises funds for humanitarian causes.

World Peace Campaign, Hill House, Cookley, Kidderminster DY10 3UW, Worcs (+44-1562-851101) (fax 851824) (office@worldpeacecampaign.co.uk) (www.worldpeacecampaign.co.uk).

World Peace Prayer Society [WPPS] (RP PO EL RE), Allanton Sanctuary, Auldgirth, Dumfries DG2 0RY (+44-1387-740642) (allanton@worldpeace-uk.org) (www.worldpeace-uk.org). Promote the message "May peace prevail on earth".

XR Peace (EL RA), via Trident Ploughshares, c/o Edinburgh Peace & Justice Centre, Central Methodist Church, 25 Nicolson Sq, Edinburgh EH8 9BX (+44-1547-520929) (xrpeace@gn.apc.org) (xrpeace.org). Peace activists supporting Extinction Rebellion.

Yorkshire CND (ND), The Deaf Centre, 25 Hallfield Rd, Bradford BD1 3RP, W Yorks (+44-1274-730795) (info@yorkshirecnd.org.uk) (www.yorkshirecnd.org.uk). *Action for Peace*.

Youth and Student CND [YSCND] (ND RA), 162 Holloway Rd, London N7 8DQ (+44-20-7700 2393) (yscnd@riseup.net) (www.yscnd.org).

BURKINA FASO

Action des Chrétiens pour l'Abolition de la Torture [ACAT] (HR), 02 BP 5093, Ouagadougou 02 (+226-5043 7029) (acatburkina@gmail.com)

BURMA

Peace Way Foundation (HR), see under Thailand.

CAMBODIA

Centre for Peace and Conflict Studies (RE CR), PO Box 93066, Siem Reap City - 17252, Siem Reap Province (centrepeaceconflictstudies@gmail.com) (www.centrepeaceconflictstudies.org).

CANADA

Action by Christians Against Torture / Action des Chrétiens pour l'Abolition de la torture [ACAT-Canada] (HR), 2715 chemin de la Côte-Ste-Catherine, Montréal, QC, H3T 1B6 (+1-514-890 6169) (fax 890 6484) (acat@acatcanada.org) (www.acatcanada.org).

Amnesty International Canadian Section - English Speaking (AI), 312 Laurier Ave E, Ottawa, ON, K1N 1H9 (+1-613-744 7667) (fax 746 2411) (members@amnesty.ca) (www.amnesty.ca). *The Activist*.

Amnistie Internationale - Section Canadienne Francophone (AI), 50 rue Ste-Catherine Ouest - bureau 500, Montréal, QC, H2X 3V4 (+1-514-766 9766) (fax 766 2088) (www.amnistie.ca). *Agir*.

Artistes pour la Paix (PA ND AT), CP 867 - Succursale C, Montréal, QC, H2L 4L6 (artistespourlapaix.org).

Baptist Peace Fellowship of North America - Bautistas por la Paz (RP), see under USA.

Boundary Peace Initiative (FR), Box 2572, Grand Forks, BC, V0H 1H0 (+1-250-442 0434) (l4peace@telus.net) (boundarypeaceinitiative.ca)

Canadian Centres for Teaching Peace (RE PO), 230 Belle Isle St, Shediac, NB, E4P 1G8 (+1-403-461 2469) (fax 309-407 6576) (stewartr@peace.ca) (www.peace.ca).

Canadian Coalition for Nuclear Responsibility / Regroupement pour la Surveillance du Nucléaire [CCNR] (ND EL CD), 53 Dufferin Rd, Hampstead, QC, H3X 2X8 (+1-514-489 5118) (ccnr@web.ca). (www.ccnr.org).

Canadian Peace Congress (WP), PO Box 73593, Wychwood Post Office, Toronto, ON, M6C 4A7 (info@CanadianPeaceCongress.ca) (www.canadianpeacecongress.ca).

Canadian School of Peacebuilding (RE CR), Canadian Mennonite University, 500 Shaftesbury Blvd, Winnipeg, Manitoba, R3P 2N2 (+1-204-487 3300) (fax 837 7415) (csop@cmu.ca) (csop.cmu.ca).

Canadian Secular Alliance [CSA] (HR), 802 - 195 St Patrick St, Toronto, ON, M5T 2Y8

Centre de Ressources sur la Non-violence [CRNV] (WR EL), 1945 rue Mullins - bureau 160, Montréal, QC, H3K 1N9 (+1-514-504 5012) (crnv@nonviolence.ca) (nonviolence.ca).

Christian Peacemaker Teams [CPT Canada] (RP PA RA), 103 Bellevue Ave, Torontoo, ON, M5T 2N8 (+1-647-339 0991) (canada@cpt.org) (cpt.org). Also based in USA.

Civilian Peace Service Canada (CD PO), 2106-1025 Richmond Rd, Ottawa, ON, K2B 8G8 (+1-613-721 9829) (gbreedyk@civilianpeaceservice.org) (civilianpeaceservice.ca).

Coalition for Gun Control, PO Box 90062, 1488 Queen St West, Toronto, ON, M6K 3K3 (+1-416-604 0209) (coalitionforguncontrol@gmail.com) (guncontrol.ca). Also in Montreal (+1-514-528 2360).

Coalition to Oppose the Arms Trade [COAT] (AT), 191 James St, Ottawa, ON, K1R 5M6 (+1-613-231 3076) (overcoat@rogers.com) (coat.ncf.ca).

Collectif Échec À la Guerre (PA RE DA), c/o AQOCI, 1001 Rue Sherbrooke Est - Bur 540, Montréal, QC, H2L 1L3 (+1-514-919 7249) (info@echecalaguerre.org) (echecalaguerre.org).

Conscience Canada (TR), 515 Langs Dr - Unit J, Cambridge, ON, N3H 5E4 (+1-250-537 5251) (info@consciencecanada.ca) (www.consciencecanada.ca).

Edmonton Peace Council (WP), 392 Meadowview Drive, Fort Saskatchewan, Alberta T8L 0N9 (+1-587-873 9739) (canadianpeace@gmail.com). *Alberta Peace News*.

Friends of the Earth / Les Ami(e)s de la Terre [FoE] (FE), 150 - 18 Louisa St, Ottawa, ON, K1R 6Y6 (+1-613-241 0085) (foe@foecanada.org) (www.foecanada.org).

Greenpeace Canada (GP), 33 Cecil St, Toronto, ON, M5T 1N1 (+1-416-597 8408) (fax 597 8422) (supporter.ca@greenpeace.org) (www.greenpeace.ca).

IPPNW Canada (IP IB), 30 Cleary Ave, Ottawa, ON, K2A 4A1 (+1-613-233 1982) (info@ippnwcanada.ca) (www.ippnwcanada.ca).

Mennonite Central Committee Canada (RP HR EL), 134 Plaza Dr, Winnipeg, MB, R3T 5K9 (+1-204-261 6381) (fax 269 9875) (canada@mcccanada.ca) (www.mcccanada.ca).

Pace e Bene Canada (PA RP), 4058 Rivard, Montreal, Quebec, H2L 4H9 (veronow@sympatico.ca).

Peace Brigades International - Canada [PBI-Canada] (CR RE SD), 211 Bronson Ave - Suite 220, Ottawa, ON, K1R 6H5 (+1-613-237 6968) (direction@pbicanada.org) (pbicanada.org).

Peace Magazine (PA AT CR), Box 248, Toronto P, Toronto, ON, M5S 2S7 (+1-416-789 2294) (office@peacemagazine.org) (www.peacemagazine.org). 4 yrly, Can$20 (Can$24 US, Can$35 elsewhere).

Peace Studies Program (RE), McMaster University, Togo Salmon Hall 721, 1280 Main St West, Hamilton, Ontario L8S 4M2 (+1-905-525 9140) (peacestudies.humanities.mcmaster.ca). Formerly Centre for Peace Studies.

PeaceWorks, c/o MSCU Centre for Peace Advancement, CGUC, University of Waterloo, 140 Westmount Road North, Waterloo, ON, N2L 3G6 (+1-519-591 1365) (mail@peaceworks.tv) (peaceworks.tv). Youth movement.

Project Ploughshares (RE AT ND RP DA), 140 Westmount Rd North, Waterloo, ON, N2L 3G6 (+1-519-888 6541) (fax 888 0018) (plough@ploughshares.ca) (www.ploughshares.ca).

Project Save the World, c/o Box 248, Toronto P, Toronto, ON, M5S 2S7 (+1-416-789 2294) (project@peacemagazine.org) (peacemagazine.org). A project of Peace Magazine.

Religions for Peace - Canada / Religions pour la Paix - Canada (RP RE PA), 3333 Queen Mary Rd 490-1, Montréal, QC, H3Z 1A2 (pascale.fremond@videotron.ca).

Servas Canada (SE), c/o Christine Fernie, PO Box 147, Rimbey, AB, T0C 2J0 (canada@servas.org) (www.canadaservas.org).

Trudeau Centre for Peace, Conflict and Justice (RE), Monk School of Global Affairs, University of Toronto, 1 Devonshire Place, Toronto, ON, M5S 3K7 (+1-416-946 0326) (pcj.programme@utoronto.ca) (www.munkschool.utoronto.ca/trudeaucentre).

United Nations Association in Canada / Association canadienne pour les Nations-Unies [UNAC/ACNU] (UN EL RE HR CD), 400 - 30 Metcalfe St, Ottawa, ON, K1P 5L4 (+1-613-232 5751) (fax 563 2455) (info@unac.org) (unac.org).

USCC Doukhobors (RP CD PA), Box 760, Grand Forks, BC, V0H 1H0 (+1-250-442 8252) (fax 442 3433) (info@usccdoukhobors.org) (www.usccdoukhobors.org). *Iskra*. Union of Spiritual Communities of Christ.

Voice of Women for Peace / La Voix des Femmes pour la Paix [VOW] (IB UN PA), 25 Cecil St - Suite 310, Toronto, ON, M5T 1N1 (+1-416-603 7915) (info@vowpeace.org) (www.vowpeace.org).

Women's International League for Peace and Freedom [WILPF] (WL), PO Box 365,

CANADA

916 West Broadway, Vancouver, BC, V5Z 1K7 (+1-604-224 1517) (judydavis@telus.net).
World Federalist Movement - Canada / Mouvement Fédéraliste Mondial (Canada) (WF), Suite 207, 110 - 323 Chapel St, Ottawa, ON, K1N 7Z2 (+1-613-232 0647) (wfcnat@web.ca) (www.worldfederalistscanada.org). *Mondial.*

CENTRAL AFRICAN REPUBLIC

ACAT-Centrafrique (HR), BP 527, Bangui (acat_rca@yahoo.fr).

CHAD

ACAT Tchad (HR), BP 2231, N'Djamena (acatchad2017@gmail.com).
Tchad Non-Violence [TNV] (WR FR), BP 1266, N'Djamena (astnv@yahoo.fr).

CHILE

Greenpeace Chile (GP), Argomedo 50, Santiago (+56-2-2634 2120) (fax 2634 8580) (info-chile@greenpeace.org) (www.greenpeace.org/chile/).
Grupo de Objeción de Conciencia "Ni Casco Ni Uniforme" (WR), Bremen 585, Ñuñoa, Santiago (+56-2-556 6066) (objetores@yahoo.com) (nicasconiuniforme.wordpress.com).
Grupo de Objeción de Conciencia - Rompiendo Filas (WR), Prat 289 - Oficina 2-A, Temuco (rompiendofilas@entodaspartes.org).
Servicio Paz y Justicia - Chile [SERPAJ] (FR), Orella Nº 1015, Valparaíso (+56-32-215 8239) (serpaj@serpajchile.cl) (serpajchile.cl).

CHINA

China Committee on Religion and Peace [CCRP] (RP), 23 Taipingqiao St, Xichen District, Beijing 100811 (+86-10-6619 1655) (fax 6619 1645) (ccrp1994@hotmail.com) (www.cppcc.gov.cn/ccrp).
Friends of Nature [FON] (EL), Rm 406, Building C, Huazhan Guoji Gongyu, 12 Yumin Road, Chaoyang District, Beijing 100029 (+86-10-6523 2040) (office@fonchina.org) (www.fon.org.cn).

CONGO, DEMOCRATIC REPUBLIC OF

Association pour les Nations Unies de la RDC [ANU-RDC] (UN), BP 2214, Kinshasa 1 (www.unadrcongo.org).
Cercle des Jeunes Leaders pour la Paix / Circle of Young Leaders for Peace (RP), Av Kwango - No 7, Kintambo Magasin, Ngaliema, Dist Lukunga, Kinshasa (+243-81-514 0938) (jcsaki2000@yahoo.fr).
Congo Peace Network (DA CR), 42 Ave Bunagana, Q Katindo, Commune de Goma (+243-85-222 4225) (info@congopeacenetwork.org) (cpn.congopeacenetwork.org).
Groupe Interconfessionnel de la Réconciliation / Kinshasa [GIR] (FR), see under Belgium.
Life & Peace Institute (CR RP), Bukavu (for postal address see under Rwanda) (pieter.vanholder@life-peace.org).
Peace & Conflict Resolution Project (CR), for postal address see under Rwanda (+243-993-463279) (peacecrp@yahoo.com) (www.peaceconflictresolutionproject.webs.com). Based in Bukavu.

COSTA RICA

Centro de Estudios Para la Paz [CEPPA] (RE), Apdo 8-4820, 1000 San José (+506-2234 0524) (fax) (info@ceppacr.org) (www.ceppacr.org).
Liga Internacional de Mujeres pro Paz y Libertad [LIMPAL] (WL), Avenida sexta Bis No 1336 - por Calle 15, Costado Oeste de los Tribunales San José (limpalcr@yahoo.es).
Monteverde Friends Meeting (SF), Monteverde 5655, Puntarenas (+506-2645 5530) (fax 2645 5302) (MonteverdeQuakers@gmail.com) (MonteverdeQuakers.org).

CROATIA

Centar za Zene Zrtve Rata / Centre for Women War Victims - ROSA [CZZR] (CR HR), Kralja Drzislava 2, 10000 Zagreb (+385-1-455 1142) (fax 455 1128) (cenzena@zamir.net) (www.czzzr.hr). Feminist, anti-militarist.
Centar za Mirovne Studije / Centre for Peace Studies [CMS] (WR CR RE HR), Selska cesta 112a, 10000 Zagreb (+385-1-482 0094) (fax) (cms@cms.hr) (www.cms.hr).

CUBA

Movimiento Cubano por la Paz y la Soberanía de los Pueblos (WP), Calle C No 670, e/ 27 y 29, Vedado, Habana (+53-7-831 9429) (secretariat@movpaz.cu) (www.movpaz.cu).

CYPRUS

Hands Across the Divide - Women Building Bridges in Cyprus (HR CD CR DA), Ellispontos 10, Dasoupolis 2015, Nicosia (handsacrossthedivide@gmail.com) (www.handsacrossthedivide.org). Supports feminist values and demilitaristion.
Oikologiki Kinisi Kyprou / Ecological Movement of Cyprus (EL), TK 28948, Nicosia 2084 (+357-2251 8787) (fax 2251 2710) (ecological_movement@cytanet.com.cy)

(www.ecologicalmovement.org.cy). *Ecologiki Enimerosi.*

Philoi tes Ges (Kypros) / Friends of the Earth (Cyprus) [FOE] (FE), 361 Saint Andrews St, Lemesos 3035 (+357-2534 7042) (office@foecypus.org) (www.foecypus.org).

United Nations Association of Cyprus [UNAC] (UN), TK 21508, 1510 Nicosia(+357-2465 6318) (c.a.theodoulou@cytanet.com.cy).

CYPRUS (NORTHERN)

Hands Across the Divide - Women Building Bridges in Cyprus (HR CD CR DA), see under Cyprus (www.handsacrossthedivide.org). Supports feminist values and demilitaristion.

CZECH REPUBLIC

České Mírové Hnutí / Czech Peace Movement (WP), Josefa Houdka 123, 15531 Praha (mirovehnuti@email.cz) (www.mirovehnuti.cz).

Hnutí DUHA (FE RA), Údolní 33, 60200 Brno (+420-5 4521 4431) (fax 5 4521 4429) (info@hnutiduha.cz) (hnutiduha.cz). *Evergreen.*

Lékaři za Bezpečný Život na Zemi / Physicians for Global Security (IP), c/o Vaclav Stukavec, Jizní 222, 46801 Jablonec nad Nisou 8 (+420-603 364224) (stukav@volny.cz).

Nezávislé Sociálne Ekologické Hnutí / Independent Socio-Ecological Movement [NESEHNUTÍ] (WR EL HR AT), Krízová 463/15, 60300 Brno (+420-5 4324 5342) (brno@nesehnuti.cz) (nesehnuti.cz). Social Ecological Movement.

Památník Mohyla Míru / Cairn of Peace Memorial (RE), K Mohyle Míru 200, 66458 Peace (+420-54 424 4724) (www.muzeumbrnenska.cz).

DENMARK

Aldrig Mere Krig / No More War [AMK] (WR AT IB), Nørremarksvej 4, 6880 Tarm (+45-9737 3163) (info@aldrigmerekrig.dk) (aldrigmerekrig.dk). *Ikkevold.*

Amnesty International (AI), Gammeltorv 8 - 5 sal, 1457 København K (+45-3345 6565) (amnesty@amnesty.dk) (www.amnesty.dk).

Center for Konfliktløsning / Danish Centre for Conflict Resolution (CR RE), Dronning Olgas Vej 30, 2000 Frederiksberg (+45-3520 0550) (center@konfliktloesning.dk) (www.konfliktloesning.dk).

Danske Laeger Mod Kernevåben [DLMK] (IP), Langdalsvej 40, 8220 Brabrand, Aarhus (+45-8626 4717) (povl.revsbech@gmail.com) (www.danskelaegermodkernevaaben.dk). *Läkare mot Kärnvapen.*

FN-Forbundet (UN WF), Tordenskjoldsgade 25 st th, 1055 København K (+45-3346 4690) (fnforbundet@fnforbundet.dk) (www.fnforbundet.dk).

Klimabevaegelsen i Danmark / Climate Movement Denmark (EL), c/o Thomas Meinart Larsen, JC Christensens Gade 2A - 3TV, 2300 København S (sek@klimabevaegelsen.dk) (www.klimabevaegelsen.dk).

Kvindernes Internationale Liga for Fred og Frihed [KILFF] (WR), Vesterbrogade 10 - 2, 1620 København V (wilpfdk@gmail.com) (kvindefredsliga.dk).

NOAH / Friends of the Earth Denmark (FE), Nørrebrogade 39 - 1, 2200 København N (+45-3536 1212) (fax 3536 1217) (noah@noah.dk) (www.noah.dk).

Plums Fond for Fred, Økologi og Baeredygtighed / Plums Foundation for Peace, Ecology and Sustainability (DA HR EL), Dronningensgade 14, 1420 København K (+45-3295 4417) (plumsfond@plumsfond.dk). Previously Danish Peace Foundation / Fredsfonden.

Servas Danmark (SE), c/o Jan Degrauwe, Højbakkevej 32, 9440 Aabybro (+45-2048 5087) (info@servas.dk) (www.servas.dk).

EAST TIMOR

Haburas Foundation / Friends of the Earth Timor Leste (FE), PO Box 390, Dili (+670-331 0103) (haburaslorosae@yahoo.com) (www.haburasfoundation.org).

ECUADOR

Servicio Paz y Justicia del Ecuador [SER-PAJ] (WR RP), Casilla 17-03-1567, Quito (+593-22-257 1521) (fax) (serpaj@ecuanex.ec) (www.serpaj.org.ec).

EGYPT

Arab Organisation for Human Rights [AOHR] (HR), 91 Merghani St, Heliopolis, Cairo 11341 (+20-2-2418 1396) (fax 2418 5346) (alaa.shalaby@aohr.net) (www.aohr.net).

No to Compulsory Military Service Movement (WR), [post should be sent via the WRI office in London] (+49-1763-141 5934) (NoMilService@gmail.com) (www.nomilservice.com).

FINLAND

Ålands Fredsinstitut / Åland Islands Peace Institute (RE HR CR), PB 85, 22101 Mariehamn, Åland (+358-18-15570) (peace@peace.ax) (www.peace.ax).

Greenpeace Finland (GP), Iso Roobertinkatu 20-22 A (5 frs), 00120 Helsinki (+358-9-6229 2200) (fax 6229 2222) (info.finland@greenpeace.org) (www.greenpeace.fi).

Kansainvälinen Vapaaehtoistyö [KVT] (SC), Rauhanasema, Veturitori 3, 00520 Helsinki (kvt@kvtfinland.org) (www.kvtfinland.fi).

FINLAND

Laajan Turvallisuuden Verkosto / Wider Security Network [WISE] (CR DA), Siltasaarenkatu 4 - 7th floor, 00530 Helsinki (+358-44-972 4669) (info@widersecurity.fi) (www.widersecurity.fi).
Formerly Civil Society Conflict Prevention Network.

Maan Ystävät / Friends of the Earth (FE), Mechelininkatu 36 B 1, 00260 Helsinki (+358-45-886 3958) (fax -2-237 1670) (toimisto@maanystavat.fi) (www.maanystavat.fi).

Peace Union of Finland / Suomen Rauhanliitto / Finlands Fredsförbundet (IB FR ND AT RE), Peace Station, Veturitori, 00520 Helsinki (+358-9-7568 2828) (fax 147297) (rauhanliitto@rauhanliitto.fi).

Physicians for Social Responsibility / Lääkärin Sosiaalinen Vastuu / Läkarens Sociala Ansvar [PSR/LSV] (IP HR PA EL), Caloniuksenkatu 9 D 64, 00100 Helsinki (+358-45-350 8516) (lsv@lsv.fi) (www.lsv.fi).

Sadankomitea / Committee of 100 (WR IB ND AT), Rauhanasema, Veturitori 3, 00520 Helsinki (sadankomitea@sadankomitea.fi) (www.sadankomitea.fi).

SaferGlobe (RE AT CR), Siltasaarenkatu 4 - 7th floor, 00530 Helsinki (+358-40-778 8523) (toimisto@saferglobe.fi) (www.saferglobe.fi).
Peace and security think-tank.

Sitoutumaton Vasemmisto / Independent Left (WR EL HR), Mannerheimintie 5B 7krs, 00100 Helsinki (sitvas-hallitus@helsinki.fi) (sitvasfi.wordpress.com).

Siviilipalveluskeskus / Civiltjänstcentralen (PA), Latokartanontie 97, 07810 Ingermaninkylä (+358-295-029500) (etunimi.sukunimi@ely-keskus.fi) (www.siviilipalveluskeskus.fi).
Centre for Non-Military Service.

Suomen Luonnonsuojeluliitto / Finnish Association for Nature Conservation [FANC] (EL), Itälahdenkatu 22-b A, 00210 Helsinki (+358-9-2280 8224) (toimisto@sll.fi) (www.sll.fi).

Suomen Rauhanpuolestajat / Finnish Peace Committee (IB WP TW), Hämeentie 48, 00500 Helsinki (+358-50-358 1441) (pulut@rauhanpuolustajat.fi) (www.rauhanpuolustajat.org).
Rauhan Puolesta.

Taiteilijat rauhan puolesta / Artister för Fred / Performers and Artists for Nuclear Disarmament [PAND] (ND), Pengerkatu 1, 00750 Helsinki (+358-50-522 2748) (pandtalo@hotmail.fi).

Union of Conscientious Objectors / Aseistakieltäytyjäliitto [AKL] (WR), Rauhanasema, Veturitori 3, 00520 Helsinki (+358-40-836 2786) (toimisto@akl-web.fi) (www.akl-web.fi).

Women's International League for Peace and Freedom - Finnish Section [WILPF] (WL), PL 1174, 00101 Helsinki (wilpf@wilpf.fi) (wilpf.fi).

FRANCE

Abolition des Armes Nucléaires - Maison de Vigilance (ND), 21 ter rue Voltaire, 75011 Paris (abolitiondesarmesnucleaires@orange.fr) (abolitiondesarmesnucleaires.org).
Formerly Maison de Vigilance.

Action des Chrétiens pour l'Abolition de la Torture [ACAT] (HR), 7 rue Georges Lardennois, 75019 Paris (+33-14040 4243) (fax 14040 4244) (acat@acatfrance.fr) (www.acatfrance.fr).

Action des Citoyens pour le Désarmement Nucléaire [ACDN] (ND), 31 Rue du Cormier, 17100 Saintes (+33-673 507661) (contact@acdn.net) (www.acdn.net).
Opposes both military and civilian nukes.

***Alternatives Non-Violentes* [ANV]** (PA RE CR), Centre 308, 82 rue Jeanne d'Arc, 76000 Rouen (+33-235 752344) (contact@alternatives-non-violentes.org) (alternatives-non-violentes.org).

Amis de la Terre - France (FE), Mundo M, 47 ave Pasteur, 93100 Montreuil (+33-14851 3222) (fax 14851 9512) (france@amisdelaterre.org) (www.amisdelaterre.org).

Association des Médecins Français pour la Prévention de la Guerre Nucléaire [AMF-PGN] (IP), 5 Rue Las Cases, 75007 Paris (+33-14336 7781) (revue@amfpgn.org) (amfpgn.org). *Médecine et Guerre Nucléaire.*

Association française pour les Nations Unies (UN), 26 Av Charles Floquet, 75007 Paris (+33-17716 2454) (contact@afnu.fr) (afnu.fr).

Brigades de Paix Internationales [PBI-France] (HR PO RE CD), 21 ter, rue Voltaire, 75011 Paris (+33-14373 4960) (pbi.france@free.fr) (pbi-france.org).
Presence Internationale.

Centre de Documentation et de Recherche sur la Paix et les Conflits & Observatoire des Armements [CDRPC] (RE AT DA), 187 Montée de Choulans, 69005 Lyon (+33-478 369303) (www.obsarm.info).

Centre de Ressources sur la Non-violence de Midi-Pyrénées (RE CR), 2 Allée du Limousin, 31770 Colomiers (+33-561 786680) (crnv.midi-pyrenees@wanadoo.fr) (www.non-violence-mp.org).

Centre mondial de la Paix, des Libertés et des Droits de l'Homme (RE), Place Monseigneur, BP 10183, 55100 Verdun (+33-329 865500) (contact@cmpaix.eu) (www.cmpaix.eu).

Cesser d'Alimenter la Guerre / Stop Fuelling War [SFW] (AT RA), c/o Centre

Quaker de Paris, 114 rue de Vaugirard, 75006 Paris (stopfuellingwar@gmail.com) (stopfuellingwar.org). Countering the normalisation of the trade in arms.

Coordination pour l'Éducation à la Non-violence et la Paix (NE), 148 rue du Faubourg Saint-Denis, 75010 Paris (+33-14633 4156) (education-nvp.org).

Greenpeace (GP), 13 rue d'Enghien, 75010 Paris (+33-18096 9696) (fax) (contact.fr@greenpeace.org) (www.greenpeace.org/france).

Groupe Non-Violent Louis Lecoin (DA PA), Maison de l'Environnement, 106 Ave du Casino, 59240 Dunkerque (+33-328 591233) (groupnonviolentlouislecoin@laposte.net).

Groupement pour les Droits des Minorités [GDM] (HR), 212 rue St-Martin, 75003 Paris (+33-14575 0137) (fax 14579 8046) (yplasseraud@wanadoo.fr). *La Lettre du GDM.*

Institut de Recherche sur la Résolution Non-violente des Conflits [IRNC] (RE SD CR PA), 14 rue des Meuniers, 93100 Montreuil-sous-Bois (+33-14287 9469) (fax) (irnc@irnc.org) (www.irnc.org). *Alternatives Non-violentes.*

Ligue d'Amitié Internationale (CD), Les Champs Fleuris - Nº 4, 14 rue Maurice Boyau, 91220 Bretigny-sur-Orge (+33-160 853407) (www.ifl-france.org). Affiliate of the International Friendship League.

Mémorial de Caen Museum - Cité de l'Histoire pour la Paix / Centre for History and Peace (PO RE), Esplanade Eisenhower, BP 55026, 14050 Caen Cedex 4 (+33-231 060644) (fax 231 060670) (contact@memorial-caen.fr) (www.memorial-caen.fr).

Mouvement de la Paix (IB WP ND PA AT), 9 Rue Dulcie September, 93400 Saint-Ouen (+33-14012 0912) (national@mvtpaix.org) (www.mvtpaix.org). *Planète Paix; La Paix en Mouvement.*

Mouvement International de la Réconciliation [MIR] (FR WR), 68 rue de Babylone, 75007 Paris (+33-14753 8405) (mirfr@club-internet.fr) (www.mirfrance.org). *Cahiers de la Réconciliation.*

Mouvement pour une Alternative Non-violente [MAN] (WR SD CR AT RA), 47 ave Pasteur, 93100 Montreuil (+33-14544 4825) (man@nonviolence.fr) (www.nonviolence.fr).

Non-Violence Actualité [NVA] (CR HR RE), Centre de Ressources sur la Gestion non-violente des Relations et des Conflits, BP 241, 45202 Montargis cedex (+33-238 936722) (fax 975 385985) (Nonviolence.Actualite@wanadoo.fr) (www.nonviolence-actualite.org). 6 yrly, Eu43 pa.

Non-Violence XXI (PA RE), 47 Ave Pasteur, 93100 Montreuil (+33-14548 3762) (fax 14544 4825) (coordination@nonviolence21.org) (www.nonviolence21.com).

Pax Christi France (PC), 5 rue Morère, 75014 Paris (+33-14449 0636) (accueil@paxchristi.cef.fr) (www.paxchristi.cef.fr). *Journal de la Paix.*

Réseau "Sortir du Nucléaire" / Network for a Nuclear Phase-Out (EL RA PO), 9 rue Dumenge, 69317 Lyon cedex 04 (+33-47828 2922) (fax 47207 7004) (contact@sortirdunucleaire.org) (www.sortirdunucleaire.org). Network of groups in France against nuclear energy.

Service Civil International [SCI-F] (SC), 75 rue du Chevalier Français, 59800 Lille (+33-320 552258) (sci@sci-france.org) (www.sci-france.org).

Société Religieuse des Amis (SF), Centre Quaker International, 114 Rue de Vaugirard, 75006 Paris (+33-14548 7423) (assembleedefrance@gmail.com) (www.QuakersEnFrance.org). *Lettre des Amis.*

Sortir de la Violence - France (FR CR RE), 11 rue de la Chaise, 75007 Paris (sdv-France@sortirdelaviolence.org) (www.sortirdelaviolence.org).

Stop Fuelling War - Cessez d'alimenter la Guerre (WR AT), Centre Quaker International, 114 rue de Vaugirard, 75006 Paris (+33-676 879173) (direction@stopfuellingwar.org) (www.stopfuellingwar.org). Campaigns against Paris arms fairs.

Union Pacifiste de France [UPF] (WR AT), 66 Bld Vincent Auriol, 75013 Paris (unionpacifiste@riseup.net) (www.unionpacifiste.org). *Union Pacifiste.*

FRENCH POLYNESIA

Ligue Internationale des Femmes pour la Paix et la Liberté - Section Polynésienne [LIFPL] (WL), Faaone pk 49.2, Côté Montagne, 98713 Faaone, Tahiti (+689-264729) (wilpf.polynesie@gmail.com).

GEORGIA

Sakhartvelos Mtsvaneta Modzraoba / Green Movement of Georgia (FE), 55 Kandelaki St, 0160 Tbilisi (+995-32-386978) (info@greens.ge) (www.greens.ge).

War Resisters' International - Georgian Section (WR), 45 Kavtaradze St - Apt 45, Tbilisi 0186 (+995-577-117878) (uchananua@yahoo.com).

GERMANY

Aktion Sühnezeichen Friedensdienste [ASF] (WC RP HR CD), Auguststr 80, 10117 Berlin-Mitte (+49-30-2839 5184) (fax 2839 5135) (asf@asf-ev.de) (www.asf-ev.de). *Zeichen.*

Aktion Völkerrecht / International Law Campaign (WF ND CD), c/o Peter Kolbe, Werderstr 36, 69120 Heidelberg (buero@a-vr.org) (www.aktion-voelkerrecht.de).

GERMANY

Aktionsgemeinschaft Dienst für den Frieden [AGDF] (WC PA RP), Endenicher Str 41, 53115 Bonn (+49-228-249990) (fax 249 9920) (agdf@friedensdienst.de) (www.friedensdienst.de).
Voluntary service co-ordination agency.

Amnesty International (AI), Zinnowitzer Str, 10115 Berlin (+49-30-420 2480) (fax 4202 48488) (info@amnesty.de) (www.amnesty.de). *ai-Journal*.

Anti-Kriegs-Museum / Anti-War Museum (WR), Brüsseler Str 21, 13353 Berlin (+49-30-4549 0110) (Anti-Kriegs-Museum@gmx.de) (www.anti-kriegs-museum.de).

Arbeitsgemeinschaft für Friedens- und Konfliktforschung / German Association for Peace and Conflict Studies [AFK] (RE), c/o Fakultät Gesellschaft und Ökonomie, Hochschule Rhein-Waal, 47533 Kleve (+49-2821-806739793) (fax 8067 3162) (afk-gf@afk-web.de) (afk-web.de).

Archiv Aktiv für gewaltfreie Bewegungen (WR RE EL), Normannenweg 17-21, 20537 Hamburg (+49-40-430 2046) (email@archiv-aktiv.de) (www.archiv-aktiv.de).

ausgestrahlt (EL RA ND), Grosse Bergstr 189, 22767 Hamburg (+49-40-2531 8940) (fax 2531 8944) (info@ausgestrahlt.de) (www.ausgestrahlt.de). *.ausgestrahlt-magazin*. Anti-nuclear direct action network.

Bürgermeister für den Frieden in Deutschland und Österreich (CD ND DA), c/o Landeshauptstadt Hannover, Büro Oberbürgermeister, Trammplatz 2, 30159 Hannover (+49-511-1684 1446) (fax 1684 4025) (mayorsforpeace@hannover-stadt.de) (www.mayorsforpeace.de).

Berghof Foundation (CR RE), Lindenstr 34, 10969 Berlin (+49-30-844 1540) (fax 8441 5499) (info@berghof-conflictresearch.org) (www.berghof-conflictresearch.org).
Works to prevent political and social violence.

Bund für Soziale Verteidigung [BSV] (WR SD CR), Schwarzer Weg 8, 32423 Minden (+49-571-29456) (fax 23019) (office@soziale-verteidigung.de) (www.soziale-verteidigung.de). *Soziale Verteidigung*.

Bund für Umwelt und Naturschutz Deutschland [BUND] (FE), Am Köllnischen Park 1, 10179 Berlin (+49-30-275 8640) (fax 2758 6440) (info@bund.net) (www.bund.net).

Connection eV - International Support of Conscientious Objectors and Deserters (PA HR), Von-Behring-Str 110, 63075 Offenbach (+49-69-8237 5534) (office@Connection-eV.org) (www.Connection-eV.org).

Deutsche Friedensgesellschaft - Vereinigte Kriegsdienstgegner [DFG-VK] (WR IB RE), Hornbergstr 100, 70188 Stuttgart (+49-711-6529 6246) (verwaltung@dfg-vk.de) (www.dfg-vk.de).

Deutsche Gesellschaft für die Vereinten Nationen [DGVN] (UN), Zimmerstr 26/27, 10969 Berlin (+49-30-259 3750) (fax 2593 7529) (info@dgvn.de) (www.dgvn.de). *Vereinte Nationen*.

Deutsche Sektion der IPPNW / Ärzte in sozialer Verantwortung (IPPNW Germany) (IP AT DA), Körtestr 10, 10967 Berlin (+49-30-698 0740) (fax 693 8166) (kontakt@ippnw.de) (www.ippnw.de). *Forum*.

Deutscher Friedensrat / German Peace Council (WP), Platz der Vereinten Nationen 7, 10249 Berlin (+49-30-426 5290) (fax 4201 7338) (saefkow-berlin@t-online.de) (www.deutscher-friedensrat.de).

DFG-VK Hessen (WR), Mühlgasse 13, 60486 Frankfurt/Main (+49-69-431440) (dfgvkhessen@t-online.de) (www.dfg-vk-hessen.de).

Evangelische Arbeitsgemeinschaft für Kriegsdienstverweigerung und Frieden [EAK] (RP), Endenicher Str 41, 53115 Bonn (+49-228-249 9929) (fax 249 9920) (weber@eak-online.de) (www.eak-online.de).
Supports peace work in Protestant churches.

Forum Ziviler Friedensdienst / Civil Peace Service Forum [forumZFD] (SF CR RE), Am Kölner Brett 8, 50825 Köln (+49-221-912 7320) (fax 9127 3299) (kontakt@forumZFD.de) (www.forumZFD.de).
Offers conflict transformation training & courses.

Frauennetzwerk für Frieden eV / Women's Network for Peace (IB CR), Kaiserstr 201, 53113 Bonn (+49-228-626730) (fax 626780) (info@frauennetzwerk-fuer-frieden.de) (www.frauennetzwerk-fuer-frieden.de).

Friedensausschuss der Religiösen Gesellschaft der Freunde (Quäker) (SF PA CR DA RA), via Helga Tempel, Föhrenstieg 8, 22926 Ahrensburg (+49-4102-53337) (helga.tempel@gmx.de). *Quäker*.

Gandhi Information Centre / Gandhi-Informations-Zentrtum (RA PE), Postfach 210109, 10501 Berlin (mkgandhi@snafu.de) (www.nonviolent-resistance.info).

GandhiServe Foundation (RE HR), Rathausstr 51a, 12105 Berlin (+49-1523-398 7220) (fax 3212-100 3676) (mail@gandhimail.org) (www.gandhiservefoundation.org).

Gewaltfreie Aktion Atomwaffen Abschaffen / Nonviolent Action to Abolish Nuclear Weapons [GAAA] (ND RA), c/o Marion Küpker, Beckstr 14, 20357 Hamburg (+49-40-430 7332) (marion.kuepker@gaaa.org) (www.gaaa.org).

Graswurzelrevolution (WR AL RA), Breul 43, 48143 Münster (+49-251-482 9057) (fax 482 9032) (redaktion@graswurzel.net) (www.graswurzel.net).

Greenpeace (GP), Hongkongstr 10, 20457 Hamburg (+49-40-306180) (fax 3061 8100) (mail@greenpeace.de) (www.greenpeace.de). Berlin: +49-30-308 8990.

Haus der Demokratie und Menschenrechte / House of Democracy and Human Rights Foundation (HR EL), Greifswalder Str 4, 10405 Berlin (+49-30-2016 5522) (fax 204 1263) (kontact@hausderdemokratie.de) (www.hausderdemokratie.de).

Heidelberger Institut für Internationale Konfliktforschung [HIIK] (RE), Bergheimer Str 58, 69115 Heidelberg (+49-6221-542863) (info@hiik.de) (www.hiik.de). *Conflict Barometer*.

Initiative Musiker/innen gegen Auftritte der Bundeswehrmusikkorps (PA), c/o Dietmar Parchow, Austr 77, 72669 Unteringen (musikergegenmilitaermusik@idk-berlin.de) (musiker-gegen-militaermusik.jimdo.com). Against public and church use of military bands.

Institut für Friedensarbeit und Gewaltfreie Konfliktaustragung [IFGK] (WR RE CR), Hauptstr 35, 55491 Wahlenau/Hunsrück (+49-6543-980096) (info@dr-barbara-mueller.com) (www.ifgk.de). *IFGK Working Papers*.

Institut für Friedenspädagogik Tübingen/ Institute for Peace Education Tübingen (RE CR), Corrensstr 12, 72076 Tübingen (+49-7071-920510) (fax 920 5111) (info-tuebingen@berghof-foundation.org) (www.friedenspaedagogik.de). A branch of the Berghof Foundation.

Internationale der Kriegsdienstgegner/innen [IDK] (WR AL), Postfach 280312, 13443 Berlin (info@idk-berlin.de) (www.idk-info.net).

Internationale Frauenliga für Frieden und Freiheit [IFFF] (WL), Haus der Demokratie und Menschenrechte, Greifswalder Str 4, 10405 Berlin (info@wilpf.de) (wilpf.de).

Internationale Jugendgemeinschaftsdienste [IJGD] (WC EL CD), Kasernenstr 48, 53113 Bonn (+49-228-228 0014) (fax 228 0010) (workcamps@ijgd.de) (www.ijgd.de). Workcamps and volunteering in Germany and abroad.

Juristen und Juristinnen gegan Atomare, Biologische und Chemische Waffen - IALANA Deutschland (ND), Marienstr 19-20, 10117 Berlin (+49-30-2065 4857) (fax 2065 4858) (info@ialana.de) (www.ialana.de).

Komitee für Grundrechte und Demokratie (HR CD RA PA), Aquinostr 7-11 (HH), 50670 Köln (+49-221-972 6920) (fax 972 6931) (info@grundrechtekomitee.de) (www.grund-drechtekomitee.de).

Kooperation für den Frieden (DA ND RE), Römerstr 88, 53111 Bonn (+49-228-692905) (fax 692906) (info@koop-frieden.de) (www.koop-frieden.de). Networking organisation in German peace movement.

KURVE Wustrow - Bildungs- und Begegnungsstätte für gewaltfreie Aktion (FR PA CR HR RE), Kirchstr 14, 29462 Wustrow (+49-5843-98710) (fax 987111) (info@kurvewustrow.org) (www.kurvewustrow.org).

Martin-Luther-King-Zentrum (PA), Stadtgutstr 23, 08412 Werdau (+49-3761-760284) (fax 760304) (info@martin-luther-king-zentrum.de) (www.king-zentrum.de).

Netzwerk Friedenskooperative (ND PA AT), Römerstr 88, 53111 Bonn (+49-228-692904) (fax 692906) (friekoop@friedenskooperative.de) (www.friedenskooperative.de). *Friedensforum*.

Netzwerk Friedenssteuer [NWFS] (TR), Krennerweg 12, 81479 München (+49-8062-725 2395) (fax 725 2396) (info@netzwerk-friedenssteuer.de) (www.netzwerk-friedenssteuer.de). *Friedenssteuer-Nachrichten*.

Ohne Rüstung Leben (AT CR PA ND DA), Arndtstr 31, 70197 Stuttgart (+49-711-608396) (fax 608357) (orl@gaia.de) (www.ohne-ruestung-leben.de). *Ohne Rüstung Leben-Informationen*.

Pax Christi Deutsche Sektion (PC), Hedwigskirchgasse 3, 10117 Berlin (+49-30-2007 6780) (fax 2007 67819) (sekretariat@paxchristi.de) (www.paxchristi.de).

Peace Brigades International Deutscher Zweig [PBI] (CR HR PA), Bahrenfelder Str 101 A, 22765 Hamburg (+49-40-3890 4370) (fax 3890 43729) (info@pbi-deutschland.de) (www.pbideutschland.de).

Peace Museum (RE), Kaulbachstr 2, 90408 Nürnberg (+49-911-360 9577) (na3745@fen-net.de) (www.friedensmuseum.odn.de).

Projekt Alternativen zur Gewalt / AVP Germany [PAG] (CR), Kaliweg 31, 30952 Ronnenberg (+49-5109-7695) (fax 1014) (info@pag.de) (www.pag.de). Part of Alternatives to Violence network.

RüstungsInformationsBüro [RIB-Büro] (AT PA RE), Stühlinger Str 7, 79016 Freiburg (+49-761-767 8088) (fax 767 8089) (rib@rib-ev.de) (www.rib-ev.de). Campaign against small arms.

RfP Deutschland / Religions for Peace (RP), c/o Franz Brendle, Im Schellenkönig 61, 70184 Stuttgart (+49-711-539 0209) (fax 505 8648) (rfp@r-f-p.de) (www.religionsforpeace.de). *Informationen*.

Servas Germany (SC), O'Swaldstr 32, 22111 Hamburg (mail@servas.de) (www.servas.de).

Service Civil International - Deutscher Zweig [SCI-D] (SC PA EL), Blücherstr 14, 53115 Bonn (+49-228-212086) (fax 264234) (info@sci-d.de) (www.sci-d.de).

GERMANY

Stiftung die schwelle / Schwelle Foundation - Beiträge zum Frieden (CR TW RE HR), Wachmannstr 79, 28209 Bremen (+49-421-303 2575) (stiftung@dieschwelle.de) (www.dieschwelle.de).
Versöhnungsbund [VB] (FR IB PA), Schwarzer Weg 8, 32423 Minden (+49-571-850875) (fax 829 2387) (vb@versoehnungsbund.de) (www.versoehnungsbund.de).

GHANA

Anam Foundation for Peacebuilding [AF4PB] (CR PO), Box TL 392, Tamale (+233-20-276 8844) (info@anam4peace.org) (www.anam4peace.org).

GREECE

Diethnis Amnistia / Amnesty International (AI), 30 Sina Street, 10672 Athinai (+30-210 3600 628) (fax 210 3638 016) (athens@amnesty.org.gr) (www.amnesty.org.gr). *Martyries.*
Elliniki Epitropi gia ti Thiethni Yphesi kai Eirene / Greek Committee for International Detente and Peace [EEDYE] (WP), Themistokleous 48, 10681 Athinai (+30-210 3844 853) (fax 210 3844 879) (eedye@otenet.gr) (eedye.gr).
Enomenes Koinonies ton Valkanion / United Societies of the Balkans [USB] (CD CR HR PO), Adamanas 9, Agios Paulos, 55438 Thessaloniki (+30-231 0215 629) (fax) (info@usbngo.gr) (www.usbngo.gr).
Greenpeace Greece (GP), Kolonou 78, 10437 Athinai (+30-210 3840 774) (fax 210 3804 008) (gpgreece@greenpeace.org) (www.greenpeace.org/greece).
Syndhesmos Antirrision Syneidhisis / Association of Greek Conscientious Objectors [SAS] (WR), Tsamadou 13A, 10683 Athinai (+30-694 4542 228) (fax 210 4622 753) (greekCO@hotmail.com) (www.antirrisies.gr).

GRENADA

Friends of the Earth Grenada [FOE-G] (FE TW), PO Box 521, Lucas St, Queen's Park, St George's (+1473-416 1247) (friendsoftheearthgrenada@gmail.com).

HONG KONG

Alternatives to Violence Project - AVP Hong Kong (CR PO), 12a Shun Ho Tower, 24-30 Ice House St, Central (avphongkong@gmail.com) (www.avphongkong.org).
Amnesty International Hong Kong (AI), Unit 3D, Best-O-Best Commercial Centre, 32-36 Ferry St, Kowloon (+852-2300 1250) (fax 2782 0583) (admin-hk@amnesty.org.hk) (www.amnesty.org.hk).
Association for the Advancement of Feminism [AAF] (HR), Flats 119-120, Lai Yeung House, Lei Cheng Uk Estate, Kowloon (+852-2720 0891) (fax 2720 0205) (aaf@aaf.org.hk) (www.aaf.org.hk). *Nuliu.*
Greenpeace China (GP), 8/F Pacific Plaza, 410-418 Des Voeux Rd West (+852-2854 8300) (fax 2745 2426) (enquiry.hk@greenpeace.org) (www.greenpeace.org/china).
Also Beijing office: see under China.

HUNGARY

Bocs Foundation (FR EL TW), Pf 7, 8003 Székesfehérvár (m@bocs.hu) (www.bocs.hu). *Bocsmagazin.*
Magyar Orvosmozgalom a Nukleáris Háború Megelőzéséért (IP), c/o Zita Makoi, Hegedus Gy u 48, 1133 Budapest (zita.makoi@gmail.com).
Magyar Természetvédők Szövetsége [MTVSZ] (FE), Ulloi U 91B - III/21, 1091 Budapest (info@mtvsz.hu) (www.mtvsz.hu).

ICELAND

Amnesty International (AI), Thingholtsstraeti 27, 101 Reykjavík (+354-511 7900) (fax 511 7901) (amnesty@amnesty.is) (www.amnesty.is).
Peace 2000 Institute (CR RE), Vogasel 1, 109 Reykjavík (+354-557 1000) (fax 496 2005) (info@peace2000.org) (peace2000.org).
Offices also in Britain, USA.
Samtök Hernadarandstaedinga / Campaign Against Militarism (WR ND DA), Njalsgata 87, 101 Reykjavík (+354-554 0900) (sha@fridur.is) (fridur.is). *Dagfari.*

INDIA

All India Peace and Solidarity Organisation [AIPSO] (WP), c/o AIPSO West Bengal, 5 Sarat Ghosh St (behind Entally Market), Kolkota 700014 (bengalaipso@gmail.com) (www.aipsowb.org).
Anglican Pacifist Fellowship [APF] (RP), c/o John Nagella, Opp SBI Colony, AT Agraharam, Guntur 552004, Andhra Pradesh.
Anuvrat Global Organisation [ANUVIBHA] (IB EL ND PO CR), B01-02, Anuvibha Jaipur Kendra, opp Gaurav Tower, Malviya Nagar, Jaipur 302017, Rajasthan (+91-141-404 9714) (slgandhi@hotmail.com) (www.anuvibha.in).
Bombay Sarvodaya Friendship Centre (FR WC SF), 701 Sainath Estate, Opp Lokmanya Vidyalay, Nilam Nagar-II, Mulund East, Mumbai 400081 (+91-22-2563 1022) (danielm@mtnl.net.in).
Christavashram - Fellowship of Reconciliation India [FORI] (FR), Manganam PO, Kottayam - 686018, Kerala (+91-481-257 0701) (manganam.tripod.com/ashram).

Coalition for Nuclear Disarmament and Peace [CNDP] (ND), A-124/6 - First Floor, Katwaria Sarai, New Delhi 110016 (+91-11-6566 3958) (fax 2651 7814) (cndpindia@gmail.com) (www.cndpindia.org). Network of 200 organisations.

Control Arms Foundation of India [CAFI] (AT DA), B5 / 146 - First Floor, Safdarjung Enclave, New Delhi 110029 (+91-11-4601 8541) (cafi.communique@gmail.com) (cafi-online.org).

Ekta Parishad (HR PO TW), 2/3A - Second Floor - Jungpura-A, New Delhi 10014 (+91-11-2437 3998) (ektaparishad@gmail.com) (www.ektaparishad.com). Federation of thousands of community organisations.

Friends of the Gandhi Museum (RE EL PO), B-4 Puru Society, Airport Rd, Lohegaon, Pune 411032 (+91-937 120 1138) (satyagrahi2000@gmail.com).

Gandhi Book Centre / Mumbai Sarvodaya Mandal (PO), 299 Tardeo Rd, Nana Chowk, Mumbai 400007 (+91-22-2387 2061) (info@mkgandhi.org) (www.mkgandhi.org).

Gandhi Research Foundation (RE), Gandhi Teerth, Jain Hills PO Box 118, Jalgaon 425001, Maharashtra (+91-257-226 0011) (fax 226 1133) (gandhiexam@gandhifoundation.net) (www.gandhifoundation.net).

Gandhian Society Villages Association (WR), Amaravathy Pudur PO, Pasumpon District, Tamil Nadu 623301 (+91-8645-83234).

Greenpeace India (GP), 60 Wellington Rd, Richmond Town, Bangalore 560025, Karnataka (+91-80-2213 1899) (fax 4115 4862) (supporter.services.in@greenpeace.org) (www.greenpeace.org/india). Regional Office in Delhi (+91-11-6666 5000).

Gujarat Vidyapeeth (RE), Ashram Rd (near Income tax), Ahmedabad 380014 (+91-79-2754 0746) (fax 2754 2547) (registrar@gujaratvidyapith.org) (www.gujaratvidyapith.org). Gandhian study centre.

Indian Campaign for Nuclear Disarmament (IB ND EL), 11 Chetla Central Rd, Alipore, Kolkata 700027, West Bengal (+91-33-466 5659) (manabendranathmandal@ymail.com).

Indian Doctors for Peace and Development [IDPD] (IP), 139-E Kitchlu Nagar, Ludhiana 141001, Punjab (+91-161-230 0252) (fax 230 4360) (idpd2001@yahoo.com) (www.idpd.org).

National Gandhi Museum and Library (RE), Rajghat, New Delhi 110002 (+91-11-2331 1793) (fax 2332 8310) (gandhimuseumdelhi@gmail.com) (www.gandhimuseum.org). Has collection of original relics, books, etc.

People's Movement Against Nuclear Energy - WISE India [PMANE] (EL ND), 42/27 Esankai Mani Veethy, Prakkai Road Jn, Nagercoil 629002, Tamil Nadu (drspudayakumar@yahoo.com). Linked to World Information Service on Energy.

Swadhina / Independence (WR), 34/C Bondel Rd, Ballygunge, Kolkata 700019 (+91-33-3245 1730) (mainoffice.swadhina@gmail.com) (www.swadhina.org.in).

Tibetan Centre for Human Rights and Democracy (FR HR), Narthang Building - Top Floor, Gangchen Kyishong, Dharamsala, HP 176215 (+91-1892-223363) (fax 225874) (office@tchrd.org) (www.tchrd.org). Works for human rights of Tibetans in Tibet.

War Resisters of India/West (WR), c/o Swati & Michael, Juna Mozda, Dediapada, Dt Narmada, Gujarat 393040 (+91-2649-290249) (mozdam@gmail.com).

Women's International League for Peace and Freedom - India [WILPF] (WL), c/o Peace Research Centre, Gujatat Vidyapith, Ahmedabad 380014.

INDONESIA

Institute for Democracy and Peace [SETARA] (HR CR), Jl Hang Lekiu II - No 41, Kebayoran Baru, Jakarta Selatan 12120 (62-21-720 8850) (fax 2277 5683) (setara@setara-institute.org) (setara-institute.org).

IRAN

Iran Human Rights (HR), see under Norway (mail@iranhr.net) (www.iranhr.net). Main focus is on death penalty.

Iranian Physicians for Social Responsibility [PSR-Iran] (IP), PO Box 11155-18747, Tehran Peace Museum, Parke shahr, Tehran (+98-21-6675 6945) (fax 6693 9992) (info@irpsr.org).

IRELAND, NORTHERN

NOTE: Organisations working on an all-Ireland basis (ie covering both the Republic of Ireland and Northern Ireland), with their office address in the Irish Republic, will be found listed there. Similarly, groups operating on a United Kingdom-wide basis (ie covering both Britain and Northern Ireland), with a British-based office, will be found listed under Britain.

Amnesty International - NI Region [AI-NI] (AI), 397 Ormeau Rd, Belfast BT7 (+44-28-9064 3000) (fax 9069 0989) (nireland@amnesty.org.uk) (www.amnesty.org.uk).

Bahá'í Council for Northern Ireland (RP), Apt 4, 2 Lower Windsor Ave, Belfast BT9 (+44-28-9016 0457) (bcni@bahai.org.uk) (www.bahaicouncil.ni.org.uk).

IRELAND, Northern

Centre for Democracy and PeaceBuilding [CDPB] (HR CR), 46 Hill St, Belfast BT1 2LB (info@democracyandpeace.org) (democracyandpeace.org). Sharing peace-building expertise internationally.

Children are Unbeatable! Alliance (HR), Unit 9, 40 Montgomery Rd, Belfast BT6 (+44-28-9040 1290) (carolconlin@btinternet.com) (www.childrenareunbeatable.org.uk). For abolition of all physical punishment.

Christian Aid Ireland (TW), Linden House, Beechill Business Park, 96 Beechill Rd, Belfast BT8 7QN (+44-28-9064 8133) (belfast@christian-aid.org) (www.christianaid.ie).

Co-operation Ireland (CD), 5 Weavers Court Business Park, Linfield Rd, Belfast BT12 (+44-28-9032 1462) (info@cooperationireland.org) (www.cooperationireland.org). Works for tolerance and acceptance of differences.

Committee on the Administration of Justice [CAJ] (HR), Community House, Citylink Business Park, 6A Albert St, Belfast BT12 (+44-28-9031 6000) (info@caj.org.uk) (www.caj.org.uk). *Just News.*

Corrymeela Community (RP), 83 University St, Belfast BT7 1HP (+44-28-9050 8080) (fax 9050 8070) (belfast@corrymeela.org) (www.corrymeela.org). *Corrymeela.*

Friends of the Earth - NI [FOE-NI] (FE), Gordon House, 22-24 Lombard St, Belfast BT1 1RD (+44-28-9023 3488) (friendsoftheearth.uk/northern-ireland).

Global Peacebuilders (CR), c/o Springboard Opportunities, 2nd Floor, 7 North St, Belfast BT1 1NH (+44-28-9031 5111) (fax 9031 3171) (james@springboard-opps.org) (www.globalpeacebuilders.org).

Green Party in Northern Ireland (EL), 1st Floor, 76 Abbey St, Bangor BT20 4JB (+44-28-9145 9101) (info@greenpartyni.org) (www.greenpartyni.org).

Healing Through Remembering [HTR] (RE), Unit 2.2, Bryson House, 28 Bedford St, Belfast BT2 7FE (+44-28-9023 8844) (info@healingthroughremembering.org) (www.healingthroughremembering.org).

Institute for Conflict Research [ICR] (RE CR HR), North City Business Centre - Unit 12-14, 2 Duncairn Gdns, Belfast BT15 2GG (+44-28-9074 2682) (info@conflictresearch.org.uk) (www.conflictresearch.org.uk).

Institute for the Study of Conflict Transformation and Social Justice [ISCT-SJ] (RE CR), Queen's University Belfast, 19 University Sq, Belfast BT7 (+44-28-9097 3609) (ctsj@qub.ac.uk).

Integrated Education Fund [IEF] (PO HR), Forest View, Purdy's Lane, Belfast BT8 7AR (+44-28-9069 4099) (info@ief.org.uk) (www.ief.org.uk).

Irish Network for Nonviolent Action Training and Education [INNATE] (WR RA FR), c/o 16 Ravensdene Park, Belfast BT6 0DA (+44-28-9064 7106) (fax) (innate@ntlworld.com) (www.innatenonviolence.org). *Nonviolent News.*

Northern Ireland Community Relations Council [CRC] (CR PO RE), 2nd Floor, Equality House, 7-9 Shaftesbury Sq, Belfast BT2 7DP (+44-28-9022 7500) (info@nicrc.org.uk) (www.community-relations.org.uk).

Northern Ireland Council for Integrated Education [NICIE] (PO HR CD RE), 25 College Gdns, Belfast BT9 (+44-28-9097 2910) (fax 9097 2919) (info@nicie.org.uk) (www.nicie.org.uk).

Oxfam Ireland (TW), 115 North St, Belfast (+44-28-9023 0220) (fax 9023 7771) (info@oxfamireland.org) (www.oxfamireland.org).

Pat Finucane Centre (HR RE CR), Unit B8, Ráth Mór Centre, Bligh's Lane, Derry BT48 0LZ (+44-28-7126 8846) (fax 7126 6453) (info@patfinucanecentre.org) (www.patfinucanecentre.org). Armagh Office: 028-3751 5191.

Peace People (FR CD HR), 224 Lisburn Rd, Belfast BT9 6GE (+44-28-9066 3465) (info@peacepeople.org) (www.peacepeople.com).

Quaker Service (SF), 541 Lisburn Rd, Belfast BT9 7GQ (+44-28-9020 1444) (info@quakerservice.org) (www.quakerservice.com).

Swords to Ploushares [StoP] (AT), c/o INNATE, 16 Ravensdene Park, Belfast BT6 0DA. Irish anti-arms trade network.

The Junction (CR PO), 8-14 Bishop St, Derry/Londonderry BT48 6PW (+44-28-7136 1942) (info@thejunction-ni.org) (thejunction-ni.org). Community relations, civic empowerment.

TIDES Training (CR), 174 Trust, Duncairn Complex, Duncairn Ave, Belfast BT14 6BP (+44-28-9075 1686) (info@tidestraining.org) (www.tidestraining.org).

Tools for Solidarity - Ireland (TW PO), 55A Sunnyside St, Belfast BT7 (+44-28-9543 5972) (fax) (tools.belfast@myphone.coop) (www.toolsforsolidarity.com). *Solidarity.*

Transitional Justice Institute [TJI] (RE), Ulster University - Jordanstown Campus, Shore Rd, Newtownabbey BT37 (+44-28-9036 6202) (fax 9036 8962) (transitionaljustice@ulster.ac.uk) (www.transitionaljustice.ulster.ac.uk). Also Magee Campus, Londonderry.

IRELAND, REPUBLIC OF

Alternatives to Violence Project [AVP Ireland] (CR), Quaker House, Stocking Lane, Rathfarnham, Dublin 16 (info@avpireland.ie) (avpireland.ie).

Amnesty International Ireland (AI), Sean MacBride House, 48 Fleet St, Dublin 2 (+353-1-863 8300) (fax 671 9338) (info@amnesty.ie) (www.amnesty.ie). *Amnesty Ireland*.

Chernobyl Children International (PO EL HR), 1A The Stables, Alfred St, Cork City (+353-21-455 8774) (fax 450 5564) (info@chernobyl-ireland.com) (www.chernobyl-international.com).

Co-operation Ireland [CI] (CD), Port Centre, Alexandra Rd, Dublin 1 (+353-1-819 7692) (fax 894 4962) (info@cooperationireland.org) (www.cooperationireland.org). Works for tolerance and acceptance of differences.

Dublin Quaker Peace Committee (SF), c/o Quaker House, Stocking Lane, Rathfarnham, Dublin 16 (info@dublinquakerpeace.ie) (www.dublinquakerpeace.org).

Eco-Congregation Ireland (EL), c/o 13 The Pinnacles, Broomfield, Midleton, Co Cork (info@ecocongregationireland.com) (www.ecocongregationireland.com). Interdenominational project.

Educate Together (HR RE PO CR), 11-12 Hogan Place, Dublin 2 (+353-1-429 2500) (fax 429 2502) (info@educatetogether.ie) (www.educatetogether.ie).

Friends of the Earth (FE), 9 Upper Mount St, Dublin 2 (+353-1-639 4652) (info@foe.ie) (www.foe.ie).

Friends of the Irish Environment (EL), Kilcatherine, Eyeries, Co Cork (+353-27-74771) (admin@friendsoftheirishenvironment.org) (www.friendsoftheirishenvironment.org).

Glencree Centre for Peace and Reconciliation (CR RE), Glencree, Enniskerry, Co Wicklow (+353-1-282 9711) (info@glencree.ie) (glencree.ie).

Ireland Palestine Solidarity Campaign [IPSC] (HR), 35 North Lotts, Dublin 1, D01 A3E0, Co Offaly (+353-1-872 7798) (info@ipsc.ie) (www.ipsc.ie).

Irish Anti-War Movement, PO Box 9260, Dublin 1 (+353-1-872 7912) (info@irishantiwar.org) (www.irishantiwar.org).

Irish Campaign for Nuclear Disarmament / Feachtas um Dhí-armáil Eithneach [ICND] (IB ND), PO Box 6327, Dublin 6 (irishcnd@gmail.com) (www.irishcnd.org). *Peacework*.

Irish Centre for Human Rights (HR), National University of Ireland, University Rd, Galway (+353-91-493948) (fax 494575) (humanrights@nuigalway.ie) (www.nuigalway.ie/human_rights).

Irish Council for Civil Liberties / An Chomhairle um Chearta Daonna [ICCL] (HR), Unit 11, 34 Ushers Quay, Dublin 8 (+353-1-912 1640) (info@iccl.ie) (www.iccl.ie).

Irish United Nations Association [IUNA] (UN), 14 Lower Pembroke St, Dublin 2 (+353-1-661 6920) (irelandun@gmail.com).

Mediators' Institute Ireland [MII] (CR), Suite 112, The Capel Building, Mary's Abbey, Dublin 7 (+353-1-609 9190) (info@themii.ie) (www.themii.ie).

Pax Christi Ireland (PC HR AT), 52 Lower Rathmines Rd, Dublin 6 (+353-1-496 5293) (www.paxchristi.ie).

Peace and Neutrality Alliance / Comhaontas na Síochána is Neodrachta [PANA] (ND AT), 17 Castle St, Dalkey, Co Dublin (+353-1-235 1512) (info@pana.ie) (www.pana.ie).

Peace Brigades International - Ireland [PBI] (HR), 12 Parliament St, Temple Bar, Dublin 2 (pbiireland@peacebrigades.org) (www.pbi-ireland.org).

People's Movement / Gluaiseacht an Phobail (HR DA), 25 Shanowen Crescent, Santry, Dublin 9 (post@people.ie) (people.ie). Opposes increased EU centralisation and militarism.

Servas (SE), c/o Donal Coleman, 53 Glengara Park, Glenageary, Co Dublin A96 TOF6 (+353-87-915 9635) (ireland@servas.org) (www.servas.org).

ShannonWatch (DA HR), PO Box 476, Limerick DSU, Dock Rd, Limerick (+353-87-822 5087) (shannonwatch@gmail.com) (www.shannonwatch.org). Monitors foreign military use of Shannon Airport.

Swords to Ploushares [StoP] (AT), for address see under Ireland, Northern. Irish anti-arms trade network.

Vegetarian Society of Ireland [VSI] (EL PO), c/o Dublin Food Coop, 12 Newmarket, Dublin 8 (info@vegetarian.ie) (www.vegetarian.ie). *The Irish Vegetarian*.

Voluntary Service International [VSI] (SC), Carmichael House, 4-7 North Brunswick St, Dublin 7 (info@vsi.ie) (www.vsi.ie).

ISLE OF MAN

Shee Nish! / Peace Now! (AT PA DA), c/o Stuart Hartill, Eskdale Apartments - Apt 10, Queens Drive West, Ramsey IM8 2JD (+44-1624-803157) (stuarth@manx.net). Widely-based coalition of peace campaigners.

ISRAEL (see also Palestine)

NOTE: Territories allocated to Israel in the United Nations partition of Palestine in 1947, together with further areas annexed by Israel prior to 1967, are included here. Other parts of Palestine occupied by Israel in 1967 or later are listed under Palestine.

ISRAEL

Al-Beit - Association for the Defence of Human Rights in Israel (HR CD TW), PO Box 650, Arara 30026 (+972-6-635 4370) (fax 635 4367) (uridavis@actcom.co.il). Concentrates on right of residence and housing.

Alternative Information Centre [AIC] (HR RE TW AL AT), POB 31417, West Jerusalem 91313 (+972-2-624 1159) (fax 3-762 4664) (connie.hackbarth@alternativenews.org) (www.alternativenews.org). *Economy of the Occupation.*
See also Palestine.

Amnesty International Israel (AI), PO Box 5239, Tel-Aviv 66550 (+972-3-525 0005) (fax 525 0001) (info@amnesty.org.il) (amnesty.org.il).

B'Tselem - Israeli Information Centre for Human Rights in the Occupied Territories (HR), PO Box 53132, West Jerusalem 9153002 (+972-2-673 5599) (fax 674 9111) (mail@btselem.org) (www.btselem.org).

Bimkom - Planners for Planning Rights (HR), 13 Ebenezra St - PO Box 7154, West Jerusalem 9107101 (+972-2-566 9655) (fax 566 0551) (bimkom@bimkom.org) (www.bimkom.org).

Coalition of Women for Peace [CWP] (HR CD), POB 29214, Tel Aviv - Jaffa 61292 (+972-3-528 1005) (fax) (cwp@coalitionofwomen.org) (www.coalitionofwomen.org).

Combatants for Peace (CD CR), 12 Yad Harutsim St, Tel Aviv - Jaffa 6770005 (office@cfpeace.org) (www.cfpeace.org). Israeli and Palestinian ex-fighters for peace.

Defence for Children International - Israel [DCI-Israel] (HR), POB 2533, West Jerusalem 91024 (+972-2-563 3003) (fax 563 1241) (dci@dci-il.org).

Geneva Initiative (CD CR), c/o HL Education for Peace, 33 Jabotinsky Rd, Ramat-Gan 525108 (+972-3-693 8780) (fax 691 1306) (www.geneva-accord.org).
See also Palestine.

Gisha: Legal Centre for Freedom of Movement (HR), Harakevet 42, Tel Aviv - Jaffa 67770 (+972-3-624 4120) (fax 624 4130) (info@gisha.org) (gisha.org).

Givat Haviva Jewish-Arab Centre for Peace [JACP] (CR HR RE), MP Menashe 37850 (+972-4-630 9289) (fax 630 9305) (givathaviva@givathaviva.org.il) (www.givathaviva.org.il).

Greenpeace Mediterranean - Israel (GP HR), PO Box 20079, Tel Aviv 61200 (+972-3-561 4014) (fax 561 0415) (gpmedisr@greenpeace.org) (www.greenpeace.org/israel).

Gush Shalom / Peace Bloc (CD CR HR RE RA), PO Box 2542, Holon 58125 (+972-3-556 5804) (info@gush-shalom.org) (www.gush-shalom.org).

Hamerkaz Hamishpati L'zkhuyot Hami-ut Ha'aravi Beyisrael / Legal Centre for Arab Minority Rights in Israel [Adalah] (HR), 94 Yaffa St, PO Box 8921, Haifa 31090 (+972-4-950 1610) (fax 950 3140) (adalah@adalah.org) (www.adalah.org). Works for equal rights for Arab citizens in Israel.

HaMoked - Centre for the Defence of the Individual (HR), 4 Abu Obeidah St, Jerusalem 97200 (+972-2-627 1698) (mail@hamoked.org.il) (www.hamoked.org.il).

Hand in Hand - Centre for Jewish-Arab Education in Israel (PO CD RE), PO Box 10339, Jerusalem 91102 (+972-2-673 5356) (info@handinhand.org.il) (www.handinhandk12.org).
Supports integrated, bilingual education.

Interfaith Encounter Association [IEA] (RP CD), PO Box 3814, West Jerusalem 91037 (+972-2-651 0520) (fax 651 0557) (yehuda@interfaith-encounter.org) (www.interfaith-encounter.org). *IEA Stories.*

Israel-Palestine Creative Regional Initiatives [IPCRI] (RE CR EL CD), see under Palestine (+972-52-238 1715) (www.ipcri.org).

Israeli Committee for a Middle East Free from Atomic, Biological and Chemical Weapons (ND HR), PO Box 16202, Tel Aviv 61161 (+972-3-522 2869) (fax) (spiro@bezeqint.net).

Mossawa Center - Advocacy Center for Arab Citizens in Israel (HR), 5 Saint Lucas St, PO Box 4471, Haifa 31043 (+972-4-855 5901) (fax 855 2772) (programs.mossawa@gmail.com) (www.mossawa.org).

New Profile - Movement for the Demilitarisation of Israeli Society (WR), c/o Sergeiy Sandler, POB 48005, Tel Aviv 61480 (+972-3-696 1137) (newprofile@speedy.co.il) (www.newprofile.org).
Feminist movement of women and men.

Ometz Le'sarev / Courage to Refuse, PO Box 16238, Tel Aviv (+972-3-523 3103) (info@seruv.org.il) (www.seruv.org.il). (Zionists) refusing deployment in the Territories.

OneVoice Movement - Israel [OVI] (CD CR), PO Box 29695, Tel Aviv 66881 (+972-3-516 8005) (info@OneVoice.org.il) (www.onevoicemovement.org).
See also Palestine.

Palestinian-Israeli Peace NGO Forum (Israeli Office) (CD), c/o The Peres Center for Peace, 132 Kedem St, Jaffa 68066 (+972-3-568 0646) (fax 562 7265) (info@peres-center.org) (www.peacengo.org).
See also under Palestine.

Parents' Circle - Families' Forum: Bereaved Israeli and Palestinian Families Supporting

Peace and Tolerance (CD CR), 1 Hayasmin St, Ramat-Efal 52960 (+972-3-535 5089) (fax 635 8367) (contact@theparentscircle.org) (www.theparentscircle.com). See also under Palestine.

Physicians for Human Rights - Israel [PHRI] (HR PO), 9 Dror St, Jaffa-Tel Aviv 68135 (+972-3-513 3100) (fax 687 3029) (mail@phr.org.il) (www.phr.org.il).

Public Committee Against Torture in Israel [PCATI] (HR), POB 4634, West Jerusalem 91046 (+972-2-642 9825) (fax 643 2847) (pcati@stoptorture.org.il) (www.stoptorture.org.il).

Rabbis for Human Rights [RHR] (HR), 9 HaRechavim St, West Jerusalem 9346209 (+972-2-648 2757) (fax 678 3611) (info@rhr.israel.net) (www.rhr.israel.net).

Sadaka-Reut - Arab-Jewish Partnership (CR RE HR GR), 35 Shivtey Israel St, PO Box 8523, Jaffa - Tel-Aviv 61084 (+972-3-518 2336) (fax) info@reutsadaka.org) (www.reutsadaka.org).

Seeds of Peace (CD CR PO), PO Box 42365, Salah Eddin Street (Herod's Gate Branch), Jerusalem 97200 (+972-3-527 3740) (fax 527 3741) (jerusalem@seedsofpeace.org) (www.seedsofpeace.org). Trains people for conflict transformation.

Shatil (CD HR), PO Box 53395, West Jerusalem 91533 (+972-2-672 3597) (fax 673 5149) (shatil@shatil.nif.org.il) (www.shatil.org.il). Also 4 other regional offices.

Shovrim Shtika / Breaking the Silence (HR), PO Box 51027, 6713206 Tel Aviv (info@breakingthesilence.org.il) (www.breakingthesilence.org.il). Former soldiers opposing the occupation.

Wahat al-Salam - Neve Shalom [WAS-NS] (HR RE CR PO CD), Doar Na / Mobile Post, Shimshon 9976100 (+972-2-999 6305) (fax 991 1072) (info@wasns.info) (wasns.org). "Oasis of Peace".

Windows - Israeli-Palestinian Friendship Centre (CD), PO Box 5195, Tel Aviv - Jaffa (+972-3-620 8324) (fax 629 2570) (office@win-peace.org) (www.win-peace.org). *Windows*. Chlenov 41. See also in Palestine.

Zochrot / Remembering (HR), Ben Tzvi 2, POB 8412, Tel Aviv - Yaffa 6818164 (zochrot@zochrot.org) (www.zochrot.org). Supports Palestinians' right of return.

ITALY

Amnesty International - Sezione Italiana (AI), Via Magenta 5, 00185 Roma (+39-06 4490210) (fax 06 449 0222) (infoamnesty@amnesty.it) (www.amnesty.it).

Archivio Disarmo [IRIAD] (IB RE AT), Via Paolo Mercuri 8, 00193 Roma (+39-06 3600 0343) (fax 06 3600 0345) (archiviodisarmo@pec.it) (www.archiviodisarmo.it).

Associazione Italiana Medicina per la Prevenzione della Guerra Nucleare [AIMPGN] (IP), Via Bari 4, 64029 Silvi Marina (TE) (+39-085 935 1350) (fax 085 935 3333) (mdipaolantonio55@gmail.com) (www.ippnw-italy.org).

Associazione Memoria Condivisa (CR), Viale 1º Maggio 32, 71100 Foggia (+39-0881 637775) (fax) (info@memoriacondivisa.it) (www.memoriacondivisa.it). Supports non-violence as a response to terrorism.

Associazione Museo Italiano per la Pace / Association of Italian Museums for Peace (RE), Via Ezio Andolfato 1, 20126 Milano (museoitalianoperlapace@gmail.com). Promotes culture of peace in schools.

Azione dei Cristiani per l'Abolizione della Tortura [ACAT] (HR), c/o Rinascita Cristiana, Via della Trasportina 15, 00193 Roma (+39-06 686 5358) (posta@acatitalia.it) (www.acatitalia.it).

Centro Studi Sereno Regis - Italian Peace Research Institute / Rete CCP [IPRI] (RE CR EL), Via Garibaldi 13, 10122 Torino (+39-011 532824) (fax 011 515 8000) (www.serenoregis.org). *IPRI Newsletter*.

Gesellschaft für Bedrohte Völker / Associazione per i Popoli Minacciati / Lia por i Popui Manacês (HR), CP 233, 39100 Bozen/Bolzano, Südtirol (+39-0471 972240) (fax) (gfbv.bz@ines.org) (www.gfbv.it). Part of international GFBV network.

Greenpeace (GP), Via Della Cordonata 7, 00187 Roma (+39-06 6813 6061) (fax 06 4543 9793) (info.it@greenpeace.org) (www.greenpeace.org/italy). *GP News*.

International School on Disarmament and Research on Conflicts [ISODARCO] (RE CR DA), c/o Prof Carlo Schaerf, via della Rotonda 4, 00186 Roma (+39-06 689 2340) (isodarco@gmail.com) (www.isodarco.it).

Lega degli Obiettori di Coscienza [LOC] (WR), Via Mario Pichi 1, 20143 Milano (+39-02 837 8817) (fax 02 5810 1220) (locosm@tin.it) (ospiti.peacelink.it/loc/).

Movimento Internazionale della Riconciliazione [MIR] (FR), via Garibaldi 13, 10122 Torino (+39-011 532824) (fax 011 515 8000) (segretaria@miritalia.org) (www.miritalia.org).

Movimento Nonviolento [MN] (WR TR EL), Via Spagna 8, 37123 Verona (+39-045 800 9803) (fax) (azionenonviolenta@sis.it) (www.nonviolenti.org). *Azione Nonviolenta*.

Operazione Colomba / Operation Dove (RP CD CR), Via Mameli 5, 47921 Rimini (+39-0541 29005) (fax) (info@operazionecolomba@it) (www.operationdove.org). A project of Associazione Papa Giovanni XXIII.

Pax Christi Italia (PC), via Quintole per le Rose 131, 50029 Tavarnuzze, Firenze (+39-055 202 0375) (fax) (info@paxchristi.it) (www.paxchristi.it). *Mosaico di Pace*.

ITALY

PBI Italia (PA RA HR), Via Asiago 5/a, 35010 Cadoneghe (PD) (+39-345 269 0132) (info@pbi-italy.org) (www.pbi-italy.org).
Religioni per la Pace Italia (RP), Via Pio VIII 38-D-2, 00165 Roma (+39-333 273 1245) (info@religioniperlapaceitalia.org) (www.religioniperlapaceitalia.org).
Rete Italiana Pace e Disarmo / Italian Peace and Disarmament Network [RIPD] (DA RE), c/o Casa per la Nonviolenza, via Spagna 8, 37123 Verona (+39-045 800 9803) (segretaria@retepacedisarmo.org) (www.retepacedisarmo.org).
Servas Italia (SE), c/o Centro Studi Sereno Regis, Via Garibaldi 13, 10122 Torino (segretario@servas.it) (www.servas.it).
Servizio Civile Internazionale [SCI-I] (SC), Via Alessandro Cruto 43, 00146 Roma (+39-06 5964 8311) (info@sci-italia.it) (sci-italia.it).
Società Italiana per l'Organizzazione Internazionale [SIOI] (UN), Piazza di San Marco 51, 00186 Roma (+39-06 692 0781) (fax 06 678 9102) (sioi@sioi.org) (www.sioi.org). *La Comunità Internazionale*.

IVORY COAST

Centre de Recherche et d'Action pour la Paix [CERAP] (RE HR), 15 Ave Jean Mermoz Cocody, 08 BP 2088, Abidjan 08 (+225-2244 4720) (fax 2244 8438) (info@cerap-inades.org) (www.cerap-inades.org).
WILPF Côte d'Ivoire (WL), 08 BP 2237, Abidjan (+225-747 0491) (wilpfcotedivoire@gmail.com).

JAPAN

Chikyu no Tomo / Friends of the Earth (FE), 1-21-9 Komone, Itabashi-ku, Tokyo 173-0037 (+81-3-6909 5983) (fax 6909 5986) (info@foejapan.org) (www.foejapan.org).
Goi Peace Foundation / May Peace Prevail on Earth International - Japan Office (CD PO), Heiwa-Daiichi Bldg, 1-4-5 Hirakawa-Cho, Chiyoda-ku, Tokyo 102-0093 (+81-3-3265 2071) (fax 3239 0919) (info@goipeace.or.jp) (www.goipeace.or.jp).
Green Action (EL), Suite 103, 22-75 Tanaka Sekiden-cho, Sakyo-ku, Kyoto 606-8203 (+81-75-701 7223) (fax 702 1952) (info@greenaction-japan.org) (www.greenaction-japan.org). Campaigns especially against nuclear fuel cycle.
Greenpeace Japan (GP), N F Bldg 2F 8-13-11, Nishi-Shinjuku, Shinjuku, Tokyo 160-0023 (+81-3-5338 9800) (fax 5338 9817) (www.greenpeace.or.jp).
Himeyuri Peace Museum (RE), 671-1 Ihara, Itoman-shi, Okinawa 901-0344 (+81-98-997 2100) (fax 997 2102) (himeyuri1@himeyuri.or.jp) (www.himeyuri.or.jp).
Hiroshima Peace Culture Foundation [HPCF] (PA ND RE), 1-2 Nakajima-cho, Naka-ku, Hiroshima 730-0811 (+81-82-241 5246) (fax 542 7941) (p-soumu@pcf.city.hiroshima.jp) (www.pcf.city.hiroshima.jp/hpcf). *Peace Culture*.
Hiroshima Peace Memorial Museum (RE), 1-2 Nakajima-cho, Naka-ku, Hiroshima 730-0811 (+81-82-241 4004) (fax 542 7941) (hpcf@pcf.city.hiroshima.jp) (www.pcf.city.hiroshima.jp).
Japan Association of Lawyers Against Nuclear Arms [JALANA] (ND), 20-4-906 Araki-cho, Shinjuku-ku, Tokyo 160-0007 (+81-4-2998 2866) (fax 2998 2868) (jalana.office@gmail.com) (www.hankaku-j.org).
Japan Council Against A & H Bombs - Gensuikyo (IB ND PA), 2-4-4 Yushima, Bunkyo-ku, Tokyo 113-8464 (+81-3-5842 6034) (fax 5842 6033) (antiatom@topaz.plala.or.jp) (www.antiatom.org). *No More Hiroshimas*; *Gensuikyo Tsushin*. National federation.
Japanese Physicians for the Prevention of Nuclear War [JPPNW] (IP), c/o Hiroshima Prefectural Medical Association, 3-2-3 Futabanosato, Higashi-ku, Hiroshima 732-0057 (+81-82-568 1511) (fax 568 2112) (ippnw-japan@hiroshima.med.or.jp) (www.hiroshima.med.or.jp).
Kyoto Museum for World Peace (RE), Ritsumeikan University, 56-1 Kitamachi, Toji-in, Kyoto 603-8577 (+81-75-465 8151) (fax 465 7899) (peacelib@st.ritsumei.ac.jp) (www.ritsumei.ac.jp/mng/er/wp-museum).
Network Against Japan Arms Trade [NAJAT] (AT), 311 Shimin Plaza - 302 Heisei Building - 3-12, Shimomiyabi Cho, Shinjuku, Tokyo 162-0822 (anti.arms.export@gmail.com) (najat2016.wordpress.com).
Nihon Hidankyo / Japan Confederation of A- and H-Bomb Sufferers' Organisations (ND CR HR), Gable Bldg 902, 1-3-5 Shiba Daimon, Minato-ku, Tokyo 105-0012 (+81-3-3438 1897) (fax 3431 2113) (kj3t-tnk@asahi-net.or.jp) (www.ne.jp/asahi/hidankyo/nihon). *Hidankyo*.
Organising Committee - World Conference Against A and H bombs (ND), 2-4-4 Yushima, Bunkyo-ku, Tokyo 113-8464 (+81-3-5842 6034) (fax 5842 6033) (intl@antiatom.org).
Peace Depot - Peace Resources Cooperative (ND PA RE), Hiyoshi Gruene 1st Floor, 1-30-27-4 Hiyoshi Hon-cho, Kohoku-ku, Yokohama 223-0062 (+81-45-563 5101) (fax 563 9907) (office@peacedepot.org) (www.peacedepot.org). *Nuclear Weapon & Nuclear Test Monitor*.

Service Civil International - Japan (SC), Char House 101, 5-30-3 Minami-Karasuyama, Setagaya-ku, Tokyo 157-0062 (+81-3-6750 2383) (fax 6750 3858) (sci-japan@sci-japan.org) (www.sci-japan.org).

Toda Peace Institute (RE CR PA WF ND), Samon Eleven Bldg - 5th floor, 3-1 Samon-cho, Shinjuku-ku, Tokyo 160-0017 (contact@toda.org) (www.toda.org).

United Nations Association (UN), Nippon Building - Rm 427, 2-6-2 Ohtemachi, Chiyoda-ku, Tokyo 100-8699 (+81-3-3270 4731) (info@unaj.or.jp) (www.unaj.or.jp).

WRI Japan (WR HR AL), 666 Ukai-cho, Inuyama-shi, Aichi-ken 468-0085 (+81-568-615850).

JORDAN

Generations for Peace (CR), Al-Hussein Youth Sport City, PO Box 963772, Amman 11196 (+962-6-500 4600) (fax 568 2954) (feedback@gfp.ngo) (www.generationsforpeace.org). Grassroots empowerment and advocacy.

KAZAKHSTAN

Chalyqaralyq qauipsizdik Zhenye Sayasat Optalyghy / Centre for International Security and Policy [CISP] (RE), PO Box 257, 37/9 Turan Ave, 010088 Astana (+7-717-225 0544) (info@cisp-astana.kz) (www.cisp-astana.kz).

KENYA

Centre for Research and Dialogue - Somalia [CRD] (CR RE), PO Box 28832, Nairobi (www.crdsomalia.org). Based in Mogadishu, Somalia.

International Friendship League - Kenya [IFL] (CD), PO Box 9929, 00200 Nairobi. Part of international network of groups.

KOREA, REPUBLIC OF

Greenpeace East Asia - Seoul Office (GP), 2/F - 358-121 Seogyo-dong, Mapo-gu, Seoul (+82-2-3144 1994) (fax 6455 1995) (greenpeace.kr@greenpeace.org) (www.greenpeace.org/eastasia).

World Without War (WR), 422-9 Mangwon-dong, Mapo-gu, Seoul 121-230 (+82-2-6401 0514) (fax) (peace@withoutwar.org) (www.withoutwar.org).

LATVIA

Latvijas Zemes Draugi (FE), Lapu iela 17, Zemgales Priekšpilseta, Riga 1002 (+371-6722 5112) (zemesdraugi@zemesdraugi.lv) (www.zemesdraugi.lv).

LEBANON

Fighters for Peace (CR RE), Zico House - 2nd Floor, Spears Street, Beirut (+961-3-971242) (info@fightersforpeace.org) (fightersforpeace.org). Ex-combatants from various factions.

Greenpeace Mediterranean (GP), PO Box 13-6590, Beirut (+961-1-361255) (fax 36 1254) (supporters@greenpeace.org.lb) (www.greenpeace.org/lebanon). See also Israel, Turkey.

WILPF (WL), c/o Nouha Ghosn, PO Box 14-6725, Beirut.

LIBERIA

Sustainable Development Institute (FE), PO Box 5678, Duarzon Village, 1000 Monrovia 10 (+231-330-641355) (managementteam@sdiliberia.org) (www.sdiliberia.org).

LITHUANIA

Mizhnarodniy Tsenter Gramadsyanskich Initsiyatiy "Nash Dom" / International Centre of Civil Initiatives (WR HR), Aušros Vartu St 3 - office 2, Vilnius (+370-60-765718) (feedack@nash-dom.info) (nash-dom.info). Belarusian organisation in exile.

United Nations Association (UN HR), Lithuanian Culture Research Institute, Saltoniskiu St 58, 08015 Vilnius (+370-5-275 1898) (jurate128@yahoo.de).

LUXEMBOURG

Action des Chrétiens pour l'Abolition de la Torture [ACAT] (HR), 5 Av Marie-Thérèse, 2132 Luxembourg (+352-4474 3558) (fax 4474 3559) (contact@acat.lu) (www.acat.lu).

Association Luxembourgeoise pour les Nations Unies [ALNU] (UN), 3 Rte d'Arlon, 8009 Strassen (+352-461468) (fax 461469) (alnu@pt.lu) (www.alnu.lu).

Iwerliewen fir Bedreete Volleker (HR), BP 98, 6905 Niederanven (+352-2625 8687) (info@iwerliewen.org) (iwerliewen.org).

Mouvement Écologique (FE), 6 Rue Vauban, 2663 Luxembourg (+352-439 0301) (fax 4390 3043) (meco@oeko.lu) (www.meco.lu).

Schengen Peace Founation (RE), 14 Rue Mathias Hardt, 1717 Luxembourg (+352-223294) (dominicusrohde@schengenpeacefoundation .org) (schengenpeacefoundation.org). Organises annual World Peace Forum.

Servas (SE), see under Belgium.

MALAWI

International Friendship League - Malawi [IFL] (CD), PO Box 812, Mzuzu (menardkamabga@yahoo.com).

MALAYSIA

Malaysian Physicians for Peace and Social Responsibility [MPPSR] (IP), c/o Academy of Medicine, 50480 Kuala Lumpur (+60-3-7956 8407) (rsmcoy@sternyx.com) (www.ppsr.org).

For explanation of codes and abbreviations, see introduction

MALAYSIA

Sahabat Alam Malaysia / Friends of the Earth Malaysia [SAM] (FE), 258 Jalan Air Itam, George Town, 10460 Penang (+60-4-228 6930) (fax 228 6932) (sam_inquiry@yahoo.com) (www.foe-malaysia.org).

Service Civil International [SCI] (SC), c/o Stephen Nah, 58 Lorong Lintang Zooview Taman Zooview, 68000 Ampang, Kuala Lumpur (+60-3-4161 1581) (sci_malaysia@yahoo.com) (www.scimalaysia.org).

MALI

ACAT-Mali (HR), BP 165, Bamako (mali.acat96@gmail.com). Action by Christians for the Abolition of Torture.

MALTA

John XXIII Peace Laboratory [Peacelab] (IB RP RE), Triq Hal-Far, Zurrieq ZRQ 2609 (+356-2168 9504) (fax 2164 1591) (info@peacelab.org) (www.peacelab.org). *It-Tieqa*.

Moviment ghall-Ambient / Friends of the Earth Malta (FE), PO Box 1013, South Street, Valletta VLT 1000 (+356-7996 1460) (info@foemalta.org) (www.foemalta.org).

MAURITIUS

Lalit (SF WL PA), 153 Main Rd, Grand River North West, Port-Louis (+230-208 2132) (lalitmail@intnet.mu) (www.lalitmauritius.org). Anti-militarist party and campaign.

MEXICO

Médicos Mexicanos para la Prevención de la Guerra Nuclear (IP), Antiguo Claustro - Hospital Juarez - PA, Plaza San Pablo, 06090 Mexico - DF (fromow@servidor.unam.mx).

MONACO

Organisation pour la Paix par le Sport - Peace and Sport (CD), L'Aigue Marine, 24 Ave de Fontvieille - Bloc B, 98000 (+377-9797 7800) (fax 9797 1891) (contact@peace-sport.org) (www.peace-sport.org).

MONGOLIA

Blue Banner (ND), Post Office 49 - Box 35, Ulaanbaatar 13381 (enkhee53@yahoo.com). Promotes nuclear non-proliferation.

Oyu Tolgoi Watch (EL HR), POB 636, Ulaanbaatar 46A (+976-9918 5828) (otwatch@gmail.com). Opposing devastation by Rio Tinto mining project.

MONTENEGRO

UN Association Montenegro (UN), Gradina bb, Danilovgrad 81410 (+382-69-522144) (una.mne@gmail.com).

NAMIBIA

Alternatives to Violence Project [AVP Namibia] (CR), PO Box 50617, Bachbrecht, Windhoek (+264-61-371554) (fax 371555) (vicky@peace.org.na).

Earth Life (Namibia) [ELN] (EL), PO Box 24892, Windhoek 9000 (+264-61-227913) (fax 305213) (earthl@iway.na).

NEPAL

Human Rights and Peace Foundation [HURPEF] (HR), GPO 8975, Epc 5397, Kathmandu (+977-1-438 5231) (hurpef@hons.com.np) (www.hurpef.org.np).

Human Rights Without Frontiers - Nepal (WR HR), PO Box 10660, Maitidevi-33, Kathmandu (+977-1-444 2367) (fax 443 5331) (hrwfnepal@mail.com.np) (www.hrwfnepal.net.np). *Human Rights Monitor*.

National Land Rights Forum (WR HR), Bhumi-Ghar, Tokha-10, Dhapasi Kathmandu (+977-1-691 4586) (fax 435 7033) (land@nlrfnepal.org) (www.nlrfnepal.org).

Nepal Physicians for Social Responsibility (IP), PO Box 19624, Bagbazar, Kathmandu (psrn@healthnet.org.np).

Peace Museum Nepal [PMN] (RE), 29 Anamnagar, Kathmandu (+977-1-425 4409) (peacemuseumnepal@gmail.com) (www.peacemuseumnepal.com).

People's Forum for Human Rights - Bhutan (HR), Anarmani 4, Birtamod, Jhapa (+977-23-540824) (rizal_pfhrb@ntc.net.np).

United Nations Association of Nepal (UN), PO Box 306, Baluwatar, Kathmandu (+977-1-442 6444) (fax 441 3637) (info@unanp.org) (unanp.org).

NETHERLANDS

Amsterdamse Catholic Worker / Ploughshares Support Group (PA AT RP HR RA), Postbus 12622, 1100 AP Amsterdam (+31-20-699 8996) (noelhuis@antenna.nl) (noelhuis.nl). *A Pinch of Salt*.

Anti-Militaristies Onderzoekskollectief - VD AMOK (WR RE AT ND), Lauwerecht 55, 3515 GN Utrecht (+31-30-890 1341) (info@vdamok.nl) (www.vdamok.nl).

Campagne tegen Wapenhandel (AT), Anna Spenglerstr 71, 1054 NH Amsterdam (+31-20-616 4684) (fax) (info@stopwapenhandel.org) (www.stopwapenhandel.org). Campaign against arms trade.

Christian Peacemaker Teams - Nederland [CPT-NL] (RP RA PA), c/o Irene van Setten, Bredasingel 70, 6843 RE Arnhem (+31-26-848 1706) (info@cpt-nl.org) (www.cpt-nl.org).

Doopsgezind Wereldwerk / Mennonite Worldwork (FR CR TW), Amersfoortweg 11, 1324 PE Almere (+31-63-846 1996) (secretariaat@dgwereldwerk.nl) (www.dgwereldwerk.nl).

Greenpeace Nederland (GP), NDSM-Plein 32, 1033 WB Amsterdam (+31-20-626 1877) (fax 622 1272) (info@greenpeace.nl) (www.greenpeace.nl).

Kerk en Vrede (FR PA RE), Joseph Haydnlaan 2a, 3533 AE Utrecht (+31-30-231 6666) (secretariaat@kerkenvrede.nl) (kerkenvrede.nl).

Museum voor Vrede en Geweldloosheid [MVG] (RE PA), Ezelsveldlaan 212, 2611 DK Delft (+31-15-785 0137) (info@vredesmuseum.nl) (www.vredesmuseum.nl). *De Vredesboot.*

Musicians Without Borders (CD), Tolhuisweg 1, 1031 CL Amsterdam (+31-20-330 5012) (info@mwb.ngo) (www.musicianswithoutborders.org).

Nederlandse Vereniging voor de Verenigde Naties [NVVN] (UN), Eisenhowerlaan 128, 3573 HJ Utrecht (info@nvvn.nl) (nvvn.nl).

Nederlandse Vereniging voor Medische Polemologie [NVMP] (IP), PO Box 199, 4190 CD Geldermalsen (+31-6-4200 9559) (office@nvmp.org) (nvmp.org).

Pax (PC AT RE CD), Sint Jacobsstr 12, 3511 BS Utrecht (+31-30-233 3346) (info@paxvoorvrede.nl) (www.paxvoorvrede.nl). Also www.paxforpeace.nl.

Peace Brigades Nederland [PBI] (RA PO CR RE), Oudegracht 36, 3511 AP Utrecht (+31-6-1649 8221) (info@peacebrigades.nl) (www.peacebrigades.nl).

Religieus Genootschap der Vrienden - Quakers Nederland (SF), Quaker Centrum, Stadhouderslaan 8, 2517 HW 's-Gravenhage (secretariaat@dequakers.nl) (www.quakers.nu).

Stichting Voor Aktieve Geweldloosheid [SVAG] (SD PO RE), Postbus 288, 5280 AG Boxtel (+31-40-244 4707) (info@geweldloosactief.nl) (www.geweldlozekracht.nl). *Geweldloze Kracht.*

Stichting Vredesburo Eindhoven (PA RE), Grote Berg 41, 5611 KH Eindhoven (+31-40-244 4707) (info@vredesburo.nl) (www.vredesburo.nl). *Vredesburo Nieuwsbrief.*

Vredesbeweging Pais (WR EL), Ezelsveldlaan 212, 2611 DK Delft (+31-15-785 0137) (info@vredesbeweging.nl) (www.vredesbeweging.nl). *vredesmagazine.nl.*

Vrijwillige Internationale Aktie [VIA] (SC), Eastonstr 174, 1068 JE Amsterdam (info@stichtingvia.nl) (www.stichtingvia.nl).

Vrouwen en Duurzame Vrede (CR ND SD), Haaksbergerstr 317, 7545 GJ Enschede (+31-53-434 0559) (info@vrouwenenduurzamevrede.nl) (www.vrouwenenduurzamevrede.nl).

Women's International League for Peace and Freedom - Netherlands [WILPF-IVVV] (WL), Laan van Nieuw Oost Indië 252, 2593 CD Den Haag (+31-345-615105) (info@wilpf.nl) (www.wilpf.nl).

NEW ZEALAND / AOTEAROA

Abolition 2000 Aotearoa New Zealand [A2000 ANZ] (ND), c/o Pax Christi, PO Box 68419, Newton, Aukland 1145 (+64-9-377 5541) (abolition2000@ymail.com) (www.a2000.org.nz).

Amnesty International (AI), PO Box 5300, Wellesley St, Auckland 1141 (+64-9-303 4520) (fax 303 4528) (info@amnesty.org.nz) (www.amnesty.org.nz).

Anabaptist Association of Australia and New Zealand (RP), see under Australia (anabaptist.asn.au).

Anglican Pacifist Fellowship [APF] (RP AT TR), c/o Indrea Alexander, 9 Holmes St, Waimate 7924 (apfnzsecretary@gmail.com) (converge.org.nz/pma/apf). *The Anglican Pacifist of Aotearoa New Zealand.*

Anti-Bases Campaign [ABC] (PA RE), Box 2258, Christchurch 8140 (abc@chch.planet.org.nz) (www.converge.org.nz/abc). 2 yrly.

Aotearoa Lawyers for Peace (ND), c/o Matt Robson, PO Box 11-648, Ellerslie, Auckland 1051 (+64-9-524 8403).

Campaign Against Foreign Control of Aotearoa [CAFCA], PO Box 2258, Christchurch 8140 (cafca@chch.planet.org.nz) (www.cafca.org.nz). *Foreign Control Watchdog.*

Disarmament and Security Centre [DSC] (IB WL RE ND CR), PO Box 8390, Christchurch 8440 (+64-22-067 3517) (lucy@disarmsecure.org) (www.disarmsecure.org).

Engineers for Social Responsibility [ESR] (EL ND AT), PO Box 6208, Wellesley Street, Auckland 1141 (www.esr.org.nz).

Green Party of Aotearoa/NZ (EL), PO Box 11652, Wellington 6142 (+64-4-801 5102) (fax 801 5104) (greenparty@greens.org.nz) (www.greens.org.nz). *Te Awa.*

Greenpeace Aotearoa New Zealand (GP), 11 Akiraho St, Mount Eden, Auckland (+64-9-630 6317) (fax 630 7121) (info@greenpeace.org.nz) (www.greenpeace.org/new-zealand). *Kakariki.*

Pax Christi Aotearoa/NZ (PC), PO Box 99380, Auckland Central (+64-9-377 5541) (paxchristiaotearoa@gmail.com) (www.paxchristiaotearoa.nz).

Peace Action Wellington (DA AT RA), PO Box 9263, Wellington (peacewellington@riseup.net) (peacewellington.org). Work includes direct action against arms fairs.

Peace Foundation (CR RE), PO Box 8055, Symonds Street, Auckland 1150 (+64-9-373 2379) (fax 379 2668) (peace@peacefoundation.org.nz) (kiaora.peace.net.nz).

NEW ZEALAND

Peace Movement Aotearoa [PMA] (AT HR PA RE), PO Box 9314, Wellington 6141 (+64-4-382 8129) (fax 382 8173) (pma@xtra.co.nz) (www.converge.org.nz/pma). National networking body.

Quaker Peace and Service Aotearoa/New Zealand [QPSANZ] (SF), Quaker Meeting House, 72 Cresswell Ave, Christchurch 8061 (+64-3-980 4884) (www.quaker.org.nz/groups/qpsanz).

Stop the Arms Trade NZ (AT DA), PO Box 9843, Wellington (stop-the-arms-trade@riseup.net) (www.stopthearmstrade.nz). Actions against weapons expos.

United Nations Association of New Zealand [UNANZ] (UN), PO Box 24494, Wellington 6142 (+64-4-496 9638) (office@unanz.org.nz) (unanz.org.nz).

West Papua Action Auckland [WPAA] (HR TW), PO Box 68419, Wellesley St, Auckland 1141 (+64-9-815 9000) (fax) (westpapuaactionauckland.wordpress.com).

Women's International League for Peace and Freedom [WILPF] (WL), PO Box 2054, Wellington (wilpfaotearoa@gmail.com) (www.wilpf.nz).

NICARAGUA

Centro de Prevención de la Violencia [CEPREV] (HR PO DA), Villa Fontana - casa 23, Club Terraza 1/2 c al lago, Managua (fax +505-2278 1637) (www.ceprev.org). Promotes a culture of peace.

NIGERIA

Alternatives to Violence Project [AVP Nigeria] (WR), 5 Ogunlesi St, off Bode Thomas Rd, Onipanu, Lagos (+234-1-497 1359) (prawa@linkserve.com.ng).

Anglican Pacifist Fellowship - Nigeria [APF] (RP), c/o Peter U James, Akwa Ibom Peace Group, PO Box 269, Abak, Akwa Ibom State.

Centre for Global Nonviolence Nigeria (RE PA), 20 Ogunka Eruwa Rd, Rumuoke Newlayout (off Ada George Road), Mgbuoba, Port Harcourt, Rivers State (cgnv_ngr@yahoo.com) (cgnv.edublogs.org).

Peace Initiative Network [PIN] (CR CD RE), PO Box 14937, Kano (info@peaceinitiativenetwork.org) (peaceinitiativenetwork.org).

United Nations Association of Nigeria (UN), PO Box 54423, Falomo, Ikoyi, Lagos (+234-802-319 8698).

NORTH MACEDONIA

Dzivenje na ekologistitje na Makedonija / Ecologists' Movement of Macedonia [DEM] (FE), Ul Vasil Gjorgov 39 - 6, 1000 Skopje (+389-2-220518) (fax) (dem@dem.org.mk) (www.dem.org.mk).

Mirovna Aktsiya / Aksioni Paqësor / Peace Action (WR), Dimo Narednikot A1/2/31, 7500 Prilep (+389-48-401888) (office@mirovnaakcija.org) (www.mirovnaakcija.org). Also in Tetovo (+389-44-520808).

United Nations Association of Macedonia (UN), St Zorz Bize 9-b, 1000 Skopje (+389-2-244 3751) (fpesevi@mt.net.mk) (www.sunamk.org).

NORWAY

Amnesty International (AI), PO Box 702, Sentrum, 0106 Oslo (+47-2240 2200) (fax 2240 2250) (info@amnesty.no) (www.amnesty.no).

Centre for Peace Studies - Senter for Fredsstudier [CPS] (RE), UiT - The Arctic University of Norway, PO Box 6050 Langnes, 9037 Tromsø (+47-7764 4000) (mail@peace.uit.no) (uit.no/enhet/peace).

Folkereisning Mot Krig [FMK] (WR AT), PO Box 2779, Solli, 0204 Oslo (+47-2246 4670) (fax) (fmk@ikkevold.no) (www.ikkevold.no). *Ikkevold.*

Fred og Forsoning - IFOR Norge (FR), Fredshuset, Møllergata 12, 0179 Oslo (contact@ifor.no) (www.ifor.no).

Informasjonsarbeidere for Fred [IF] (IB AT ND DA), c/o Heffermehl, Stensgaten 24B, 0358 Oslo (+47-9174 4783) (fredpax@online.no) (peaceispossible.info).

Iran Human Rights (HR), Box 2635 Solli, 0204 Oslo (mail@iranhr.net) (www.iranhr.net). Iranian organisation in exile.

Nansen Centre for Peace and Dialogue [NCPD] (CR RE HR), Bjømstjerne Bjørnsons gate 2, 2609 Lillehammer (+47-6125 5500) (post@peace.no) (www.peace.no).

Narviksenteret - Nordnorsk Fredssenter (IB), Postboks 700, 8509 Narvik (+47-9154 7078) (fax 7694 4560) (fred.no).

Nei til Atomvåpen / No to Nuclear Weapons (ND), Postboks 8838, Youngstorget, 0028 Oslo (post@neitilatomvapen.org) (www.neitilatomvapen.no).

Nobel Peace Prize Watch (DA RE), for postal address see under Sweden (mail@nobelwill.org) (www.nobelwill.org). Promotes original purpose of Nobel Prize.

Nobels Fredssenter / Nobel Peace Centre (RE), PO Box 1894 Vika, 0124 Oslo (+47-4830 1000) (fax 9142 9238) (post@nobelpeacecenter.org) (www.nobelpeacecenter.org).

Norges Fredslag (DA AT ND RE), Grensen 9B, Postboks 8922, Youngstorget, 0028 Oslo (www.fredslaget.no). Norwegian Peace Association.

Norges Fredsråd / Norwegian Peace Council (IB), Postboks 8940 Youngstorget, 0028 Oslo (+47-9527 4822) (fax 2286 8401) (post@norgesfredsrad.no) (norgesfredsrad.no).

Norges Naturvernforbund (FE), Mariboes gate 8, 0183 Oslo (+47-2310 9610) (fax 2293 1802) (medlem@naturvernforbundet.no) (naturvernforbundet.no).

Norwegian Nobel Institute / Det Norske Nobelinstitutt (RE DA CR), Henrik Ibsens gate 51, 0255 Oslo (+47-2212 9300) (fax 9476 1117) (postmaster@nobel.no) (nobelpeaceprize.org).

Peace Brigades Norge [PBI-Norge] (CR HR PA), c/o Sentralen, Postboks 183, 0102 Oslo (kontakt@pbi.no) (www.pbi.no).

WILPF Norge - Internasjonal Kvinneliga for Fred og Frihet [IKFF] (WL), Storgata 11, 0155 Oslo (+47-9308 9644) (ikff@ikff.no) (www.ikff.no). *Fred og Frihet*.

PAKISTAN

Human Rights Commission of Pakistan [HRCP] (HR), Aiwan-i-Jamhoor, 107 Tipu Block, New Garden Town, Lahore 54600 (+92-42-3586 4994) (fax 3588 3582) (hrcp@hrcp-web.org) (hrcp-web.org).

Revolutionary Association of the Women of Afghanistan [RAWA] (HR), PO Box 374, Quetta (+92-300-554 1258) (rawa@rawa.org) (www.rawa.org).

Servas Pakistan [SE-PK] (SE), c/o Muhammad Naseem, GPO Box 516, Lahore 54000 (+92-321-444 4516) (fax 42-3532 2223) (servaspakistan@yahoo.com) (pages.intnet.mu/servas/Pakistan/). *Servas Pakistan Newsletter*.

PALESTINE (see also Israel)

NOTE: Because all of Palestine is under Israeli control (including areas not under day-to-day occupation), it is advisable to add 'via Israel' to addresses here (as well as 'Palestine').

Al-Haq (RE PC), PO Box 1413, Ramallah, West Bank (+970-2-295 4646) (fax 295 4903) (www.alhaq.org).

Al-Watan Centre (CR HR RE), PO Box 158, Hebron, West Bank (+970-2-222 3777) (fax 222 0907) (info@alwatan.org) (www.alwatan.org). Supports popular resistance and nonviolence.

Alternative Information Centre [AIC] (HR RE TW AL AT), Building 111, Main Street, Beit Sahour, West Bank (+972-2-277 5444) (fax 277 5445) (www.alternativenews.org). See also Israel.

Arab Educational Institute - Open Windows [AEI] (HR PC), Paul VI Street, Bethlehem, West Bank (+970-2-274 4030) (fax 277 7554) (info@aeicenter.org) (www.aeicenter.org).

Combatants for Peace (CD CR), Ramallah (for postal address, see under Israel) (office@cfpeace.org) (cfpeace.org). Palestinian and Israeli ex-fighters for peace.

Ecumenical Accompaniment Programme in Palestine and Israel - Jerusalem Office [EAPPI] (RP HR CD CR), PO Box 741, East Jerusalem 91000 (+972-2-628 9402) (communications@eappi.org) (eappi.org).

Geneva Initiative (CD CR), c/o Palestinian Peace Coalition, PO Box 4252, Ramallah (+972-2-297 2535) (fax 297 2538) (www.geneva-accord.org). See also Israel.

Good Shepherd Collective (HR RA CR), Um al-Khair, South Hebron Hills, West Bank Governate, West Bank (+972-58-438 1133) (info@goodshepherdcollective.org) (goodshepherdcollective.org). Collective resisting military occupation.

International Peace and Co-operation Centre [IPCC] (TW CR), PO Box 24162, Jerusalem 91240 (+972-2-581 1992) (fax 540 0522) (info@ipcc-jerusalem.org) (home.ipcc-jerusalem.org).

Israel-Palestine Creative Regional Initiatives [IPCRI] (RE CR EL CD), PO Box 9321, Jerusalem 91092 (+970-59-856 7287) (ipcri@ipcri.org) (www.ipcri.org). Office is in Ammunition Hill, East Jerusalem.

Middle East Non-Violence and Democracy - FOR Palestine [MEND] (FR HR CR), PO Box 66558, Beit Hanina, East Jerusalem (+970-2-656 7310) (fax 656 7311) (lucynusseibeh@gmail.com) (www.mendonline.org).

Miftah - Palestinian Initiative for the Promotion of Global Dialogue and Democracy (HR), PO Box 69647, Jerusalem 95908 (+970-2-298 9490) (fax 298 9492) (administration@miftah.org) (www.miftah.org).

Movement Against Israeli Apartheid in Palestine [MAIAP] (HR), see under Israel.

OneVoice Movement - Palestine (CD CR), PO Box 2401, Ramallah, West Bank (+970-2-295 2076) (info@OneVoice.ps) (www.onevoicemovement.org). See also Israel.

Palestine-Israel Journal **(RE CD CR)**, PO Box 19839, East Jerusalem (+972-2-628 2115) (fax 627 3388) (pij@pij.org) (www.pij.org). 4 yrly.

Palestinian BDS National Committee (HR RA), c/o PACBI, PO Box 1701, Ramallah, West Bank (pacbi@bdsmovement.net) (bdsmovement.net/bnc).

Palestinian Centre for Human Rights [PCHR] (HR), PO Box 1328, Gaza City, Gaza Strip (+970-8-282 4776) (fax 282 5255) (pchr@pchrgaza.org) (www.pchrgaza.org).

Palestinian Physicians for the Prevention of Nuclear War [PPPNW] (IP), PO Box 51681, East Jerusalem (azizlabadi@yahoo.com).

Palestinian-Israeli Peace NGO Forum (Palestinian Office) (CD), c/o Panorama, Al Ahliya St, Ramallah 2045 (+970-2-295 9618) (fax 298 1824) (panorama@panoramacenter.org) (www.peacengo.org). See also under Israel.

PALESTINE

Parents' Circle - Families' Forum: Bereaved Palestinian and Israeli Families Supporting Peace and Tolerance (CD CR), 13 Jamal Abed Al-Nasser St, Al-Ram, East Jerusalem (+972-2-234 4554) (fax 234 4553) (alquds@theparentscircle.com) (www.theparentscircle.com). See also under Israel.

Wi'am - Palestinian Conflict Resolution Centre (FR CR), PO Box 1039, Bethlehem, West Bank (+970-2-277 7333) (fax) (hope@alaslah.org) (www.alaslah.org).

Windows - Israeli-Palestinian Friendship Centre (CD), PO Box 352, Ramallah (office@win-peace.org) (www.win-peace.org). See also in Israel.

PARAGUAY

Amnistía Internacional Paraguay (AI), Dr Hassler 5229 - e/ Cruz del Defensor y Cruz del Chaco, Bsrrio Villa Mora, Asunción (+595-21-604822) (fax 663272) (ai-info@py.amnesty.org) (www.amnesty.org).

SERPAJ-Paraguay (HR PA), Calle Teniente Prieto 354 - entre Dr Facundo Insfran y Tte Rodi, Asunción (+595-21-481333) (serpajpy@serpajpy.org.py) (www.serpajpy.org.py).

PHILIPPINES

Initiatives for International Dialogue [IID] (CD TW), 27 Galaxy St, GSIS Heights, Matina, 8000 Davao City (+63-82-299 2052) (iidnet.org). Manila office +63-2-911 0205.

POLAND

Lekarze Przeciw Wojnie Nuklearnej - Sekcja Polska IPPNW (IP), Ul Mokotowska 3 - lok 6, 02640 Warszawa (+48-22-845 5784) (b.wasilewski@ips.pl).

Servas Polska (SE), c/o Joanna Mozga, Ul Kasprzaka 24A m 39, 01211 Warszawa (joanna@servas.pl) (servas.pl).

Stowarzyszenie "Nigdy Wiecej" / "Never Again" Association (HR PO), PO Box 6, 03700 Warszawa 4 (redakcja@nigdywiecej.org) (www.nigdywiecej.org). Works for genocide commemoration, anti-racism.

PORTUGAL

Amnistia Internacional Portugal (AI), Rua dos Remorales 7 - 2º, 1200-370 Lisboa (+351-21 386 1664) (aiportugal@amnistia.pt) (www.amnistia.pt).

Associação das Nações Unidas Portugal (UN), Rua do Almada 679 - 1º - S 103, 4050-039 Porto (+351-22 200 7767) (anuportugal@gmail.com).

Associação Livre dos Objectores e Objectoras de Consciência [ALOOC] (WR AL), Rua D Aleixo Corte-Real 394 - 3º D, 1800-166 Lisboa (alooc.portugal@gmail.om).

Conselho Português para a Paz e Cooperação [CPPC] (WP ND DA), Rua Rodrigo da Fonseca 56-2º, 1250-193 Lisboa (+351-21 386 3375) (fax 21 386 3221) (conselhopaz@cppc.pt) (www.cppc.pt). Portuguese Council for Peace and Co-operation.

Observatório Género e Violência Armada / Observatory on Gender and Armed Violence [OGIVA] (DA HR), Centro Estudos Sociais, Colégio de S Jerónimo, Apartado 3087, 3000-995 Coimbra (+351-239 855593) (fax 239 855589) (ogiva@ces.uc.pt) (www.ces.uc.pt).

Pax Christi Portugal (PC), Basílica da Estrela, Praça da Estrela, 1200-667 Lisboa (info@paxchristiportugal.net) (www.paxchristiportugal.net).

PUERTO RICO

Humanistas Seculares de Puerto Rico (HR), 120 Ave Carlos Chardon - 123, San Juan 00918 (www.humanistaspr.org).

Pax Christi Puerto Rico (PC), c/o Randolph Rivera Cuevas, HC 3 Box 9695, Gurabo 00778 (+1787-761 1355) (fax) (clidin@bppr.com).

ROMANIA

Institutul Român pentru Actiune, Instruire si Cercetare în Domeniul Pacii [PATRIR] (RE), Strada Ion Ghica 30, 400306 Cluj-Napoca (+40-264 420298) (info@patrir.ro) (patrir.ro). Peace Action, Training and Research Institute.

RUSSIA

Dom Druzeiy v Moskvye / Friends' House Moscow (SF), Sukharevskaya M - pl 6 - str 1, 127051 Moskva (+7-903-664 1075) (dd.moskva@gmail.com) (friendshousemoscow.org).

Federatsiya Mira i Soglasiya / International Federation for Peace and Conciliation [IFPC] (WP), 36 Prospekt Mira, 129090 Moskva (+7-495-680 3576) (fax 688 9587) (vik@ifpc.ru) (www.ifpc.ru). Mir i Soglasie.

Memorial (HR CD), Malyi Karetnyi pereulok 12, 127051 Moskva (+7-495-650 7883) (fax 609 0694) (info@memo.ru) (www.memo.ru).

Nyemyetsko-Russkiy Obmyen / Deutscher-Russischer Austausch [NRO] (CD), Ligovsky Pr 87 - Ofis 300, 191040 Sankt-Peterburg (+7-812-718 3793) (fax 718 3791) (nro@obmen.org) (www.obmen.org). German-Russian Exchange.

Rossiiskaya Assotsiatsiya Sodeystviya OON / United Nations Association of Russia (UN), Vernadsky prospekt 76, 119454 Moskva (+7-495-225 4085) (fax 234 5803) (una@una.ru) (una.ru).

Soldatskiye Matyeri Sankt-Peterburg / Soldiers' Mothers of St Petersburg (HR PA PC), Ul Razyezzhaya 9, 191002 Sankt-

Peterburg (+7-812-712 4199) (fax 712 5058) (soldiersmothers@yandex.ru) (www.soldiersmothers.ru).
Tsentr Mezhnatsionalnovo Sotrudnichestva / Centre for Interethnic Co-operation (CR CD), a/ya 8, 127055 Moskva (+7-499-972 6807) (center@interethnic.org) (www.interethnic.org).

RWANDA
Life & Peace Institute - DR Congo (RE RP), PO Box 64, Cyangugu (+243-81-249 4489) (pieter.vanholder@life-peace.org) (www.life-peace.org).
Peace & Conflict Resolution Project (of Bukavu, DR Congo) [PCR] (CR), PO Box 37, Cyangugu (+243-993-463279) (peacecrp@yahoo.com) (www.peaceconflictresolutionproject.webs.com). Operates in Bukavu, eastern Congo.

SERBIA
Beogradski Forum za Svet Ravnopravnih / Belgrade Forum for a World of Equals [Beoforum] (WP), Sremska Broj 6 - IV sprat, 11000 Beograd (+381-11-328 3778) (beoforum@eunet.rs) (www.beoforum.rs).
Centar za Nenasilnu Akciju - Beograd / Centre for Nonviolent Action - Belgrade [CNA] (CR PA RE CD), Cika Ljubina 6, 11000 Beograd (+381-11-263 7603) (fax) (cna.beograd@nenasilje.org) (www.nenasilje.org). See also in Bosnia-Herzegovina.
Centre for Applied NonViolent Action and Strategies [CANVAS], Gandijeva 76a, 11070 Novi Beograd (+381-11-222 8331) (fax 222 8336) (office@canvasopedia.org) (www.canvasopedia.org).
Udruzenje za Ujedinjene Nacije Srbije / United Nations Association of Serbia (UN), Makedonska St 22, 11000 Beograd (+381-11-322 4648) (info@unaserbia.rs) (www.unaserbia.rs).
Zene U Crnom Protiv Rata / Women in Black Against War (WR), Jug Bogdanova 18/V, 11000 Beograd (+381-11-262 3225) (zeneucrnombeograd@gmail.com) (www.zeneucrnom.org).

SIERRA LEONE
Friends of the Earth Sierra Leone [FOESL] (FE), PM Bag 950, 33 Robert St, Freetown (+232-22-226577) (fax 224439) (foesl@sierratel.sl) (www.onesky.ca/foesl).

SINGAPORE
Inter-Religious Organisation - Singapore (RP), Palmer House, 70 Palmer Rd - 05-01/02, Singapore 079427 (+65-6221 9858) (fax 6221 9212) (irosingapore@gmail.com) (iro.sg). Affiliate of Religions for Peace International.
United Nations Association of Singapore [UNAS] (UN), PO Box 351, Tanglin Post Office, Singapore 912412 (+65-6792 0026) (sctham@unas.org.sg) (www.unas.org.sg). *World Forum.*

SLOVAKIA
Inštitút ľudských Práv / Human Rights Institute (HR), Karpatská 23, 81105 Bratislava (info@ludskeprava.sk) (www.ludskeprava.sk).
Pax Christi Bratislava-Pezinok (PC), Kpt Jaroša 15, 90201 Pezinok (+421-33-640 1284) (fax) (molnars@nextra.sk).
Priatelia Zeme Slovensko / Friends of the Earth Slovakia (FE), Komenského 21, 97401 Banská Bystrica (+421-48-412 3859) (fax) (foe@priateliazeme.sk) (www.priateliazeme.sk).

SLOVENIA
Zavod Voluntariat / Slovenian SCI Group (SC), Bezigrad 6, 1000 Ljubljana (+386-1-239 1623) (info@zavod-voluntariat.si) (www.zavod-voluntariat.si).

SOMALIA
Centre for Research and Dialogue [CRD] (CR RE), for postal address see under Kenya (+252-1-658666) (fax 5-932355) (crd@crdsomalia.org) (www.crdsomalia.org). Street address: K4 Airport Rd, Mogadishu.

SOUTH AFRICA
Africa4Palestine (HR RA), PO Box 2318, Houghton 2041, Johannesburg (+27-11 403 2097) (fax 86 650 4836) (info@africa4palestine.com) (www.africa4palestine.com).
African Centre for the Constructive Resolution of Disputes [ACCORD] (RE CD CR), 2 Golf Course Drive, Mount Edgecombe, Durban 4320, Kwazulu-Natal (+27-31 502 3908) (fax 31 502 4160) (info@accord.org.za) (www.accord.org.za). *Conflict Trends.*
Anglican Pacifist Fellowship [APF] (RP), c/o Victor Spencer, PO Box 54, Ficksburg 9730 (+27-51-922700) (victor.spencer@cpsanet.co.za).
Centre for Environmental Rights [CER] (EL HR), Second Floor, Springtime Studios, 1 Scott Rd, Observatory 7925, Cape Town (+27-21 447 1647) (fax 86 730 9098) (info@cer.org.za) (cer.org.za).
Centre for the Study of Violence and Reconciliation (RE CR HR), PO Box 30778, Braamfontein, Johannesburg 2017 (+27-11 403 5650) (fax 11 339 6785) (info@csvr.org.za) (www.csvr.org.za). Also in Cape Town (+27-21 447 2470).
GroundWork / Friends of the Earth South Africa (FE), PO Box 2375, Pietermaritzburg 3200 (+27-33 342 5662) (fax 33 342 5665) (team@groundwork.org.za) (www.groundwork.org.za).

SOUTH AFRICA

International Centre of Nonviolence [ICON] (RE HR), ML Sultan Campus, Durban University of Technology, PO Box 1334, Durban 4000 (+27-31 373 5499) (icon@dut.ac.za) (www.icon.org.za). Works for a culture of nonviolence.

United Nations Association of South Africa [UNA-SA] (UN), 23 Andries Pretorius St (corner of Victoria St), Somerset West 7130, Cape Town (+27-21 850 0509) (admin@unasa.org.za) (unasa.org.za).

SOUTH SUDAN

Organisation for Nonviolence and Development [ONAD] (WR CR HR), PO Box 508, Juba (+211-921-352592) (onadjuba2011@gmail.com) (www.onadev.org).

SPAIN

Acció dels Cristians per l'Abolició de la Tortura [ACAT] (HR), c/Anglí 55, 08017 Barcelona (+34-93 203 8915) (acat.montserrat2@gmail.com).

Alternativa Antimilitarista - Movimiento de Objección de Conciencia [AA-MOC] (WR RA TR), C/San Cosme y San Damián 24-2º, 28012 Madrid (+34-91 475 3782) (moc.lavapies@nodo50.org) (www.antimilitaristas.org).

Amnistía Internacional España (AI), C/ Fernando VI - 8 - 1º Izda, 28004 Madrid (+34-91 310 1277) (fax 91 319 5334) (info@madrid.es.amnesty.org) (www.es.amnesty.org).

Antimilitaristes - MOC València (WR RA TR), C/ Roger de Flor 8 - baix-dta, 46001 València (+34-96 391 6702) (retirada@pangea.org) (mocvalencia.org).

Centre d'Estudis per la Pau JM Delàs (WR RE AT RP IB), Erasme de Janer 8 - Door 9, 08001 Barcelona, Catalunya (+34-93 441 1947) (info@centredelas.org) (www.centredelas.org). *Materiales de Trabajo.*

Ekologistak Martxan Bizkaia (ND EL TW), c/ Pelota 5 - Behea, 48005 Bilbo, Euskadi (+34-94 479 0119) (fax) (bizkaia@ekologistakmartxan.org) (www.ekologistakmartxan.org). *Eco Boletín.*

Fundación Seminario de Investigación para la Paz [SIP] (RE), Centro Pignatelli, Pº de la Constitución 6, 50008 Zaragoza (+34-976 217215) (fax 976 230113) (sipp@seipaz.org) (www.seipaz.org).

Gernika Gogoratuz - Peace Research Centre [GGG] (IB RE), Artekale 1-1, 48300 Gernika-Lumo, Bizkaia (+34-94 625 3558) (fax 94 625 6765) (gernikag@gernikagogoratuz.org) (www.gernikagogoratuz.org).

Grup Antimilitarista Tortuga (PA), C/ Ametler 26 - 7ª, 03203 Elx, Alacant (tortuga@nodo50.org) (www.grupotortuga.com). Part of network Alternativa Antimilitarista - MOC.

International Institute for Nonviolent Action [NOVACT] (RE PA CD CR), Junta de Comerç 20, 08001 Barcelona (+34-93 551 4714) (communication@novact.org) (novact.org).

Justicia y Paz - España [CGJP] (RP), Rafael de Riego 16 - 3º dcha, 28045 Madrid (+34-91 506 1828) (juspax@juspax-es.org) (www.juspax-es.org).

Kontzientzi Eragozpen Mugimendua / MOC Euskal Herria [KEM-MOC] (WR AL RA TR), Calle Fika Nº 4 - lonja derecha, 48006 Bilbao, Euskadi (+34-94-415 3772) (mocbilbao@gmail.com) (www.sinkuartel.org). Part of network Alternativa Antimilitarista - MOC.

Liga Internacional de Mujeres por la Paz y la Libertad (WL), 26-28 bajo - Almería, Zaragoza (wilpf.espanya@gmail.com) (wilpf.es).

Paz y Cooperación / Peace and Co-operation (IB RE TW), Meléndez Valdés 68 - 4º izq, 28015 Madrid (+34-91 549 6156) (fax 91 543 5282) (pazycooperacion@hotmail.com) (www.peaceandcooperation.org). *Premio Escolar Paz y Cooperación.*

Servas España (SE), Calle de la Roca 5, 08319 Dosrius (servas.spain@gmail.com) (www.servas.es).

Servei Civil Internacional - Catalunya [SCI] (SC PA), c/ Carme 95 - baixos 2a, 08001 Barcelona, Catalunya (+34-93 441 7079) (info@sci-cat.org) (www.sci-cat.org).

Survival International (España) [SI] (HR), C/Príncipe 12 - 3º, 28012 Madrid (+34-91 521 7283) (fax 91 523 1420) (info@survival.es) (www.survival.es). *Boletín de Acción Urgente.*

SRI LANKA

Mahatma Gandhi Centre (PO PA RE), 22/17 Kalyani Rd, Colombo 00600 (+94-11-250 1825) (fax) (power2people@gandhiswaraj.org) (gandhiswaraj.con).

National Peace Council of Sri Lanka [NPC] (CR RE CD), 12/14 Purana Vihara Rd, Colombo 6 (+94-11-281 8344) (fax 281 9064) (npc@sltnett.lk) (www.peace-srilanka.org). *Paths to Peace.*

Nonviolent Direct Action Group [NVDAG] (FR WR IB), PO Box 2, 29 Kandy Rd, Kaithady-Nunavil, Chavakachcheri (del-smskr@eureka.lk). *NVDAG Report.*

SUDAN

Peace Desk of New Sudan Council of Churches (RP CD CR HR), see under Kenya.

SWEDEN

Greenpeace (GP), Rosenlundsgatan 29 B, 11863 Stockholm (+46-8-702 7070) (info.se@greenpeace.se) (www.greenpeace.se).

Internationella Kvinnoförbundet för Fred och Frihet [IKFF] (WL), Norrtullsgatan 45 - 1 tr, 11345 Stockholm (+46-8-702 9810) (info@ikff.se) (www.ikff.se).

Jordens Vänner / Friends of the Earth Sweden (FE TW), Box 7048, 40231 Göteborg (+46-31-121808) (fax 121817) (info@jordensvanner.se) (www.jordensvanner.se).

Kristna Fredsrörelsen (FR), Ekumeniska Centret, Box 14038, 16714 Bromma (+46-8-453 6840) (fax 453 6829) (info@krf.se) (krf.se). *Fredsnytt.*

Life & Peace Institute [LPI] (RP AT RE TW CR), Kungsängsgatan 17 - 1st floor, 75322 Uppsala (+46-18-660130) (info@life-peace.org) (life-peace.org).

Nobel Peace Prize Watch (DA RE), c/o Magnusson, Marklandsgatan 63, 41477 Göteborg (gosta.tomas@gmail.com) (www.nobelwill.org). Promotes original purpose of Nobel Prize.

Nordic Nonviolence Study Group [NORNONS] (RE PA), Sparsnäs 1010, 66891 Ed (johansen.jorgen@gmail.com) (www.nornons.org).

Ofog (WR RA AT ND AL), c/o Göteborgs Fredskommitté, Linnégatan 21, 41304 Göteborg (+46-733-815361) (info@ofog.org) (www.ofog.org).

PBI-Sverige (HR CR), Blixtåsvägen 6, 42437 Angered (+46-31-330 7509) (info@pbi-sweden.org) (www.pbi-sweden.org).

Servas Sverige (SE), c/o Eva Hartman-Juhlin, Svankärrsvägen 3B, 75653 Upsalla (sweden@servas.se) (www.servas.se).

Stockholm Centre for the Ethics of War and Peace [SCEWP] (RE), Universitetsvägen 10, 11418 Stockholm (stockholmcentre.org).

Svenska FN-Förbundet (UN), Box 15115, 10465 Stockholm (+46-8-462 2540) (fax 641 8876) (info@fn.se) (www.fn.se). *Världshorisont.*

Svenska Fredskommittén / Swedish Peace Committee [SFK] (DA ND), Tegelviksgatan 40, 11641 Stockholm (info@svenskafredskommitten.nu) (www.svenskafredskommitten.nu).

Sveriges Fredsråd / Swedish Peace Council (IB), Tegelviksgatan 40, 11641 Stockholm (info@FredNu.se) (frednu.se). National federation.

Swedish Peace and Arbitration Society / Svenska Freds- och Skiljedomsföreningen [SPAS] (WR IB AT), Polhemsgatan 4, 11236 Stockholm (+46-8-5580 3180) (info@svenskafreds.se) (www.svenskafreds.se).

Uppsala Universitet Institutionen för freds- och konfliktforskning / Dept of Peace and Conflict Research (RE AT), Box 514, 75120 Uppsala (+46-18-471 0000) (info@pcr.uu.se) (www.pcr.uu.se).

Vännernas Samfund (Kväkarna) (SF), Box 9166, 10272 Stockholm (+46-8-668 6816) (fax) (info@kvakare.se).

SWITZERLAND

Action des Chrétiens pour l'Abolition de la Torture / Aktion der Christen für die Abschaffung der Folter [ACAT-Suisse] (HR), Speichergasse 29, 3011 Berne (+41-31 312 2044) (info@acat.ch) (www.acat.ch).

Amnesty International (AI), Speichergasse 33, 3011 Bern (+41-31 307 2222) (fax 31 307 2233) (info@amnesty.ch) (www.amnesty.ch). *Amnesty Magazin(e).*

APRED - Participative Institute for the Progress of Peace (RE CD HR), Route des Siernes Picaz 46, 1659 Flendruz (+41-79 524 3574) (info@demilitarisation.org) (www.apred.org).

Ärzte/Ärztinnen für Soziale Verantwortung / Médecins pour une Résponsibilité Sociale [PSR/IPPNW] (IP), Bireggstr 36, 6003 Luzern (+41-41 240 6349) (fax) (sekretariat@ippnw.ch) (www.ippnw.ch).

Association for Inclusive Peace (RE CR), 14b Av Giuseppe Motta, 1202 Genève (info@inclusivepeace.org) (www.inclusivepeace.org). Making peace processes more sustainable.

Basel Peace Office (RE ND), c/o Swisspeace, K-Haus, Kasernenstr 8, 4058 Basel (info@baselpeaceoffice.org) (www.baselpeaceoffice.org).

Centre pour l'Action Non-Violente [CENAC] (WR RP IB), 52 rue de Genève, 1004 Lausanne (+41-21 661 2434) (fax 21 661 2436) (info@non-violence.ch) (www.non-violence.ch).

cfd - the feminist peace organisation (PA CR HR), Postfach, 3001 Berne (+41-31 300 5060) (info@cfd-ch.org) (www.cfd-ch.org). *cfd-Zeitung.*

ContrAtom - Association Antinucléaire Genevoise (EL), CP 65, 1211 Genève 8 (+41-22 321 5709) (info@contratom.ch) (www.contratom.ch). *ContrAtom.*

Eirene Suisse (RP TW EL CR), 9 Rue du Valais, 1202 Genève (+41-22 321 8556) (fax) (info@eirenesuisse.ch) (eirenesuisse.ch).

Fight for Humanity (HR), 150 route de Fernay - PO Box 2100, 1211 Genève 2 (info@fightforhumanity.org) (www.fightforhumanity.org). Supports human rights in conflict zones.

For explanation of codes and abbreviations, see introduction

SWITZERLAND

Frauen für den Frieden / Donne per la Pace / Femmes pour la Paix (IB), Oberwilerstr 50, 4054 Basel (+41-44 945 0725) (sekretariat@frauenfuerdenfrieden.ch) (www.frauenfuerdenfrieden.ch). Women for Peace.

Gender and Mine Action Programme (AT CR RE HR), c/o Geneva International Centre for Humanitarian Demining, PO Box 1300, 1211 Genève 1 (+41-22 730 9335) (fax 22 730 9362) (info@gmap.ch) (www.gmap.ch).

Grüne Partei der Schweiz / Parti écologiste suisse / Partito ecologista svizzero (EL IB), Waisenhausplatz 21, 3011 Bern (+41-31 326 6660) (fax 31 326 6662) (gruene@gruene.ch) (www.gruene.ch). *Greenfo.* Green party. Grüne / Les Verts / I Verdi.

Greenpeace (GP), Badenerstr 171, Postfach 9320, 8036 Zürich (+41-44 447 4141) (fax 44 447 4199) (gp@greenpeace.ch) (www.greenpeace.org/switzerland).

Gruppe für eine Schweiz ohne Armee / Groupe pour une Suisse sans Armée [GSoA/GSsA] (WR), Maison des Associations, Rue de Savoises 15, CP 151, 1211 Geneve 8 (+41-44 273 0100) (gsoa@gsoa.ch) (www.gsoa.ch). In Zurich, +41-44 273 0100.

Institute for Peace and Dialogue / Institut für Frieden und Dialog [IPD] (CR CD RE), Ryffstr 23, 4056 Basel (+41-76 431 6170) (fhuseynli@ipdinstitute.ch) (www.ipdinstitute.ch).

Neuer Israel Fonds Schweiz - NIF Switzerland (HR), Winkelriedplatz 4, 4053 Basel (+41-61 272 1455) (fax 61 361 2972) (info@nif.ch) (www.mif.ch).

Peace Brigades International - Schweiz/Suisse [PBI] (CD HR CR RE), Gutenbergstr 35, 3011 Bern (+41-31 372 4444) (info@peacebrigades.ch) (www.peacebrigades.ch).

Pro Natura (FE), Postfach, 4018 Basel (+41-61-317 9191) (fax 317 9266) (mailbox@pronatura.ch) (www.pronatura.ch).

Schweizerische Friedensbewegung / Moviment Svizzer da Pasch / Swiss Peace Movement (WP), Postfach 2113, 4001 Basel (+41-61 681 0363) (mail@friedensbewegung.ch) (www.friedensbewegung.ch).

Schweizerische Friedensstiftung [swisspeace] (RE CR), Sonnenbergstr 17, PO Box, 3001 Bern (+41-31 330 1212) (info@swisspeace.ch) (www.swisspeace.ch).

Schweizerischer Friedensrat / Consiglio Svizzera per pa Pace / Conseil Suisse pour la Paix [SFR] (IB AT EL), Gartenhofstr 7, 8004 Zürich (+41-44 242 9321) (info@friedensrat.ch) (www.friedensrat.ch). Swiss Peace Council.

Service Civil International - Schweizer Zweig / Branche suisse / Sede svizzera [SCI] (SC), Monbijoustr 32, Postfach 2944, 3001 Bern (+41-31 381 4620) (info@scich.org) (www.scich.org). *Service Civil International.*

Société Religieuse des Amis, Assemblée de Suisse (Quaker) [SYM] (SF), c/o Maison Quaker, 13 Av du Mervelet, 1209 Genève (+41-22 748 4800) (fax 22 748 4819) (symclerk@swiss-quakers.ch) (www.swiss-quakers.ch). *Entre Amis.*

Société Suisse - Nations Unies / Schweizerisches Versicherungsverband (UN), Postfach 762, 6431 Schwyz (info@schweiz-uno.ch) (www.schweiz-uno.ch).

Weltföderalisten Schweiz / Fédéralistes mondiaux Suisse (WF), c/o Hexagon AG, Graben 5, 6300 Zug (info@weltfoederalisten.ch) (www.weltfoederalisten.ch). Member of World Federalist Movement (WFM).

Women's Internationl League for Peace and Freedom (WL), Horensteinstr 31, 8046 Zürich (info@wilpfschweiz.ch) (www.wilpfschweiz.ch).

SYRIA

Syrian Human Rights Committee [SHRC] (HR), see under Britain. Syrian human rights group in exile in Britain.

TAIWAN

Chinese Association for Human Rights [CAHR] (HR), 4F-3 - No 23 - Sec 1 - Hangchow S Rd, Taipei 10053 (+886-2-3393 6900) (fax 2395 7399) (humanright@cahr.org.tw) (www.cahr.org.tw).

Greenpeace East Asia - Taipei Office (GP), No 10, Lane 83, Section 1, Roosevelt Rd, Zhongzheng District, Taipei City 10093 (+886-2-2321 5006) (fax 2321 3209) (inquiry.tw@greenpeace.org) (www.greenpeace.org/eastasia).

John Paul II Peace Institute / Fujen Peace Centre (RP), Fujen Catholic University, 24205 Hsinchuang, Taipei County (+886-2-2905 3111) (fax 2905 2170) (peace@mail.fju.edu.tw) (peace.fjac.fju.edu.tw).

Taiwan Alliance to End the Death Penalty (HR), 3rd Floor - No 3, Lane 1 - Zhenjiang Street, Zhongzheng District, Taipei City 100008 (+886-2-2395 1158) (info@taedp.oeg.tw).

TANZANIA

United Nations Association of Tanzania (UN), PO Box 9182, Dar es Salaam (+255-22-219 9200) (fax 266 8749) (info@una.or.tz) (una.or.tz).

THAILAND
Asian Institute for Human Rights [AIHR] (HR), 109 Soi Sithicon, Suthisarnwinichai Road, Samsennok, Huaykwang, Bangkok 10310 (+66-2 277 6882) (fax) (kalpalatad@aihr.info) (aihr.info).

TIBET
Tibetan Centre for Human Rights and Democracy (FR HR), see under India. Works for human rights of Tibetans in Tibet.

TOGO
Amis de la Terre - Togo [ADT] (FE), BP 20190, Lomé (+228-2222 1731) (fax 2222 1732) (adt-togo@amiterre.tg) (www.amiterre.tg).

TUNISIA
Coalition Nationale Tunisienne contre la Peine de Mort (HR), 56 Avenue de la Liberté, 1002 Tunis (+216-2168 7533) (abolitionpm@gmail.com). National Coalition Against the Death Penalty.

TURKEY
Insan Haklari Dernegi / Human Rights Association [IHD] (HR), Necatibey Cad 82/11-12, Kizilay, Çankaya, 06430 Ankara (+90-312-230 3567) (fax 230 1707) (posta@ihd.org.tr) (www.ihd.org.tr).
Siddetsizlik Egitim ve Arastirma Denergi / Nonviolent Education and Research Association (RE WR), Kuloglu Mah Güllabici sok no 16 - Daire 2, 34433 Cihangir, Istanbul (+90-212-244 1269) (merhaba@siddetsizlikmerkezi.org) (www.siddetsizlikmerkezi.org).
Türkiye Insan Haklari Vakfi / Human Rights Foundation of Turkey [TIHV/HRFT] (HR), Mithatpasa Cad No 49/11 - 6 Kat, 06420 Kizilay / Ankara (+90-312-310 6636) (fax 310 6463) (tihv@tihv.org.tr) (www.tihv.org.tr). In Istanbul: +90-212-249 3092.
Türkiye Çevre Vafki / Environment Foundation of Turkey [TÇV] (EL), Tunali Hilmi Cd 50/20, Kavaklidere, 06660 Ankara (+90-312-425 5508) (fax 418 5118) (cevre@cevre.org.tr) (www.cevre.org.tr). *Çevre.*
Vicdani Ret Dernegi / Conscientious Objection Association [VR-DER] (WR HR), Bahariye Cad No 92/4, Kadiköy, Istanbul (+90-216-345 0100) (dernek@vicdaniret.org) (vicdaniret.org). For legalising conscientious objection.

UGANDA
International Friendship League - Uganda [IFL] (CD), c/o Ismael Nyonyintono, PO Box 37692, Kampala (ismaeluk@yahoo.com).
Jamii Ya Kupatanisha [JYAK] (FR WR CR), PO Box 198, Kampala (+256-41-427 1435) (fax 434 7389) (jyak.peace@gmail.com).
Women's International League for Peace and Freedom [WILPF Uganda] (WL), PO Box 3556, Kampala (+256-77-240 5295) (wilpf.org/uganda).

UKRAINE
Ukrainskiy Ruch Patsifistiv / Ukrainian Pacifist Movement (WR), Tverskyi Tupik Street 9 - apt 82, Kiyiv 01042 (+380-97-317 9326) (fax 44-529 0435) (yuriy.sheliazhenko@gmail.com) (pacifism.org.ua).
Zeleniy Svit - Druzi Zemli (FE PA), A/C 61, 49000 Dnipropetrovsk (+380-56-370 9572) (fax 370 9573) (foeukraine@gmail.com) (www.zsfoe.org). Green World - Friends of the Earth.

UNITED STATES OF AMERICA
350.org (EL), 20 Jay St - Suite 732, Brooklyn, NY 11201 (+1-646-801 0759) (feedback@350.org) (350.org). Campaign on climate change.
A Rocha USA (EL), PO Box 1338, Fredricksburg, TX 78624 (+1-830-522 5319) (usa@arocha.org) (arocha.us). Christian.
About Face: Veterans Against the War [IVAW] (PA RA), PO Box 3565, New York City, NY 10008 (+1-929-430 4988) (aboutfaceveterans.org). Formerly Iraq Veterans Against the War.
Action Reconciliation Service for Peace - US [ARSP] (CD RE), 1501 Cherry St, Philadelphia, PA 19102 (+1-215-241 7249) (info@actionreconciliation.org) (actionreconciliation.org).
AJ Muste Memorial Institute (IB RE WR), 168 Canal St - 6th Flr, New York, NY 10013 (+1-212-533 4335) (info@ajmuste.org) (www.ajmuste.org). *Muste Notes.*
Al-Awda - The Palestine Right to Return Coalition (HR), PO Box 8812, Coral Springs, FL 33075 (+1-760-918 9441) (fax 918 9442) (info@al-awda.org) (al-awda.org).
Alaska Peace Center, 3535 College Rd - Suite 203, Fairbanks, AK 99709-3722 (+1-907-374 0577) (info@alaskapeace.org) (www.alaskapeace.org).
Alliance for Middle East Peace [ALLMEP] (CD), 1725 I St NW - Suite 300, Washington, DC 20006 (+1-202-618 4600) (info@allmep.org) (www.allmep.org). Promoting people-to-people coexistence.
Alliance for Nuclear Accountability [ANA] (ND DA EL), 322 4th St NE, Washington, DC 20002 (+1-202-544 0217) (sgordon@ananuclear.org) (www.ananuclear.org).
Alliance for Peacebuilding (CR RE), 1800 Massachusetts Ave NW - Suite 401, Washington, DC 20036 (+1-202-822 2047) (fax 822 2049) (afp-info@allianceforpeacebuilding.org) (www.allianceforpeacebuilding.org). Coalition of organisations and individuals.

USA

Alternatives to Violence Project - USA [AVP/USA] (CR PO), 1050 Selby Ave, St Paul, MN 55104 (+1-888-278 7820) (info@avpusa.org) (avpusa.org).

American Civil Liberties Union [ACLU] (HR), 125 Broad St - 18th Floor, New York, NY 10004 (aclu@aclu.org) (www.aclu.org).

American Committee for US-Russia Accord [ACURA] (CD), 2808 Broadway - Box 18, New York, NY 10025 (editor@eastwestaccord.com) (usrussiaaccord.com). Promotes dialogue with Russia.

American Friends of Combatants for Peace (CD CR), 48 Wall St - Suite 1100, New York, NY 10005 (office@afcfp.org).

American Friends of Neve Shalom / Wahat al-Salam (CD HR PA RE), 229 N Central Ave - Suite 401, Glendale, CA 91203-3541 (+1-818-662 8883) (afnswas@oasisofpeace.org) (www.oasisofpeace.org). Support mixed (Jewish-Palestinian) Israeli village.

American Friends Service Committee [AFSC] (SF RE CR), 1501 Cherry St, Philadelphia, PA 19102 (+1-215-241 7000) (fax 241 7275) (afscinfo@afsc.org) (www.afsc.org). *Quaker Action.*

American Jews for a Just Peace [AJJP] (RA), PO Box 1032, Arlington, MA 02474 (www.ajjp.org).

Amnesty International USA [AIUSA] (AI), 311 W 43rd St - 7th floor, New York, NY 10036 (+1-212-807 8400) (fax 627 1451) (gr@aiusa.org) (www.amnestyusa.org). Also in Washington DC (+1-202-544 0200).

Anglican Pacifist Fellowship - US [APF] (RP), c/o Nathaniel W Pierce, 3864 Rumsey Dr, Trappe, MD 21673-1722 (+1-410-476 4556) (nwpierce@verizon.net).

Arkansas Coalition for Peace and Justice (DA HR), PO Box 250398, Little Rock, AR 72225 (+1-501-666 3784) (acpj@arpeaceandjustice.org) (arpeaceandjustice.org).

Arms Control Association [ACA] (AT ND RE), 1200 18th St - Ste 1175, Washington, DC 20036 (+1-202-463 8270) (fax 463 8273) (aca@armscontrol.org) (www.armscontrol.org).

Asian Pacific Environmental Network [APEN] (EL), 426 17th St - Suite 500, Oakland, CA 94612 (+1-510-834 8920) (fax 834 8926) (apen@apen4ej.org) (apen4ej.org).

Association of Christians for the Abolition of Torture [ACAT USA] (HR), PO Box 314, Pleasant Hill, TN 38578-0314 (kcharbonnet3@outlook.com).

Baptist Peace Fellowship of North America - Bautistas por la Paz [BPFNA] (RP), 300 Hawthorne Lane - Ste 205, Charlotte, NC 28204 (+1-704-521 6051) (fax 521 6053) (bpfna@bpfna.org) (www.bpfna.org). *Baptist Peacemaker.*

Beyond Conflict (RE CR), 198 Tremont St - Suite 453, Boston, MA 02116 (+1-617-945 7187) (info@beyondconflict.org) (beyondconflict.org). Uses lessons of cognitive and behavioural science.

Beyond Nuclear (EL ND), 7304 Carroll Ave - Suite 182, Takoma Park, MD 20912 (+1-301-270 2209) (info@beyondnuclear.org) (www.beyondnuclear.org).

Brady Campaign to Prevent Gun Violence (RE HR DA PO), 840 First St NE - Suite 400, Washington, DC 20002 (+1-202-370 8100) (policy@bradymail.org) (www.bradycampaign.org).

Bruderhof Communities (RP), 101 Woodcrest Dr, Rifton, NY 12471 (+1-845-658 7700) (info@bruderhof.com) (www.bruderhof.com). Also known as Church Communities International.

Buddhist Peace Fellowship [BPF] (FR IB), PO Box 3470, Berkeley, CA 94703 (+1-510-239 3764) (info@bpf.org) (www.buddhistpeacefellowship.org).

Campaign for Peace, Disarmament & Common Security (DA ND), 2161 Massachusetts Ave, Cambridge, MA 02140 (+1-617-661 6130) (JGerson@gmail.com) (www.cpdcs.org). For nuclear weapons abolition and common security.

Campaign for Uyghurs (HR), 1101 Pennsylvania Ave NW - Suite 300, Washington, DC 20004 (+1-240-660 8877) (contact@campaignforuyghurs.org) (campaignforuyghurs.org).

Campaign to Establish a US Department of Peace (RE PO CR CD), c/o The Peace Alliance, 2108 Military Rd, Arlington, VA 22207 (1-202-684 2553) (www.thepeacealliance.org).

Catholic Mobilizing Network to End the Use of the Death Penalty [CMN] (RP), 415 Michigan Ave NE - Suite 210, Washington, DC 20017 (+1-202-541 5290) (info@catholicsmobilizing.org) (catholicsmobilizing.org). Formerly Catholics Against Capital Punishment.

Catholic Peace Fellowship (RP PA), PO Box 4232, South Bend, IN 46634 (+1-574-232 2811) (staff@catholicpeacefellowship.org) (www.catholicpeacefellowship.org). Promotes conscientious objection.

Center for Applied Conflict Management [CACM] (RE CR), Kent State University, PO Box 5190, Kent, OH 44242-0001 (+1-330-672 3143) (fax 672 3362) (cacm@kent.edu) (www.kent.edu/cacm).

Center for Artistic Activism [C4AA] (PO), PO Box 543, Beacon, NY 12508 (+1-646-832 2454) (c4aa.org).

Center for Citizen Initiatives [CCI] (CD), 820 N Delaware St - Ste 405, San Mateo, CA 94401 (+1-650-458 8115) (info@ccisf.org) (ccisf.org).
Organise US-Russia citizen exchanges.

Center for Energy Research (EL CR ND), 104 Commercial St NE, Salem, OR 97301 (pbergel@igc.org).
Dedicated to breaking the nuclear chain.

Center for Jewish Nonviolence [CJNV] (PA RA HR), c/o Nonviolence International, PO Box 39127, Friendship Station NW, Washington, DC 20016 (cjnv.org). Organises visits to Israel for nonviolent action.

Center for Nonviolence and Peace Studies [CNPS] (RE CR PO), University of Rhode Island, 74 Lower College Rd - MCC 202, Kingston, RI 02881 (+1-401-874 2875) (fax 874 9108) (nonviolence@etal.uri.edu) (www.uri.edu/nonviolence).
Become the Change.

Center for Religious Tolerance [CRT] (RP CR), 520 Ralph St, Sarasota, FL 34242 (+1-941-312 9795) (info@c-r-t.org) (www.c-r-t.org).
Supports international interfaith initiatives.

Center for the Study and Promotion of Zones of Peace (RE), 139 Kuulei Rd, Kailua, HI 96734 (+1-808-263 4015) (fax) (lop-rey.zop-hi@worldnet.att.net).

Center for Victims of Torture (HR RE), 2356 University Ave W - Suite 430, Saint Paul, MN 55114 (+1-612-436 4800) (cvt@cvt.org) (www.cvt.org).

Center on Conscience & War [CCW] (PA HR), 1830 Connecticut Ave NW, Washington, DC 20009-5706 (+1-202-483 2220) (fax 483 1246) (ccw@CenteronConscience.org) (www.centeronconscience.org).
The Reporter for Conscience' sake.

Charter for Compassion (RP), PO Box 10787, Bainbridge Island, WA 98110 (partner@charterforcompassion.org) (charterforcompassion.org).

Christian Peacemaker Teams [CPT] (RP RA), PO Box 6508, Chicago, IL 60680-6508 (+1-773-376 0550) (fax 376 0549) (peacemakers@cpt.org) (www.cpt.org).

Citizens for Global Solutions (WF), 5 Thomas Circle NW, Washington, DC 20005 (+1-202-546 3950) (info@globalsolutions.org) (globalsolutions.org).
Affiliated to World Federalist Movement.

Citizens for Peaceful Resolutions [CPR] (ND PA PO), PO Box 364, Ventura, CA 93002-0364 (www.c-p-r.net).
Committed to interconnectedess of all life.

Co-operation Ireland (USA) (CD), 1501 Broadway - Suite 2600 (Attn Richard Pino), NY 10036 (www.cooperationireland.org).

Coalition to Stop Gun Violence (DA AT), 1424 L Street NW - Suite 2-1, Washington, DC 20005 (+1-202-408 0061) (csgv@csgv.org) (www.csgv.org).

CODEPINK: Women for Peace (PA), 2010 Linden Ave, Venice, CA 90291 (+1-310-827 4320) (fax 827 4547) (info@codepink.org) (www.codepink.org).
Washington office: +1-202-248 2093.

Colgate University Peace & Conflict Studies Program (RE CR), 13 Oak Dr, Hamilton, NY 13346-1398 (+1-315-228 7806) (fax 228 7121) (peace@colgate.edu) (www.colgate.edu/departments/peacestudies/).

Colombia Support Network (TW HR CD), PO Box 1505, Madison, WI 53701-1505 (+1-608-709 9817) (csn@igc.org) (www.colombiasupport.net).
Action on Colombia.

Committee Opposed to Militarism & the Draft [COMD] (PA), PO Box 15195, San Diego, CA 92175 (+1-760-753 7518) (admin@comdsd.org) (www.comdsd.org).

Common Defense Campaign [CDC] (RE), c/o William Goodfellow, Centre for International Policy, 2000 M St NW - Suite 720, Washington, DC 20036-3327 (+1-202-232 3317) (wcg@ciponline.org) (www.ciponline.org). Previously the Project on Defense Alternatives.

Conflict Information Consortium (RE CR), UCB 580, University of Colorado, Boulder, CO 80309 (beyondintractability.org).
Previously Conflict Research Consortium.

Costs of War Project (RE), Watson Institute for International and Public Affairs, Box 1970, Brown University, Providence, RI 02912-1970 (+1-401-863 2809) (costsofwar@brown.edu) (watson.brown.edu/costsofwar).
US Peace Prize winner.

Council for Responsible Genetics [CRG] (EL HR), 5 Upland Rd - Suite 3, Cambridge, MA 02140 (+1-617-868 0870) (fax 491 5344) (crg@gene-watch.org) (www.councilforresponsiblegenetics.org).
GeneWatch.

Courage to Resist (WR HR), 484 Lake Park Ave - No 149, Oakland, CA 94610 (+1-510-488 3559) (www.couragetoresist.org).
Supports public military refusers facing court.

Creative Response to Conflict [CRC] (FR CR PO), PO Box 271, Nyack, NY 10960-0271 (+1-845-353 1796) (fax 358 4924) (inquiries@crc-global.org) (crc-global.org).

Creativity for Peace (CD), 369 Montezuma Ave - No 566, Santa Fe, NM 87501 (+1-505-982 3765) (dottie@creativityforpeace.com) (www.creativityforpeace.com).

Cultural Survival [CS] (HR), 2067 Massachusetts Ave, Cambridge, MA 02140 (+1-617-441 5400) (fax 441 5417) (culturalsurvival@cs.org) (www.cs.org).

Culture Change (EL AL PO), PO Box 3387, Santa Cruz, CA 95063 (+1-215-243 3144) (fax) (info@culturechange.org) (www.culturechange.org). 4 yrly.
Supports immediate cut in petrol consumption.

USA

Culture of Peace Corporation / Culture of Peace News Network (RE), 95 Lyon St, New Haven, CT 06511 (coordinator@cpnn-world.org) (cpnn-world.org)

Cure Violence (PO CR), 227 West Monroe St - Suite 1025, Chicago, IL 60606 (+1-312-756 8632) (cvg.org). Treating violence as a health issue.

Death Penalty Information Center (HR RE), 1015 18th St NW - Suite 704, Washington, DC 20036 (+1-202-289 2275) (dpic@deathpenaltyinfo.org) (www.deathpenaltyinfo.org).

Democratic World Federalists (WF), 55 New Montgomery St - Suite 55, San Francisco, CA 94105 (+1-415-227 4880) (dwfed@dwfed.org) (www.dwfed.org).

Earth First! Journal (EL RA), PO Box 1112, Grants Pass, OR 97528 (+1-541-244 1533) (collective@earthfirstjournal.org) (www.earthfirstjournal.org). 4 yrly.

Earthworks (EL HR), 1612 K St NW - Suite 904, Washington, DC 20006 (+1-202-887 1872) (fax 887 1875) (info@earthworksaction.org) (www.earthworksaction.org). Protecting communities from mining etc.

East Timor and Indonesia Action Network [ETAN] (HR TW), PO Box 1663, New York, NY 10035-1663 (+1-917-690 4391) (etan@etan.org) (www.etan.org).

Ecumenical Accompaniment Programme in Palestine and Israel - USA [EAPPI-USA] (RP HR), c/o Steve Weaver, Church World Service, 475 Riverside Dr - Suite 700, New York, NY 10115 (info@eappi-us.org) (www.eappi-us.org).

Ecumenical Peace Institute / Clergy and Laity Concerned [EPI/CALC] (RP HR TW), PO Box 9334, Berkeley, CA 94709 (+1-510-990 0374) (epicalc@gmail.com) (www.epicalc.org).

Education for Peace in Iraq Center [EPIC] (CD HR RE), 1140 3rd St NE - Space 2138, Washington, DC 20002 (+1-202-747 6454) (info@epic-usa.org) (www.epic-usa.org). Founded by war veterans.

Educators for Peaceful Classrooms and Communities [EPCC] (RE), 520 Calabasas Rd, Watsonville, CA 95076 (www.educatorsforpeacefulclassroomsand-communities.org)

Environmentalists Against War (EL DA ND PA AT), PO Box 27, Berkeley, CA 94701 (+1-510-843 3343) (info@envirosagainstwar.org) (www.envirosagainstwar.org).

Episcopal Peace Fellowship [EPF] (FR CD), PO Box 15, Claysburg, PA 16625 (+1-312-922 8628) (epf@epfnational.org) (epfnational.org).

Equal Justice USA (HR), 81 Prospect St, Brooklyn, NYC, NY 11201 (+1-718-801 8940) (fax 801 8947) (info@ejusa.org) (ejusa.org). Against executions.

Esperanto-USA [E-USA] (HR), 91-J Auburn St - 1248, Portland, ME 04103 (+1-510-653 0998) (fax 866-200 1108) (eusa@esperanto-usa.org) (www.esperanto-usa.org). *Usona Esperantisto.*

Everytown for Gun Safety (DA), PO Box 4184, New York, NY 10163 (+1-646-324 8250) (info@everytown.org) (everytown.org). Working to end gun violence.

Farms Not Arms - Peace Roots Alliance [PRA] (DA EL), 425 Farm Rd - Suite 5, Summertown, TN 38483 (+1-931-964 2119) (fna_info@farmsnotarms.org) (www.farmsnotarms.org). Also West Coast office (+1-415-218 9021).

Fellowship for Intentional Community [FIC] (PO CR AL), 23 Dancing Rabbit Lane, Rutledge, MO 63563 (+1-660-883 5545) (fic@ic.org) (www.ic.org). *Communities.*

Fellowship of Reconciliation [FOR] (FR WR), 521 N Broaday, Nyack, NY 10960-0271 (+1-845-358 4601) (fax 358 4924) (communications@forusa.org) (www.forusa.org). *Fellowship.*

Food Not Bombs [FnB-US] (PA PO RA), PO Box 424, Arroyo Seco, NM 87514 (+1-575-770 3377) (menu@foodnotbombs.net) (www.foodnotbombs.net).

Foundation for Middle East Peace [FMEP], 1319 18th St NW, Washington, DC 20036 (+1-202-835 3650) (fax 835 3651) (info@fmep.org) (fmep.org).

Franciscan Action Network (RP EL HR), PO Box 29106, Washington, DC 20017 (+1-202-527 7575) (fax 527 7576) (info@franciscanaction.org) (franciscanaction.org).

Free Palestine Movement (HR), 405 Vista Heights Rd, El Cerrito, CA 94530 (+1-510-232 2500) (info@freepalestinemovement.org) (www.freepalestinemovement.org). Formerly Free Gaza Movement.

Fresno Center for Nonviolence (PA PO), 1584 N Van Ness Ave, Fresno, CA 93728 (+1-559-237 3223) (info@centerfornonviolence.org) (centerfornonviolence.org).

Friends for a Nonviolent World (PA PO CR), 1050 Selby Ave, Saint Paul, MN 55104 (+1-651-917 0383) (info@fnvw.org) (www.fnvw.org).

Friends of Peace Pilgrim (PO CR), PO Box 2207, Shelton, CT 06484-1841 (+1-203-926 1581) (friends@peacepilgrim.org) (www.peacepilgrim.org).

Friends of the Earth (FE), 1100 15th St NW - 11th Floor, Washington, DC 20005 (+1-202-783 7400) (fax 783 0444) (foe@foe.org) (www.foe.org).

Friends Peace Teams [FPT] (SF CR), 1001 Park Ave, St Louis, MO 63104 (+1-314-588 1122) (Office@FriendsPeaceTeams.org) (friendspeaceteams.org). *PeaceWays*.

Friendship Force (CD PO), 279 W Crogan St, Lawrenceville, GA 30046 (+1-404-522 9490) (www.friendshipforce.org). Promotes understanding through personal friendship.

Genocide Watch (HR RE), 1405 Cola Drive, McLean, VA 22101 (+1-202-643 1405) (communications@genocidewatch.org) (www.genocidewatch.org).

Global Family (CD WF RP), 17738 Minnow Way, Penn Valley, CA 95946 (www.globalfamily.org).

Global Meditations Network (CR PO), c/o Barbara Wolf, 218 Dartmouth St, Rochester, NY 14607 (bjwolf@globalmeditations.com) (www.globalmeditations.com).

Global Security Institute [GSI] (ND RE WF), 220 East 49th St - Suite 1B, New York, NY 10017 (+1-646-289 5170) (fax 289 5171) (info@gsinstitute.org) (gsinstitute.org).

Global Witness (EL HR TW CR), 1100 17th St NW - Suite 501, Washington, DC 20036 (+1-202-827 8673) (www.globalwitness.org). Also in Britain.

GMO Free USA (EL), PO Box 458, Unionville, CT 06085 (info@gmofreeusa.org) (www.gmofreeusa.org).

Green Party of the United States (EL HR CD), PO Box 75075, Washington, DC 20013 (+1-202-319 7191) (info@gp.org) (www.gp.org).

Greenpeace USA (GP), 702 H St NW - Suite 300, Washington, DC 20001 (+1-202-462 1177) (fax 462 4507) (info@wdc.greenpeace.org) (www.greenpeace.org/usa). *Greenpeace*.

Ground Zero Center for Nonviolent Action (ND PA RA), 16159 Clear Creek Rd NW, Poulsbo, WA 98370 (+1-360-930 8697) (info@gzcenter.org) (gzcenter.org). *Ground Zero*.

Guatemala Human Rights Commission USA [GHRC] (HR), 3321 12th St NE, Washington, DC 20017 (+1-202-529 6599) (fax 526 4611) (ghrc-usa@ghrc-usa.org) (www.ghrc-usa.org). *El Quetzal*.

Hand in Hand (PO CD RE), PO Box 80102, Portland, OR 97280 (+1-503-892 2962) (info@handinhandk12.org) (www.handinhandk12.org). Supports integrated education in Israel.

Harmony for Peace Foundation (PO CD ND), PO Box 2165, Southeastern, PA 19399 (+1-484-885 8539) (info@harmonyforpeace.org) (harmonyforpeace.org). Music for peace. Works with group in Japan.

Historians for Peace and Democracy [H-PAD] (DA HR CR), c/o Van Gosse, Department of History, PO Box 3003, Franklin & Marshall College, Lancaster, PA 17604-3003 (www.historiansforpeace.org). Formerly Historians Against the War.

ICAHD-USA (HR), PO Box 81252, Pittsburgh, PA 15217 (info@icahdusa.org) (www.icahdusa.org).

Ideas Across Borders (CD HR), 244 Fifth Avenue - Suite 2594, New York, NY 10001 (+1-646-844 4076) (info@ideasbeyondborders.org) (www.ideasbeyondborders.org). Share and promote critical thinking.

Institute for Food and Development Policy / Food First (RE TW EL), 398 60th St, Oakland, CA 94618 (+1-510-654 4400) (fax 654 4551) (info@foodfirst.org) (www.foodfirst.org).

Institute for Inclusive Security (RE CR), 1615 M St NW - Suite 850, Washington, DC 20036 (+1-202-403 2000) (fax 808 7070) (info@inclusivesecurity.org) (www.inclusivesecurity.org). Promotes women's contributions to peacebuilding.

Institute for Mediation and Conflict Resolution [IMCR] (CR RE), 369 E 148th St - Lower Level, Bronx, NY 10455 (+1-718-585 1190) (TRich@imcr.org) (www.imcr.org).

Institute for Middle East Understanding [IMEU] (RE CD), 2913 El Camino Real - No 436, Tustin, CA 92782 (+1-718-514 9662) (info@imeu.org) (imeu.org). Provides research and experts about Palestine.

Institute for Nonviolence Chicago (RE), 819 N Leamington St, Chicago, IL 60651 (+1-773-417 7421) (www.nonviolencechicago.org).

Interfaith Peace-Builders (RP CD CR), 1628 16th St NW, Washington, DC 20009 (+1-202-244 0821) (fax -866-936 1650) (office@ifpb.org) (www.ifpb.org). Send delegations to Israel/Palestine.

International Center for Transitional Justice [ICTJ] (CR HR), 50 Broadway - 23rd Floor, New York, NY 10004 (+1-917-637 3800) (fax 637 3900) (info@ictj.org) (www.ictj.org). Offices in Europe, Asia, Africa, South America.

International Center on Nonviolent Conflict [ICNC] (RE SD), 600 New Hampshire Ave NW - Suite 710, Washington, DC 20037 (+1-202-416 4720) (fax 466 5918) (icnc@nonviolent-conflict.org) (www.nonviolent-conflict.org).

International Civil Society Action Network (HR), 1126 16th St NW - Suite 250, Washington, DC 20036 (+1-202-355 8220) (fax 986 0952) (info@icanpeacework.org) (icanpeacework.org). For women's rights, peace and security.

InterReligious Task Force on Central America [IRTF] (HR RP TW), 3606 Brige Ave, Cleveland, OH 44113 (+1-216-961 0003) (irtf@irtfcleveland.org) (irtfcleveland.org).

Iowa Peace Network (RP), PO Box 30021, Des Moines, IA 50310 (+1-515-255 7114) (iowapeacenetwork@gmail.com).

USA

James Martin Center for Nonproliferation Studies [CNS] (ND), Middlebury Institute, 460 Pierce Street, Monterey, CA 93940 (+1-831-647 4154) (fax 647 3519) (cns@miis.edu) (nonproliferation.org). Also in Washington DC (+1-202-601 2344).

Jeanette Rankin Peace Center [JRPC] (RE EL CR PO), 519 S Higgins Ave, Missoula, MT 59801 (+1-406-543 3955) (fax 541 3997) (peace@jrpc.org) (jrpc.org).

Jewish Peace Fellowship [JPF] (FR), PO Box 271, Nyack, NY 10960-0271 (+1-845-358 4601) (fax 358 4924) (jpf@forusa.org) (www.jewishpeacefellowship.org). *Shalom*.

Jewish Voice for Peace [JVP] (HR CR RA), PO Box 589, Berkeley, CA 94701 (+1-510-465 1777) (fax 465 1616) (info@jvp.org) (jewishvoiceforpeace.org). Promotes US policy based on human rights.

JustPeace - Center for Mediation and Conflict Transformation (CR RE RP), 100 Maryland Ave NE, Washington, DC 20002 (+1-202-488 5647) (justpeace@justpeaceumc.org) (justpeaceumc.org).

Kansas Institute for Peace and Conflict Resolution [KIPCOR] (RE CR), Bethel College, 300 E 27th St, North Newton, KS 67117 (+1-316-284 5217) (fax 284 5379) (kipcor@bethelks.edu) (www.kipcor.org). Formerly Kansas Peace Institute.

Karuna Center for Peacebuilding [KCP] (CR HR RE), 447 West St, Amherst, MA 01002 (+1-413-256 3800) (fax 256 3802) (info@karunacenter.org) (www.karunacenter.org).

Korea Peace Network [KPN], 8630 Fenton St - Ste 604, Silver Spring, MD 20910 (fax +1-301-565 0850) (www.peaceaction.org/korea-peace-network/). Network campaigning for peace on Korean peninsula.

Law Center to Prevent Gun Violence (DA), 268 Bush St - No 555, San Francisco, CA 94104 (+1-415-433 2062) (fax 433 3357) (smartgunlaws.org).

Lawyers Committee on Nuclear Policy [LCNP] (ND AT DA), 220 E 49th St - Suite 1B, New York, NY 10017-1527 (+1-212-818 1861) (contact@lcnp.org) (www.lcnp.org).

Lutheran Peace Fellowship [LPF] (RP), 1710 11th Ave, Seattle, WA 98122-2420 (+1-206-349 2501) (lpf@ecunet.org) (www.lutheranpeace.org).

Mahatma Gandhi Center for Global Nonviolence (RE), James Madison University, MSC 2604, The Annex, 725 S Mason St, Harrisonburg, VA 22807 (+1-540-568 4060) (fax 568 7251) (GandhiCenter@jmu.edu) (www.jmu.edu/gandhicenter).

Mahatma Gandhi Library (RE), c/o Atul Kothari, 4526 Bermuda Dr, Sugar Land, TX 77479 (+1-281-531 1977) (fax 713-785 6252) (info@gandhilibrary.org) (www.gandhilibrary.org).

Maryland United for Peace and Justice [MUPJ] (DA HR CR), c/o Tony Langbehn, 327 E 25th St, Baltimore, MD 21218 (+1-301-390 9684) (tonylang4peace@gmail.com) (www.mupj.org).

Matsunaga Institute for Peace and Conflict Resolution (RE CR), University of Hawaii, 2424 Maile Way - Saunders 723, Honolulu, HI 96822 (+1-808-956 4237) (fax 956 0950) (uhip@hawaii.edu) (peaceinstitute.hawaii.edu).

Megiddo Peace Project, PO Box 7213, Ann Arbor, MI 48107 (megiddo@umich.edu) (www.peacetable.org). Calls for co-operation against the war system.

Metta Center for Nonviolence (RE), 205 Keller St - Suite 202D, Petaluma, CA 94952 (+1-707-235 3176) (info@mettacenter.org) (mettacenter.org).

Mid-South Peace & Justice Center (IB ND EL), 3573 Southern Ave, Memphis, TN 38111 (+1-901-725 4990) (centre@midsouthpeace.org) (midsouthpeace.org).

Middle East Research & Information Project [MERIP] (TW HR AT), 1344 T St NW - No 1, Washington, DC 20009 (+1-202-223 3677) (fax 223 3604) (www.merip.org). *Middle East Report*.

Minds of Peace (CR), PO Box 11494, St Louis, MO 63105-9998 (peace.public@gmail.com) (mindsofpeace.org). Helps discussions in divided communities.

Minnesota Alliance of Peacemakers (FR UN WL PC), PO Box 19573, Minneapolis, MN 55419 (info@mapm.org) (www.mapm.org). Umbrella group of many local organisations.

MK Gandhi Institute for Nonviolence (RE), 929 S Plymouth Ave, Rochester, NY 14608 (+1-585-463 3266) (fax 276 0203) (kmiller@admin.rochester.edu) (www.gandhiinstitute.org).

Mothers Against Violence [MAVHM] (RP), PO Box 88124, Indianapolis, IN 46208 (+1-317-400 5511) (mavhm21@gmail.com) (mothersagainstviolence.org). Reacting to violence on streets.

National Campaign for a Peace Tax Fund [NCPTF] (TR), 2121 Decatur Pl NW, Washington, DC 20008 (+1-202-483 3751) (info@peacetaxfund.org) (www.peacetaxfund.org). *Peace Tax Fund Update*.

National Campaign for Nonviolent Resistance (RA), 431 Notre Dame Lane - Apt 206, Baltimore, MD 21212 (+1-410-323 1607) (mobuszewski2001@comcast.net). Co-ordinates anti-war trainings and actions.

**National Coalition Against Censorship
[NCAC]** (HR), 19 Fulton St - Suite 407, New
York, NY 10038 (+1-212-807 6222)
(fax 807 6245) (ncac@ncac.org) (ncac.org).
Alliance of over 50 national organisations.
**National Coalition to Abolish the Death
Penalty [NCADP]** (HR), 1620 L St NW -
Suite 250, Washington, DC 20036
(+1-202-331 4090) (info@ncadp.org)
(www.ncadp.org).
**National Network Opposing the
Militarization of Youth [NNOMY]** (DA PO),
San Diego Peace Campus, 3850 Westgate
Pl, San Diego, CA 92105 (+1-619-798 8335)
(admin@nnomy.org) (nnomy.org).
National Peace Academy [NPA] (RE), PO
Box 2024, San Mateo, CA 94401 (+1-650-
918 6901) (nationalpeaceacademy.us).
**National War Tax Resistance Coordinating
Committee [NWTRCC]** (TR RA PA), PO Box
5616, Milwaukee, WI 53205-5616
(+1-262-399 8217) (nwtrcc@nwtrcc.org)
(www.nwtrcc.org). *More Than a Paycheck.*
Natural Resources Defense Council [NRDC]
(EL), 40 West 20th St, New York, NY 10011
(+1-212-727 2700) (fax 727 1773)
(nrdcinfo@nrdc.org) (www.nrdc.org). Works
to protect planet's wildlife and wild places.
Network of Spiritual Progressives [NSP]
(RP PO), 2342 Shattuck Ave - Suite 1200,
Berkeley, CA 94704 (+1-510-644 1200)
(fax 644 1255) (www.tikkun.org). *Tikkun.*
Nevada Desert Experience [NDE] (RP NP
DA RA), 1420 West Bartlett Ave, Las Vegas,
NV 89106-2226 (+1-702-646 4814)
(info@nevadadesertexperience.org)
(www.nevadadesertexperience.org).
Desert Voices.
New Israel Fund (HR), 6 East 39th St, New
York, NY 10016-0112 (+1-212-613 4400)
(fax 714 2153) (info@nif.org) (www.nif.org).
Supports progressive civil society in Israel.
Nobel Peace Laureate Project (RE), PO Box
21201, Eugene, OR 97402
(+1-541-485 1604)
(info@nobelpeacelaureates.org)
(www.nobelpeacelaureates.org).
Promote peace by honouring peacemakers.
**North American Congress on Latin America
[NACLA]** (TW HR), c/o NYU CLACS, 53
Washington Sq South - Fl 4W, New York, NY
10012 (+1-646-535 9085) (nacla.org).
Report on the Americas.
Nuclear Age Peace Foundation [NAPF] (PA
ND IB RE), 1622 Anacapa St, Santa Barbara,
CA 93101 (+1-805-965 3443) (info@napf.org)
(www.wagingpeace.org).
Nuclear Ban - Treaty Compliance Campaign
(ND), 59 Gleason Rd, Northampton, MA 01060
(+1-413-727 3704) (info@nuclearban.us)
(www.nuclearban.us). Supportintg 2017 UN
nuclear weapons ban treaty.
Nuclear Energy Information Service [NEIS]
(EL RA), 3411 W Diversey Ave - No 13,
Chicago, IL 60647 (+1-773-342 7650)
(neis@neis.org) (neis.org).
Educates about and campaigns against
nuclear power.
**Nuclear Information and Resource Service
[NIRS]** (EL ND), 6930 Carroll Ave - Suite
340, Takoma Park, MD 20912 (+1-301-270
6477) (fax 270 4291) (timj@nirs.org)
(www.nirs.org).
WISE/NIRS Nuclear Monitor. Works with
WISE, Amsterdam, to produce information.
Nuclear Resister (ND RA TR PA), PO Box
43383, Tucson, AZ 85733 (+1-520-323 8697)
(fax) (nukeresister@igc.org)
(www.nukeresister.org).
4 yrly, $25 ($35 abroad) pa.
Nuclear Threat Initiative [NTI] (ND), 1776
Eye St NW - Suite 600, Washington, DC
20006 (+1-202-296 4810) (fax 296 4811)
(contact@nti.org) (www.nti.org).
Nuclear Watch South (EL ND), PO Box 8574,
Atlanta, GA 31106 (+1-404-378 4263)
(info@nonukesyall.org)
(www.nonukesyall.org).
Nuclear Watch Tower.
Nukewatch (EL ND RA PA RE), 740A Round
Lake Rd, Luck, WI 54853 (+1-715-472 4185)
(nukewatch1@lakeland.ws)
(www.nukewatchinfo.org).
Nukewatch Quarterly.
On Earth Peace (RP), PO Box 188, 500 Main
St, New Windsor, MD 21776
(+1-410-635 8704) (onearthpeace.org).
Linked to Church of the Brethren.
OneVoice Movement - USA (CD CR), PO
Box 1577-OCS, New York, NY 10113
(+1-212-897 3985)
(info@OneVoiceMovement.org)
(www.onevoicemovement.org).
See also under Israel, Palestine, and Britain.
Oregon Peace Institute [OPI] (RE EL),
Whitefeather Peace Community, 3315 N
Russet St, Portland, OR 97217
(+1-503-327 8250)
(Oregon.Peace.Institute@gmail.com)
(orpeace.us). Also www.peacevoice.info.
Orthodox Peace Fellowship [OPF] (RP), PO
Box 76609, Washingtpon, DC 20013
(opfnorthamerica@gmail.com)
(incommunion.org).
Pace e Bene (RP PA), PO Box 2460, Athens,
OH 45701-5260 (+1-510-268 8765)
(fax 702-648 2281) (info@paceebene.org)
(www.paceebene.org).
For nonviolence and cultural transformation.
Pastors for Peace / IFCO (RP CD), 418 West
145th St, New York, NY 10031
(+1-212-926 5757) (fax 926 5842)
(ifco@ifconews.org) (www.ifconews.org).
Pathways to Peace (CD RE), c/o 122 Demont
Ave E - No 173, St Paul, MN 55117
(info@pathwaystopeace.org)
(pathwaystopeace.org).
Operates Culture of Peace Initiative.

USA

Pax Christi USA (PC CD EL), 415 Michigan Ave NE - Suite 240, Washington, DC 20017-4503 (+1-202-635 2741) (info@paxchristiusa.org) (www.paxchristiusa.org)

Peace & Justice Center (DA HR), 60 Lake St, Burlington, VT 05401 (+1-802-863 2345) (info@pjcvt.org) (www.pjcvt.org)

Peace Abbey Foundation (RP RA RE), 16 Lavender St, Millis, MA 02054 (+1-508-655 2143) (administration@peaceabbey.org) (www.peaceabbey.org). Includes Pacifist Living History Museum.

Peace Action (IB ND AT), Montgomery Center, 8630 Fenton St - Suite 934, Silver Spring, MD 20910 (+1-301-565 4050) (fax 565 0850) (kmartin@peace-action.org) (www.peaceaction.org).

Peace Action West (ND DA), 2201 Broadway - Suite 604, Oakland, CA 94612 (+1-510-849 2272) (www.peaceactionwest.org). Main office in Maryland (+1-301-565 4050).

Peace and Justice Studies Association [PJSA] (RE), 1421 37th St NW - Suite 130, Poulton Hall, Georgetown University, Washington, DC 20057 (+1-202-681 2057) (info@peacejusticestudies.org) (www.peacejusticestudies.org).

Peace Brigades International [PBI-USA] (PA RA CR), PO Box 75880, Washington, DC 20013 (+1-202-232 0142) (fax 232 0143) (info@pbiusa.org) (pbiusa.org).

Peace Development Fund [PDF] (HR EL PA), PO Box 40250, San Francisco, CA 94140-0250 (+1-415-642 0900) (peacedevfund@gmail.com) (www.peacedevelopmentfund.org). *Peace Developments*. Also PDF Center for Peace and Justice, Amherst, MA.

Peace Education and Action Centre of Eastern Iowa (RE DA), Old Brick, 26 East Market St, Iowa City, IA 52245 (+1-319-354 1925) (information@PEACEIowa.net) (peaceiowa.org).

Peace Educators Allied for Children Everywhere [PEACE] (WR RE EL CR), c/o Lucy Stroock, 55 Frost St, Cambridge, MA 02140 (+1-617-661 8374) (1peaceeducators@gmail.com) (www.peaceeducators.org). Network of parents, teachers and others.

Peace in Ukraine (DA RE CR), 2010 Linden Ave, Venice, CA 90291 c/o Codepink, (www.peaceinukraine.org). Coalition calling for ceasefire and negotiations.

Peace Resource Center of San Diego [PRC] (RE), Peace Campus, 3850 Westgate Pl, San Diego, CA 92105 (www.prcsd.org).

PeaceJam Foundation (RE CR HR), 11200 Ralston Rd, Arvada, CO 80004 (+1-303-455 2099) (rockymoutain@peacejam.org) (peacejam.org). Also in Maine (maine@peacejam.org).

Peaceworkers (CR CD PA RA SD), 721 Shrader St, San Francisco, CA 94117 (+1-415-751 0302) (fax) (davidrhartsough@gmail.com) (www.peaceworkersus.org). Promote international peace teams.

Physicians for Human Rights [PHR] (HR), 256 W 38th St - 9th Floor, New York, NY 10018 (+1-646-564 3720) (fax 564 3750) (communications@phrusa.org) (physiciansforhumanrights.org). Also offices in Washington DC amd Boston.

Physicians for Social Responsibility [PSR] (IP), 1111 14th St NW - Suite 700, Washington, DC 20005 (+1-202-667 4260) (fax 667 4201) (psrnatl@psr.org) (www.psr.org).

Ploughshares Fund (ND), 1808 Wedemeyer St - Suite 200, The Presidio of San Francisco, San Francisco, CA 94129 (+1-415-668 2244) (fax 668 2214) (ploughshares@ploughshares.org) (www.ploughshares.org). Promoting elimination of nuclear weapons.

Plowshares Network (RP RA ND PA), c/o Jonah House, 1301 Moreland Av, Baltimore, MD 21216 (+1-410-233 6238) (disarmnnow@verizon.net) (www.jonahhouse.org).

Popular Resistance (RA HR EL), c/o Alliance for Global Justice, 225 E 26th St - Suite 1, Tucson, AZ 85713 (info@popularresistance.org) (popularresistance.org). Against corporate takeover of government.

Portland State University Conflict Resolution Department (RE), 1600 SW 4th Av - Neuberger 131, Portland, OR 97201 (+1-503-725 9173) (fax 725 9174) (conflict_resolution@pdx.edu) (www.conflictresolution.pdx.edu). Specialisation in Peace and Nonviolence Studies.

Positive Futures Network, 284 Madrona Way NE - Suite 116, Bainbridge Island, WA 98110-2870 (+1-206-842 0216) (fax 842 5208) (info@yesmagazine.org) (www.yesmagazine.org). *Yes!*.

Power Shift Network (EL), PO Box 73116, Washington, DC 20056 (www.powershift.net). Youth network against climate change.

Presbyterian Peace Fellowship [PPF] (FR), 17 Cricketown Rd, Stony Point, NY 10980 (+1-845-786 6743) (info@presbypeacefellowship.org) (www.presbypeacefellowship.org).

Project on Youth and Non-Military Opportunities [Project YANO] (RE PA), PO Box 230157, Encinitas, CA 92023 (+1-760-634 3604) (projyano@aol.com) (www.projectyano.org).

Promoting Enduring Peace [PEP] (DA EL PA), 323 Temple St, New Haven, CT 06511-

6602 (+1-202-573 7322) (coordinator@pepeace.org) (www.pepeace.org).
Proposition One Campaign (ND AT), 401 Wilcox Rd, Tryon, NC 28782 (+1-202-210 3886) (et@prop1.org) (prop1.org). For nuclear weapons abolition.
Quaker House (SF RE), 223 Hillside Ave, Fayetteville, NC 28301 (+1-910-323 3912) (qpr@quaker.org) (www.quakerhouse.org). Work includes counselling disaffected soldiers.
Rainforest Action Network [RAN] (FE RA HR), 425 Bush St - Ste 300, San Francisco, CA 94108 (+1-415-398 4404) (fax 398 2732) (answers@ran.org) (www.ran.org).
Random Acts of Kindness Foundation [RAK] (CD CR PO), 1727 Tremont Pl, Denver, CO 80202 (+1-303-297 1964) (fax 297 2919) (info@randomactsofkindness.org) (www.randomactsofkindness.org).
Rebuilding Alliance (PO CD HR TW), 50 Woodside Plaza - Ste 627, Redwood City, CA 94061 (+1-650-440 9667) (contact@rebuildingalliance.org) (www.rebuildingalliance.org). Supports rebuilding in Palestine.
Refuser Solidarity Network (PA HR), 712 H St NE - PMB 98277, Washington, DC 20002 (info@refuser.org) (www.refuser.org). Supports Israeli COs and resisters.
Religions for Peace USA (RE RP CR HR), 777 UN Plaza - 9th Floor, New York, NY 10017 (+1-212-338 9140) (fax 983 0098) (rfpusa@rfpusa.org) (www.rfpusa.org).
Renounce War Projects (RP PA), 8001 Geary Blvd, San Francisco, CA 94121 (+1-415-307 1213) (peacematters@renouncewarprojects.org) (renouncewarprojects.org). Promotes Gandhian ideals.
Reprieve US (HR), PO Box 3627, New York, NY 10163 (+1-917-855 8064) (info@reprieve.org) (www.reprieve.org). Supports people facing death penalty.
Resistance Studies Initiative - Critical Support of People Power and Social Change (RE RA WR), University of Massachusetts Department of Sociology, 200 Hicks Way - Thompson Hall, Amherst, MA 01003-9277 (+1-413-545 5957) (fax 545 3204) (resist@umass.edu) (www.umass.edu/resistancestudies).
Resource Center for Nonviolence [RCNV] (WR FR HR NV), 612 Ocean St, Santa Cruz, CA (+1-831-423 1626) (rcnvinfo@gmail.com) (rcnv.org).
Rising Tide North America [RTA] (EL RA), 268 Bush St - Box 3717, San Francisco, CA 94101 (+1-503-438 4697) (networking@risingtidenorthamerica.org) (risingtidenorthamerica.org). Network of groups working on climate change.

Rocky Mountain Peace and Justice Centre (ND PA RE), PO Box 1156, Boulder, CO 80306 (+1-303-444 6981) (rmpjc@earthlink.net) (www.rmpjc.org).
Salam Institute for Peace & Justice (RE RP CR HR), PO Box 651196, Sterling, VA 20165-1196 (+1-202-360 4955) (info@salaminstitute.org) (salaminstitute.org).
San José Peace & Justice Center, 48 South 7th St, San Jose, CA 95112 (+1-408-297 2299) (sjpjc@sanjosepeace.org) (www.sanjosepeace.org)
Sarvodaya USA (TW PO), 525 N Armistead St - No 203, Alexandria, VA 22312 (info@sarvodayausa.org) (www.sarvodayausa.org). Supports Sarvodaya movement in Sri Lanka.
Satyagraha Institute (RP PA PO), c/o Carl Kline, 825 Fourth St, Brookings, SD 57006 (www.satyagrahainstitute.org). Promotes understanding of satyagraha.
School of the Americas Watch [SOA Watch] (HR), 225 E 26th St - Ste 7, Tucson, AZ 85713 (+1-202-234 3440) (info@soaw.org) (www.soaw.org).
Secular Coalition for America (HR), 1012 14th St NW - No 205, Washington, DC 20005 (+1-202-299 1091) (www.secular.org).
Seeds of Peace (CD CR PO), 370 Lexington Ave - Suite 1201, New York, NY 10017 (+1-212-573 8040) (fax 573 8047) (info@seedsofpeace.org) (www.seedsofpeace.org). Brings together teenagers from conflict areas.
September 11th Families for Peaceful Tomorrows [PT] (CD CR RE), 20 Sussex St, PO Box 802, Port Jervis, NY 12771 (+1-212-598 0970) (info@peacefultomorrows.org) (peacefultomorrows.org). Promote nonviolent resolution of conflict.
Service Civil International / International Voluntary Service [SCI-IVS USA] (SC), PO Box 1082, Great Barrington, MA 01230 (+1-413-591 8050) (fax 434-366 3545) (sciivs.usa.ltv@gmail.com) (www.volunteersciusa.org).
Sojourners (RP HR), 408 C St NE, Washington, DC 20002 (+1-202-328 8842) (fax 328 8757) (sojourners@sojo.net) (sojo.net).
States United to Prevent Gun Violence (DA RE), PO Box 1359, New York, NY 10276-1359 (info@supgv.org) (www.ceasefireusa.com). 30 affiliates.
Stop US Arms to Mexico (AT), c/o Global Exchange, 1446 Market St, San Francisco, CA 94102 (+1-510-282 8983) (johnlindsaypoland@gmail.com) (stopusarmstomexico.org).
Students for a Free Tibet (HR), 602 East 14th St - 2nd Floor, New York, NY 10009 (+1-212-358 0071) (info@studentsforafreetibet.org) (studentsforafreetibet.org).

USA

Swarthmore College Peace Collection (RE), 500 College Ave, Swarthmore, PA 19081 (+1-610-328 8557) (fax 328 8544) (wchmiel1@swarthmore.edu) (www.swarthmore.edu/Library/peace). Also houses Global Nonviolent Action Database.

Syracuse Cultural Workers (HR PA EL PO), PO Box 6367, Syracuse, NY 13217 (+1-315-474 1132) (fax 234 0930) (scw@syracuseculturalworkers.com) (www.syracuseculturalworkers.com). *Peace Calendar; Women Artists Datebook.* Also posters, cards, T-shirts, books.

Teachers Resisting Unhealthy Children's Entertainment [TRUCE] (RE PO), 160 Lakeview Ave, Cambridge, MA 02138 (truce@truceteachers.org) (www.truceteachers.org).

The Progressive (HR), 30 W Mifflin St - Suite 703, Madison, WI 53703 (+1-608-257 4626) (editorial@progressive.org) (www.progressive.org). Mthly, $32 ($80 abroad) pa.

Torture Abolition and Survivor Support Coalition [TASSC] (HR AT CR), 4121 Harewood Rd NE - Suite B, Washington, DC 20017 (+1-202-529 2991) (fax 529 8334) (info@tassc.org) (www.tassc.org).

Training for Change (RA RE PO), PO Box 30914, Philadelphia, PA 19104 (+1-267-289 2288) (info@trainingforchange.org) (www.trainingforchange.org).

Tri-Valley CAREs (ND EL), 2582 Old First St, Livermore, CA 94550 (+1-925-443 7148) (fax 443 0177) (marylia@earthlink.net) (www.trivalleycares.org). *Citizen's Watch.* Communities Against a Radioactive Environment.

UN Global Ceasefire to Universal Global Peace Treaty Project (DA RE), c/o Center for Global Nonkilling, 3653 Tantalus Drive, Honolulu, HI 96822-5033 (johndr@kkumail.com).

United for Peace and Justice [UFPJ] (DA), 244 Fifth Ave - Suite D55, New York, NY 10001 (+1-917-410 0119) (info.ufpj@gmail.com) (www.unitedforpeace.org). Major coalition.

United Nations Association of the USA [UNA-USA] (UN RE), 1750 Pennsylvania Ave NW - Suite 300, Washington, DC 20006 (+1-202-854 2360) (membership@unausa.org) (unausa.org).

United States Institute of Peace [USIP] (RE), 2301 Constitution Ave NW, Washington, DC 20037 (+1-202-457 1700) (fax 429 6063) (www.usip.org). *Peace Watch.* Officially funded.

US Campaign for Burma (HR), PO Box 34126, Washington, DC 20043 (+1-202-702 1161) (fax 234 8044) (info@uscampaignforburma.org) (www.uscampaignforburma.org).

US Campaign for Palestinian Rights [USCPR] (HR), PO Box 3609, Washington, DC 20027 (uscpr.org). Formerly US Campaign to End the Israeli Occupation.

US Climate Action Network (EL RA), 50 F St NW - 8th floor, Washington, DC 20001 (+1-202-495 3046) (fax 547 6009) (www.usclimatenetwork.org).

US Peace Council [USPC] (WP ND AT), PO Box 3105, New Haven, CT 06515-0205 (+1-203-387 0370) (USPC@uspeacecouncil.org) (uspeacecouncil.org).

US Peace Memorial Foundation (RE PA), 334 East Lake Rd - Unit 136, Palm Harbor, FL 34685-2427 (+1-202-455 8776) (info@USPeaceMemorial.org) (www.uspeacememorial.org). Produces US Peace Registry.

US Servas (SE), PO Box 3419, Berkeley, CA 94703-0419 (+1-707-825 1714) (info@usservas.org) (usservas.org).

Utah Campaign to Abolish Nuclear Weapons (ND), c/o 549 Cortez St, Salt Lake City, UT 84103 (dsawyer@xmission.com) (www.utahcan.org).

Uyghur Human Rights Project [UHRP] (HR), 1602 L St NW - Suite 613, Washington, DC 20036 (+1-202-790 1795) (info@uhrp.org) (uhrp.org).

Vermonters for Justice in Palestine (HR CR), c/o Peace & Justice Center, 60 Lake St, Burlington, VT 05401 (vtjp@vtjp.org) (www.vtjp.org).

Veterans For Peace [VFP] (DA PA RA), 1404 North Broadway, St Louis, MO 63102 (+1-314-725 6005) (fax 227 1981) (vfp@veteransforpeace.org) (www.veteransforpeace.org).

Volunteers for Peace [VFP] (WC HR PO CD EL), 131 Main St - No 201, Burlington, VT 05401 (+1-802-598 0052) (vfp@vfp.org) (www.vfp.org).

Waging Nonviolence [WNV] (WNV), 226 Prospect Park West - No 146, Brooklyn, NY 11215 (contact@wagingnonviolence.org) (wagingnonviolence.org). Internet-based resource.

War Prevention Initiative (CR CD WF RE), 221 NW Second Ave - Suite 204, Portland, OR 97209 (warpreventioninitiative.org).

War Resisters League [WRL] (WR IB TR AT), 30 E 125 St - No 229, New York, NY 10035 (+1-212-228 0450) (wrl@warresisters.org) (www.warresisters.org).

War Resisters League - New England Regional Office (WR), PO Box 1093, Norwich, CT 06360 (+1-860-639 8834) (joanne@warresisters.org) (www.warresisters.org/new-england-office).

Washington Peace Center (HR PA RE), 1525 Newton St NW, Washington, DC 20010

(+1-202-234 2000) (fax 558 5685) (info@washingtonpeacecenter.org) (washingtonpeacecenter.net).
Western States Legal Foundation (ND IB), 655 13th St - Suite 201, Preservation Park, Oakland, CA 94612 (+1-510-839 5877) (wslf@earthlink.net) (www.wslfweb.org).
Win Without War, 2000 M St NW - Suite 720, Washington, DC 20036 (+1-202-656 4999) (info@winwithoutwar.org) (winwithoutwar.org). Coalition engaging mainstream who want a safe USA.
Witness Against Torture (RP HR), c/o New York Catholic Worker, 55 East 3rd St, New York, NY 10003 (www.witnessagainsttorture.com). Campaign to close Guantanamo and end torture.
Witness for Peace [WfP] (RP HR TW), 1616 P St NW - Suite 100, Washington, DC 20036 (+1-202-547 6112) (fax 536 4708) (witness@witnessforpeace.org) (www.witnessforpeace.org).
Women for Genuine Security (CD PA), 965 62nd St, Oakland, CA 94608 (+1-415-312 5583) (info@genuinesecurity.org) (www.genuinesecurity.org).
Women's International League for Peace and Freedom - US Section [WILPF US] (WL HR), Friends House, PO Box 13075, Des Moines, IA 50310 (+1-617-266 0999) (info@wilpfus.org) (wilpfus.org).
Working Group for Peace and Demilitarization in Asia & the Pacific (DA RE), 2161 Massachusetts Ave, Cambridge, MA 02141 (+1-617-661 6130) (info@asiapacificinitiative.org) (www.asiapacificinitiative.org).
World BEYOND War (PA DA), 513 E Main St - No 1484, Charlottesville, VA 22902 (research@worldbeyondwar.org) (worldbeyondwar.org).
World Can't Wait (DA HR), 305 West Broadway - No 185, New York, NY 10013 (+1-646-807 3259) (info@worldcantwait.org) (www.worldcantwait.org). "Putting humanity and the planet first".
World Peace Foundation [WPF] (RE), Fletcher Schhol, Tufts University, 169 Holland Street - Suite 209, Somerville, MA 02144 (+1-617-627 2255) (worldpeacefoundation@tufts.edu) (sites.tufts.edu/wpf).
World Peace Now (CD ND DA), PO Box 275, Point Arena, CA 95468 (ellen.rosser@gmail.com). Formerly Friendship and Peace Society.
Worldwatch Institute (EL AT), 1400 16th St NW - Suite 430, Washington, DC 20036 (+1-202-745 8092) (fax 478 2534) (worldwatch@worldwatch.org) (www.worldwatch.org). Europe office in Copenhagen (+45-2087 1933).

URUGUAY
Amnistía Internacional Uruguay (AI), Wilson Ferreira Aldunate 1220, Montevideo 11100 (+598-2-900 7939) (fax 900 9851) (oficina@amnistia.uy) (www.amnistia.uy).
Asociación de Lucha para el Desarme Civil [ALUDEC] (CR DA), Andes 1365 - piso 10, Montevideo 11100 (+598-94-454440) (direccion@aludec.org.uy). Concerned about increased arming of "civilians".
Red de Ecología Social - Amigos de la Tierra Uruguay [REDES] (FE TW), Maldonado 1390, 11200 Montevideo (+598-2-904 2758) (prensa@redes.org.uy) (www.redes.org.uy).
SERPAJ-Uruguay (FR RE HR), Joaquín Requena 1642, 11200 Montevideo (+598-2-408 5301) (fax 408 5701) (serpajuy@serpaj.org.uy) (www.serpaj.org.uy).

UZBEKISTAN
Xalqaro Tinchlik va Birdamlik Muzei / Internacia Muzeo de Paco kaj Solidaro (IB RE CD), PO Box 76, 140100 Samarkand (+998-66-233 1753) (fax) (imps86@yahoo.com) (peace.museum.com). International Museum of Peace and Solidarity.

VIETNAM
Vietnam Peace Committee [VPC] (WP), 105a Quan Thanh, Ba Dinh, Ha Noi (+84-4-3945 4272) (fax 3733 0201) (vietpeacecom@gmail.com).

YEMEN
Mwatana for Human Rights (HR RE), Dairi St, 0000 Sanaa (+967-1-210755) (fax) (info@mwatana.org) (www.mwatana.org).

ZAMBIA
International Friendship League - Zambia [IFL] (CD), c/o George Siluyele, PO Box 234, Chongwe, Lusaka Province (georgesiluyele@yahoo.com).
OneWorld Africa [OWA] (TW), PO Box 37011, Lusaka (+260-21-129 2740) (fax 129 4188) (priscilla.jere@oneworld.net) (africa.oneworld.net). Part of OneWorld Network, in 11 countries.

ZIMBABWE
Gays and Lesbians of Zimbabwe [GALZ] (WR HR), 35 Colenbrander Rd, Milton Park, Harare (galz.org).
WILPF Zimbabwe (WL), 8 Jasmine Msasa Park, Kwekwe (+263-785-245103) (zimbabwe@wilpf.org) (wilpf.org/zimbabwe).
Zimbabwe Human Rights NGO Forum (HR), PO Box 9077, 8th Floor, Bluebridge, Eastgate, Harare (+263-4-250511) (fax 250494) (admin@hrforum.co.zw) (www.hrforumzim.com).

Notes

Notes

Notes

PEACE DIARY 2026

The 2026 Peace Diary should be available from the organisation or bookshop where you bought this Diary, or can be ordered direct from Housmans Bookshop in September 2025.
For information about 2026 prices, and other details, contact Housmans in the summer of 2025, or see
www.housmans.com/peace-diary.